NIELS HENRIK ABEL
Mathematician Extraordinary

NIELS HENRIK ABEL

Mathematician Extraordinary

OYSTEIN ORE

CHELSEA PUBLISHING COMPANY
NEW YORK, N.Y.

International Standard Book Number 0-8284-0274-4

Library of Congress Cataloging in Publication Data

    Ore, Øystein, 1899-1968.
        Niels Henrik Abel, mathematician extra-
        ordinary.

        Bibliography: p.
        1.   Abel, Niels Henrik, 1802-1829.

    QA29.A2065 1974   510'.92'4 (B)   73-14693
    ISBN 0-8284-0274-4

Printed in the United States of America

CONTENTS

⊰§ THE RETURN §⊱

⊰§ EPILOGUE §⊱

ILLUSTRATIONS

The only authentic portrait of Niels Henrik Abel

Abel's paternal grandparents, Elisabeth and Hans Mathias Abel; silhouettes of Abel's parents, Sören Georg and Anne Marie Abel

The vicarage at Finnöy; the church and vicarage at Gjerstad

Pastor Sören Georg Abel, wearing the insignia of the Knight of the Order of Danebrog

Abel's uncle and aunt, Peder Mandrup Tuxen and Elisabeth Marie Tuxen; Abel's teachers, Sören Rasmussen, professor at the university, and Bernt Michael Holmboe, *adjunct* at the Cathedral School

The Oslo Cathedral School; the courtyard of the school

Facsimile of one of Abel's manuscripts from his school days

The main buildings of the Oslo University; the inn Noah's Ark, meeting place of the students

Professor Christoffer Hansteen, Abel's faculty adviser; Niels Treschow, rector of the university; the home of the Hansteen family

Christine Kemp

Friends of Abel's student years, Baltazar Mathias Keilhau and Christian Peter Boeck; Abel's ink pot and sand case, his travel shaving case with mirror, his pipe, and his watch

The market place in Predazzo, with the inn Nave d'oro; Carl Friedrich Gauss, the leading German mathematician; the Marquis Pierre Simon Laplace, the "Newton of France"

Mathematical doodling from one of Abel's manuscripts

Baron Augustin Louis Cauchy; Adrien Marie Legendre; Carl Gustav Jacob Jacobi; Heinrich Christian Schumacher

The Froland Ironworks; the monument erected by Abel's friends at his grave

The statue of Abel in the Royal Park in Oslo

NIELS HENRIK ABEL
Mathematician Extraordinary

THIS *is a story of more than a century ago, about a circle of young scientists, and in particular one among them, a mathematician, Niels Henrik Abel. He is well known to any mathematician of today; indeed, few men have their name associated with so many results and concepts in modern mathematics. This, however, is not our main concern here. It is rather the simple story of a scientist, his family and friends, his hopes and sorrows, his triumphs and tragedies. Many great lives, rich in outer events, have inspired biographers. But the profound humanity of a searching soul may provide the background for an equally arresting chronicle — the heart-warming tale of a young man who set out from a little Norwegian town to explore the world of science.*

Family and Childhood

1

THE PASTORS ABEL

⋙ A STORY IS A WEB of many strands, yet it must of necessity have some point of beginning in time and place. So let our narrative start in the little parish of Gjerstad in southern Norway nearly two hundred years ago. The district, although mountainous, does not belong to the wilder parts of Norway; it is located a dozen miles from the sea-coast, some distance west of the Oslo fjord. At present it is easily accessible by rail and by a good road; previously it lay quite isolated at the upper end of a long, narrow lake, whose banks were rocky and steep. The approach by wagon was extremely difficult; goods were usually transported by rowboat over the lake, but otherwise travel was mostly on foot or on horseback. Only in winter did the trip to the nearest coastal town of Risör become a hilariously fast race in sleds over the frozen surface of Gjerstad Lake.

In 1784 the parish of Gjerstad was blessed with a new minister, fully to its desire. Among all the public officials the minister stood closest to the heart of the community; much of its happiness and contentment were dependent upon his person; he was the recognized leader in matters material as well as spiritual. But in the appointment of a minister there was but little the parish could do except to hope and pray for a wise decision by the king in Copenhagen, the absolute head of the state Lutheran church in the united kingdom of Denmark-Norway.

The new minister, Hans Mathias Abel, was a middle-aged man to whom the fairly remunerative parish in Gjerstad came as a reward for faithful work for the Lord in poor and isolated mountain districts during his earlier years. He was descended from a lineage of public officials; his great-grandfather had been a Danish merchant from South Jutland who through his great ability had obtained one of the most important administrative offices in the supply service of the Norwegian army. The

5

merchant forebear came from Abild parish in South Jutland, and this seems to have been the origin of the family name.

Pastor Abel had been brought up in Bergen where his father was a merchant and an alderman. He had preserved the habits of the wealthy and conservative circles in Bergen and continued to wear wig and breeches long after such apparel went out of fashion. He was a man of order: his wigs were always hung on a special table provided with pegs so that they could rest undisturbed after having been combed and brushed. Each had its special place and function; on the tallest peg in the center rested the holiday wig reserved for the Sunday services.

Abel was a modest man; his strength lay in his simple piety and deep religious conviction combined with a strong sense of duty and genuine concern for the welfare of the common man. In addition, he was courageous and when he felt that it served a good purpose he could speak his mind bluntly, to the authorities as well as to his parishioners. His contemporaries do not seem to have considered him a highly intelligent man. And it is true that he had received his theological degree in Copenhagen with the lowest possible passing mark, yet many prominent men had shared this distinction with him in order to shorten their studies — a practice encouraged by the peculiar examination system at that time whereby each candidate specified in advance the particular mark for which he wanted to qualify.

There was an abundance of problems awaiting the new vicar, but education for the young was his primary concern. Books were scarce, teachers and funds still more so; school buildings were unheard of. The teachers wandered from farm to farm and taught for a few weeks in any available space, their salary consisting principally of free board and bed. Usually they gathered their flock of children in the kitchen, which became a combined arena for the household chores and the three R's. In winter, at least, this was the only comfortable room in the house. Mathias Abel instructed some of the teachers himself, others were sent to town for a short course. To finance these ventures he sacrificed his own salary as justice of the peace.

Next there were the problems of providing for the poor, the ever-present reminders of the basic question of how living conditions in general could be improved. Abel broke new land on the parsonage farm and encouraged the peasants to do the same; he sowed flax and demonstrated the art of making linen. But his most radical innovation was

6

ABOVE *Abel's paternal grandparents, Elisabeth and Hans Mathias Abel (from portraits in Gjerstad Church, 1788).* BELOW *Silhouettes of Abel's parents, Sören Georg and Anne Marie Abel (1809)*

the cultivation of that novel fruit the potato, or "ground apple" as the peasants called it. In Norway, as in Ireland, it was to prove more than once the people's insurance against famine.

It was a busy life for the earnest pastor, but in the long winter evenings he relaxed by writing poetry and collecting material for a history of the district (not published until after his death). His wife, Elisabeth Normand, managed the parsonage and its many servants most efficiently. The marriage was unusually harmonious. In his poetry the old minister praises his spouse in terms of deep feeling:

> My blessed beautiful wife
> You, who give solace and peace
> You, the noble crown of my house
> You, the best given me in life.

The parsonage was a center of hospitality, famed for its food. Liquor, however, was never served. Excessive drinking was a perennial problem in that cold land, and if he could do no more, the pastor wanted at least to set a good example for his parishioners. By custom, alcohol was a daily drink. It was hardly possible for the men to begin their farm work in the morning without swallowing a couple of drams of native brandy, flavored with caraway seeds, for their inner warmth and cheer. Drunkenness was so common as to appear almost the natural state.

Pastor Abel never touched a glass of any alcoholic beverage. Great was the consternation, therefore, when the minister in his cassock one Sunday morning made his way to the church, raving drunk, butting into the waiting groups and excusing himself with silly grins. He passed through the aisle with obvious difficulty and climbed the pulpit, followed by the disapproving eyes of the congregation. Then he straightened his back, banged his hands on the lectern, and thundered to his audience: "I hope you have watched me with care. Such is the way you look, so do you appear in your drunkenness, you, created in the image of the Lord, behaving worse than beasts." Unfortunately it has always taken more than a sermon to stamp out the evils of alcoholism, but whatever could be done with words was achieved by Pastor Abel's merciless castigation.

The minister's good work was recognized by his superiors, but he was loath to accept praise. Once after a visitation by the bishop, Peder Hansen, the vicars of the adjoining parishes were gathered at Abel's parsonage for a banquet in the bishop's honor. Toward the end of the meal the bishop rose ceremoniously, paid his compliments to his host, and informed those present that he intended to nominate Abel for the deanship of this part of the bishopric. Before rising to respond, Pastor Abel sat for a few moments in thought, then came his answer: "I shall not accept. If this is to be a burden, there are younger men than I, more capable of carrying it. If it is to be an honor, there are worthier men for it." The bishop was taken aback; he left the table and withdrew to his rooms. Abel's wife and his colleagues implored him to offer his apologies, but the pastor refused stubbornly: "I have uttered nothing offensive." The bishop was almost equally stubborn and remained in seclusion for two days.

Pastor Hans Mathias Abel had only two children, a somewhat unusual circumstance in those days when the offspring at the vicarages frequently numbered above a dozen. The eldest child, a daughter, Margaretha Marine, never married and spent the greater part of her life with her parents. The younger, Sören Georg Abel, born in 1772, was his father's hope and pride. In many ways Sören Georg was the direct opposite in character of old Mathias. He was eminently gifted without his father's simplicity and strength; he was enterprising and full of ideas, but without his father's deep devotion to duty. He was fond of the social life of fashionable circles, and all his life he was prodded by a passionate ambition which would have brought him much greater success and happiness had it been kept in rein by a composure like his father's.

The young Sören George received his first lessons from a tutor at home. Then, as customary, he was sent to Denmark to continue his studies, for in Norway there was no university. There were many other important institutions lacking in the northern partner of the union between Denmark and Norway — for instance, there was not even a bank — and some Norwegians were beginning to feel that their country was more a province than an ally as the original intention had been. Sören Georg first attended a Danish preparatory school in Elsinore where he won the favor of the rector Niels Treschow, a Norwegian, who was later to be known as a distinguished philosopher. When at the age of sixteen Sören Georg was graduated to the university with the highest marks, Treschow expressed his deep regret at losing such a gifted pupil. At the university in Copenhagen Sören's success continued so that at

8

Pastor Sören Georg Abel, wearing the insignia of
Knight of the Order of Danebrog

the age of twenty he had obtained a degree in philology as well as one in theology, both with excellent marks.

Returning to Gjerstad, he was appointed curate and personal assistant to his father. The two cooperated cheerfully and old Pastor Abel was grateful for relief in his work: "This office is a light burden while I have such help," he wrote. For his own part, Sören Georg received an excellent training in congregational duties. He shared his father's enthusiastic interest in education, both for children and for adults. Among his first undertakings was the formation of a reading society which he hoped would introduce its subscribers to modern trends in European literature. Since he had been infused at the university with the rationalistic ideas of the period, they undoubtedly influenced his choice of books. To the old pastor's naive faith the son's novel thoughts were appalling; one day when he found a book by that heretic Voltaire on the bookshelf in his son's study he became so agitated that he sent for the sexton, simply to have someone he could pour out his sorrow to. Still, he never criticized his son publicly; on the contrary, he took every opportunity to praise him to others.

The eloquent and witty young pastor, deeply interested in politics and literature, was rapidly becoming a popular member of the social circles in the nearby coastal towns of Risör, Kragerö, and Arendal. These were flourishing times; the Napoleonic wars had created an unprecedented business boom for Norwegian exports with urgent demands for ships and lumber. The return cargoes were grains and groceries with a liberal sprinkling of luxuries and fineries for the merchants' wives and daughters, to be exhibited in the splendor of balls and assemblies during the winter season. Young Pastor Abel moved easily in this society; his best friend was Sivert Nicolai Smith, whose father, Hans Smith, was a magistrate and also the sole owner of the ironworks at Froland some miles north of the coastal town of Arendal. Here Sivert served as manager. Another prominent friend was Henrik Carstensen in Risör, one of the wealthiest men in the country.

Among the rich merchants and shipowners in Risör was Niels Henrik Saxild Simonsen, whose residence stood dominatingly on the pier. He had inherited the business from his father, who had sent him to England in his youth for education and business training. Highly respected for his fair dealings in business, Simonsen was very influential in community affairs and could at times show a magnificent generosity. Other-

9

wise he was a conservative man with a good deal of stubbornness in his opinions. The stay in Britain had greatly influenced his habits; he spent a good deal of time in his club and dressed like an Englishman of bygone days. He could be seen walking through the streets of Risör in breeches, pounding his tall walking staff against the round cobblestones, while on his head he carried the last surviving peruke with queue in town. He addressed everyone in the third person, in the Italian manner.

Simonsen married three times. His first wife, Magdalena Andrea Kraft, died early, and at the time young Pastor Abel came to know the family he was married to Magdalena's sister Christine. His oldest daughter of the first marriage, Anne Marie, was a beautiful girl with several talents: she played the pianoforte, she danced well, and her voice was greatly applauded when she could be prevailed upon to sing before the assemblies. The young Pastor Abel fell in love with her and his engagement to Fröken Simonsen was publicly announced a few months after they met. After having made the decision to marry, he had to look around for a parish of his own and so in the summer of 1799 he accepted a call to Finnöy on the southwestern coast of Norway, but still within the boundaries of Bishop Hansen's wide Christiansand diocese to which his father's parish belonged. Finnöy was considered a laborious parish, consisting as it did of a number of islands which could be visited only by boat. Nor was the call very remunerative. Still a pastor at the beginning of his career could not with reason expect anything better. The wedding was celebrated with great pomp in Risör; soon afterward the young Pastor Abel set out in a small sloop with his nineteen-year-old bride and all their household goods.

Travel conditions were poor. Abel described the voyage in a letter to his friend Sivert Smith: "Our trip was not as agreeable as one might have expected and frequently I experienced the truth of the words of the Apostle: 'Women are weak vessels.' My wife's seasickness and excessive fears made it necessary for us to leave the sloop at Lista and continue our travel on land along the coast. This roaming around, it is true, yielded us much knowledge about the districts, and many new acquaintances, but we could easily have spared them. They were connected with many difficulties, which we, however, safely surmounted. But our desire to reach our destination increased, and Finnöy became as dear to us as the land of Canaan to the children of Israel after their long

ABOVE *The vicarage at Finnöy (1826)*. BELOW *The church and vicarage at Gjerstad (water color by P. M. Tuxen, 1804)*

roving in the desert. We landed here, safe in soul, body, and goods January 22, 1800, after the birth of Christ."

Finnöy was obviously a pleasant surprise. "Here we are," he wrote to Sivert Smith, "and with pleasure, yes, I candidly confess that Finnöy exceeds my expectations. True, the parish is small, but the quality is good and the peasants are exceedingly kind. They share all their good things with the minister and so one can subsist here without concern for one's livelihood. The vicarage farm is in good condition; usually it yields about 100 bushels for 10 bushels seed." It had thirty cows, three horses, and a large flock of sheep, which to his surprise remained outside without shelter in winter as well as in summer. The manor was at least habitable and there were six servants, three girls and three young men. The pay was ten daler a year for the men, five to six for a girl, "and with this they manage quite well." The grain prices were high because of the wars and on Finnöy every farmer, including the pastor, had something to spare for sale.

Abel was familiar with the tasks in the congregation and tackled them with all the energy of youth. Again he organized a library and a reading society; after a year he had more than sixty members. "Many of them read with understanding and discrimination. To my mind this organization, although quite new, has been of greater use than all the dogmatic sermons preached here during the last ten years: more power to Bishop Hansen, a friend of education and an enemy of all prejudices."

After a good deal of argument he induced the congregation to exchange the old hymnbook for a new one, but this required a considerable number of sermons and numerous peregrinations to the farms to discuss the advantages of the more modern psalms. The peasants were conservative and doubtful, but Abel through these visits at least came to know them quite well.

"The people around here are superstitious, but they are filled with knowledge of the Bible; they support every erroneous opinion by misunderstood divine authority; they may not be invincible, but there is room for much improvement. Fortunately they are well situated and so they all have a few shillings which they can use for the support of a good purpose.

"Why are they so well-to-do? Undoubtedly because they make their living out of farming and husbandry. They drink only beer, Finnöy Porter, from their own homemade malt, and they dress in cloth which

11

they have spun themselves. This is quite different from the peasant in eastern Norway, who wants to become rich by selling lumber. He neglects his soil, drinks himself to death in brandy, and finally reaches a wonderful goal, to become the subservient scamp of the merchants. My observation is this: 'Finnöy is the happiest place in Norway.' "

A minister's concerns were many. Even though the landowners were prosperous there were always paupers to care for. In addition Pastor Abel became justice of the peace and public vaccinator. Yet all these tasks appeared small compared with the perennial problem of improving the schools. The driving force behind this movement was again Bishop Hansen, who established a training school for teachers at the episcopal see in Christiansand. Abel succeeded in sending some of the teachers in his own district to this center, but when they came back it turned out that several of them had had such scant training that they could not even understand their own notes, and the big boatshed belonging to the vicarage at Finnöy was transformed into an emergency school for the teachers where they could learn the rudiments of book knowledge. Most of the children could neither read nor write and Abel placed a good deal of the blame on his predecessor who had cared less to feed his flock than to shear it. The great day for the demonstration of the attainments of the pupils was Confirmation Sunday; the young were ranged in order in the church aisle according to ability, and it was a never-to-be-forgotten honor for a lad to be placed at the head of his confirmation class, nearest the altar. According to Abel's statement, the previous minister had evidently been far from incorruptible: "He abused those who did not bring him enough gifts and when he disliked the parents he ridiculed the children on the church floor."

The minister was obviously satisfied with the challenge of his new post, but for young Anne Marie the adjustment was more difficult. There were unaccustomed duties, the vicarage had to be run impeccably, there were servant problems, and she must forever set a good example, at home and in the parish. She was lonesome and she longed for the gay circles in Risör; the nearest town of Stavanger was at best several hours distant by oar or by sail. Fortunately Abel had brought a lady companion for her from the vicarage at Gjerstad, the experienced Elisabeth Luth, who could assist with the household chores.

"Now comes the best of it all," wrote Sören Abel to his good friend Sivert Smith. "My domestic joy has recently been increased, for on the third day of Christmas my wife presented me with a healthy son. Everything went wonderfully well, both because Finnöy has a capable midwife and because I happened to be away that day at the annex of Jelsa, fifteen miles distant. Both mother and son are doing nicely. If you happened to see this little man you would believe him to be a descendant of Ogier le Danois rather than that such a weakling as myself should be his father.

"He is being brought up à la Salzmann [the German pedagogue]. His mother's milk is and shall remain his only nourishment for the first year; he shall neither be rocked, nor swaddled; cold water, fresh air, and motion are his only medicines. As a consequence he thrives wonderfully well, so that if Salzmann's pedagogical rules prove valid also in the future I bless the hours which I spent in studying his works. I wanted to call the child Buonaparte, but my wife's concern prevented this and he is now named for my unforgettable father. I may add, just for fun, that the five farmers I invited to be his godfathers each presented him with four dalers, a sign that they are not empty boasters and can be very generous."

Unfortunately, Hans Mathias, Pastor Abel's first-born, would prove to be a poor example for the efficacy of Salzmann's pedagogical rules.

About a year and a half later, on August 5, 1802, a second son was born, the future mathematician Niels Henrik Abel, the principal figure of this story.

Little Niels Henrik was of delicate health and during his first few years he required his mother's undivided attention; thus it seems most likely that he was spared the rigors of the Salzmann system. His older brother had been named for the paternal grandfather, so according to custom the maternal grandfather, Niels Henrik Simonsen in Risör, had to be similarly honored. It was a signal distinction in the parish to become godparents to the children of the minister; for the first-born Pastor Abel selected the sheriff, the sexton, and five of the wealthiest farmers; for Niels Henrik the choice fell upon the nine peasants next in line and the wife of a magistrate living nearby.

At the turn of the century dark war clouds chased over Europe's political skies and no one knew when the storm would break. The Danish-Norwegian government was precariously balanced between the great powers. Because of its shipping interests the country had, next to

England, the strongest navy in Europe, a most valuable asset in any alliance. When England tightened its blockade of the Continent the Danish-Norwegian government responded with a declaration of the freedom of the seas and began to convoy its merchant vessels. One incident succeeded another and to protect their mutual interests the Scandinavian countries were driven into a league of armed neutrality with Russia and Prussia. The British response was swift and forceful; on April 2, 1801, a flotilla of fifty-three ships under the command of Admiral Nelson sailed into the roads of Copenhagen and engaged the Danish-Norwegian fleet. In spite of the surprise blow the action was indecisive, but the Danish-Norwegian government agreed to withdraw from the league.

An uneasy armistice reigned but no one considered it anything but the lull before the storm. In Denmark and Norway coastal defenses were organized in feverish haste; fleet and armies were built up as fast as ships and men could be procured. To take charge of the enlistment in the Stavanger district, the Admiralty in Copenhagen dispatched a young second lieutenant, eighteen-year-old Peder Mandrup Tuxen, who had already smelled the first whiffs of gunpowder during the battle in the roads of Copenhagen; despite his youth he had proved himself a capable and daring officer.

Shortly after Tuxen's arrival in Stavanger he appeared at the vicarage in Finnöy and quickly gained the friendship of the minister and his wife. It may not appear a suitable task for a priest to mobilize military powers, but now as well as on several subsequent occasions, Pastor Abel showed a glowing patriotic spirit and threw himself enthusiastically into the activities for Norway's defense. "There are again repeated rumors in circulation about impending war with England," he wrote. "My condolences to my country if it happens, and also to Finnöy, because it is very conveniently located for plunder. Let us hope that this bird of prey shall have its wings clipped. The enlistment officer has been very severe, but my Finnöy children do not easily leave their porridge and pea-pots. I console them, however, with the fact that they will find these matters just as well on board His Majesty's ships."

This first meeting with Lieutenant Tuxen was brief; after several months the "severe" young officer received orders to return to Copenhagen for advanced training.

In this tense period for the nation the years at Finnöy were ripe with work and achievements for Pastor Abel. He earned the recognition of his colleagues and superiors. Bishop Hansen did not spare his praise and after a visitation he reported: "In very few words, I found the enlightenment and order which attest to a noble people and the most admirable conduct of his office by their present tutor, the Reverend Abel." But Abel longed for greater spheres; Finnöy was much too isolated for his taste. "Although I am really contented with my lot," he confessed to Sivert Smith, "I should wish for a transfer for the sake of the future. Who does not desire the greatest measure of happiness? How wonderful it would be to arrive early at some position where one could feel: 'Here I want to live and die' and thus be able to harvest the fruits of one's efforts."

Scarcely a year after the birth of Niels Henrik the sorrowful message arrived from Gjerstad that the paternal grandfather, Pastor Mathias Abel, had died suddenly at the age of sixty-five. The families at Gjerstad and Finnöy were deeply saddened; his congregation mourned the loss of its wise and sympathetic spiritual leader. He was buried near the church, on a slope with a wide view over Gjerstad Lake and the valley he loved so well. His colleagues expressed their condolences by poetic eulogies in the pedantic style of the day; the bishop took the unusual step of making public in the little newspaper in Christiansand his own lament, describing the departed as

> Upright like the apostle Nathaniel
> Kind as St. John
> Modest and warm for all good, like St. Paul.

Sören Abel and his wife had grown homesick for Gjerstad, for their friends, and for the gay life in Risör. But chances appeared small for Pastor Abel to receive an appointment to his father's parish; he had been too short a time at Finnöy. A central call like Gjerstad should by right go to an older man as a reward for long and faithful service, as had been the case in his father's appointment. Abel did apply, however; he presented his qualifications and added that since Finnöy was the least remunerative service in the diocese it was becoming difficult, with his increasing family, to make a satisfactory living. Although the bishop praised him, he nevertheless found that an older minister in a mountain district should be given preference. But the congregation in Gjerstad firmly supported Abel, whom they had known so favorably from his service with his father; at last their insistent representations to the bishop carried so much weight that he reluctantly conceded to the congregation's wishes and recommended to the king that Abel be appointed.

During the summer of 1804, after more than four years' absence, Pastor Abel with his wife and two small sons returned to the vicarage at Gjerstad. Once more the familiar field of activity lay before Pastor Abel and the cooperation of the congregation appeared excellent. John Aas, his successor as minister, related: "Herr Abel was received with deep satisfaction by the Gjerstad congregation. Everyone favored him from earlier days. By his many gifts he was able to charm all. He commenced by changing and improving many things and the congregation met him halfway with the greatest willingness."

Again there were the old tasks: schools, library, work for the poor; he even continued as vaccinator, inoculating all children in the district, including little Niels Henrik. But he also tackled new problems. Encouraged by Bishop Hansen he tried his hand as a religious writer, publishing a collection of prayers and devotions and more important, a new commentary on Luther's catechism: *Religious Questions and Answers, Arranged for Young People*. The book, designed to replace an antiquated predecessor, was widely used and printed in many editions. From some quarters it was attacked as being too rationalistic, but it was also warmly defended by prominent clerics.

The seed sown by father and son began to flower; a visitation report from 1806 relates: "The minister, Herr Abel, preached personally; his sermon was as beautiful as it was clear and warm, scaled to the level of the congregation. A large number of youths were present, almost more than the church could hold, and here one found more than literal learning. Many distinguished themselves, particularly among those to be confirmed. Even the teacher stepped forward for examination."

All these spiritual concerns, properly within the sphere of Abel's pastoral activities, were almost overshadowed by his interest in the economic progress of his community. In this he was only one contributor among many to a larger stream of thought and action which gradually engulfed the country during these critical years. The ideas of the American and French revolutions were beginning to sift into the minds of thinking men, but as yet there was no conscious effort toward an independent and democratic government. Instead there was a strong feeling that economic self-sufficiency was essential for Norway and that the country's natural resources should be developed. Many shared in these undertakings; the clergy played such an exuberant part that today one has the impression that their spiritual duties had become only a sideline. Abel himself encouraged home industries, built a brick kiln, and improved the methods of burning charcoal and distilling tar; he urged the construction of magazines for grain reserves to ensure a seed supply and to relieve famine in years of crop failure. While his father had introduced the potato to Gjerstad, Abel improved the methods of its cultivation.

Most pleasant among his activities were the social gatherings and parties in Risör, and the family visits with friends in the nearby estates and towns. At Christmas time long lines of sleds would wind toward the vicarage for its gay annual ball. For daily home life there was not much time, but Abel loved to play with the children, and could charm everyone at the vicarage when he wanted to make the effort.

Two silhouette portraits of himself and his wife, cut by an itinerant artist, have been preserved. Under his own picture Abel wrote a little poem:

> "I preach, I love, I eat and drink and laugh.
> My finery: a well-worn hat and ditto coat.
> Don't ask me, reader, what else I am
> Since this is all that I in truth can say."

Under his wife's picture:

> "I have my portion in this world
> Joined to such a peculiar patron
> But, charming reader, thank the Lord in Heaven
> If you shall never experience worse."

The flock of children finally totaled five sons and one daughter. Pastor Abel named each in honor of some friend: Thomas Hammond, for the customs director in Risör; Peder Mandrup Tuxen, for the Danish naval officer; the daughter Elisabeth Magdalene, for her grandmother; Thor Henrik Carstensen, for the wealthy merchant in Risör.

One of the first guests after the return of the Abel family to Gjerstad was Second Lieutenant Tuxen, who by volunteering as an aide to a high-ranking officer had succeeded in obtaining an opportunity for a brief visit to Risör. He was a charming and cultivated visitor with literary and scientific interests. He was fond of playing the flute and

MATHEMATICIAN EXTRAORDINARY

entertained the children with drawings and silhouettes of the family members. In the social circles in Risör he was a favored guest. When he arrived there was already another visitor at the vicarage, Fru Abel's younger sister, the eighteen-year-old Elisabeth Marie Simonsen. No sooner had Lieutenant Tuxen entered the drawing room in his resplendent uniform than the two youngsters fell hopelessly and happily in love, and not many days had passed before he formally addressed to her a letter proposing marriage which she, equally formal, responded to with a letter of acceptance.

The call of duty came much too quickly and at Tuxen's departure the great secret was shared with Pastor Abel and his wife. But the young love did not long remain unobserved, according to Tuxen's first letter to his fiancée, describing his return crossing to Copenhagen. It had been a pleasant trip. "Every day we had Rhine wine, Madeira, Champagne and sweet wine, and every day the commissar of war and I tarried at the table after dinner, drinking toasts and cheering. The cheers were invariably these: 1. Old Simonsen, three cheers. 2. You, my girl, for whom they all show much sympathy — they continue to bother me but I always keep straight countenance — you always received nine cheers. 3. Henrik Carstensen, the commissar's host, three cheers. 4. All friends in Risör, three cheers. 5. The commissar's wife, nine cheers. Then followed a raft of others. It was a ridiculous idea for two men to sit alone and shout hurrahs at the top of their lungs, and you may believe, it amused those who were listening to us."

The cheers for old Simonsen ended abruptly; the old merchant violently opposed the engagement. In his opinion a penniless second lieutenant was no suitable match for his daughter. The two were forbidden to see each other, even letters were prohibited. So the vicarage at Gjerstad became the center of the romance, Pastor Abel served as *postillon d'amour*, and several times Lieutenant Tuxen came to Gjerstad to meet his bride in secret; once he was there even without the permission of the Admiralty in Copenhagen.

During the summer of 1807 the long-simmering political crisis in Scandinavia exploded into full-scale war. Napoleon was at the height of his power and had long exerted pressure on the Danish-Norwegian government to join him in military alliance; a French army under General Bernadotte stood poised in Hamburg to underline the threats.

Meanwhile the British worked frantically for alliances and had already succeeded in concluding a pact with Sweden. Without formal declaration of war a British fleet began landing troops near Copenhagen. An intense bombardment of the city from land and sea followed. After three days the government surrendered to avoid complete destruction of the town, and the great prize and pride of the country, its fleet, was delivered intact into British hands. Thus in an instant, Denmark-Norway had become an ally of Napoleon and was at war with England and Sweden.

At first the surprise British attack created near panic. The British fleet blockaded the Norwegian coast and chased the few remaining warships which by chance had not been in the harbor at Copenhagen. Landings and lootings were expected everywhere. From the coastal towns many moved inland with their families and valuables. Young Fröken Simonsen sought refuge with her sister's family at Gjerstad and remained with them during the winter; in February 1808 she wrote to her beloved Lieutenant Tuxen: "Since Christmas we have not had a single visitor, but I am not homesick since I have plenty to do. I get up at seven or a little earlier in the morning and read a little until it gets light. Then Abel calls me: 'Come down, Elisabeth.' My first task is to pour tea, then I become school madam for about an hour, since I teach little Henrik to read. Then I sew, work in the kitchen, or do some knitting. Toward dusk I play the pianoforte or if the weather is good, take a walk with Abel. At night when everyone in the house has gone to bed Abel and I remain until eleven o'clock when I go to my chamber. So one day runs after the other and time passes quickly. I help my sister all I can while I am here, and it benefits us both."

For Lieutenant Tuxen the war was a period of many vicissitudes. When the news of the bombardment of Copenhagen reached him he was in Holland on a technical mission. At the time there were forty Norwegian merchant vessels with crews totaling three hundred men cooped up in the harbor of Amsterdam, cut off from their homeland. Tuxen suggested that he should lead them on a march by foot to Denmark and proposed the plan in a letter to the government in Copenhagen. However, the government was slow in coming to a decision, as many governments are known to be, and when permission finally arrived the sailors' enthusiasm for the plan had evaporated.

In a letter to his fiancée Tuxen told about his adventures: "Now no one wanted to march and I had unbelievable rows with your dear countrymen — for they were all Norwegians. Partly by force, partly by threats, I finally gathered two hundred and sixty-three men and as the only officer in this large company we traveled the long road to Altona. On the way I became reconciled with the men and even the greatest rebels now loved me as a mother is loved by her children. In all the difficulties and fatigues which such a transport entails it was a true reward to see only contented faces around me and to be cheered loudly upon every occasion."

After this episode Tuxen was ordered to active sea duty. The large ships of the navy were gone and the Admiralty was compelled to rely upon gun *chaloups,* vessels which were usually rowed into action with as many as fifty to sixty men at the oars. They were almost useless for seagoing expeditions, but they could be constructed quickly and proved effective in coastal defense. They were difficult to hit and their long pair of guns fore and aft carried a considerable sting. Tuxen improved the construction of the *chaloups* and their gun emplacements and then was entrusted with one of the most important tasks of the navy: to protect communications and the provisions going to Norway.

His flotilla was stationed at Fredrikshavn, near the Skaw. By quick forays he succeeded in cutting out a number of merchant vessels from the English convoys on the way to Sweden. English men-of-war lying becalmed in the Skagerak were also tackled, and in some instances the warships were forced to surrender under the fiery attacks of the *chaloups.* These achievements not only made Tuxen famous as one of the bravest commanders in the navy; they also netted him large amounts of prize money. When he arrived at Risör in 1809 after a mission he was received with ovations in town and embraced by his dear Elisabeth. Even old Simonsen could not hide his emotion; he cleared his throat and exclaimed to Tuxen in his old-fashioned manner: "He shall be my son-in-law. God bless him and my Elisabeth."

The wedding took place in Risör the next year. Tuxen bought a house in Copenhagen, raised a large family, and served the navy and the Danish royal family in many positions of trust. A share of his prize money was used to purchase a pharmacy in Arendal for his younger brother Ole Tuxen, who, a little later, became the brother-in-law of Abel's friend Sivert Smith.

For Abel the war meant an intensification of his many activities. The

British blockade had proved very effective. It necessitated the creation of a deputy government in Norway, one of whose prime concerns was procuring food supplies for the country. One year of crop failure followed another during the war and with the usual grain shipments from Denmark reduced to a trickle famine stalked many districts. Fortunately, Gjerstad was a fertile community; potatoes served as a mainstay and the grain magazines proved useful. The minister urged the collection of herbs and the consumption of horse meat, but he probably had little success; peasants everywhere are conservative in their eating habits.

All the activities to encourage agriculture and trade were channeled into a more systematic frame in 1809 through the creation of a central "Society for the Norwegian Weal." Abel became the local chairman for Gjerstad and the surrounding districts; probably nowhere did the society have a more eager member. He offered loans free of interest to farmers breaking new soil; he awarded prizes for gardens and orchards, for the greatest number of fruit trees planted, for the cultivation of flax, hemp, and hops, and for home industry. He did not hide his achievements; all the while he was publishing his reports in the little Oslo newspaper.

Some proposals were doubtless impractical. Rather characteristic of these idealistic, nationalistic projects were a number of prizes offered by Henrik Carstensen in Risör: "A prize of 40 daler to be awarded to the first couple of Gjerstad and Söndeled who on the day of their wedding shall appear in clothes produced from materials harvested, prepared, and dyed in these districts and who use these garments every Sunday for a year. For the second and third couples the prizes are respectively 30 and 20 daler. Ribbons and kerchiefs only are excepted, but if these also are produced here, the prizes are augmented by one-half." The women took their full share in the patriotic enterprises. There were daily distributions to the hungry and the poor, collections for suffering districts and for the sailors imprisoned in England. Bandages and warm clothing must be prepared for the brave army which so far had succeeded in beating off all Swedish forays.

In 1811 the Society for the Norwegian Weal took a momentous step by making a national appeal for funds for the creation of a Norwegian university in Oslo. Abel was again the leader in his district. In his enthusiasm he promised a personal contribution which was later to prove too

21

great for him to fulfill: 100 daler in cash immediately and annually 10 daler and a quantity of grain from the little farm at Lunde which he had inherited from his father. Old Simonsen in Risör gave 2000 daler, a large sum, but relatively a smaller sacrifice since his income had been enormous.

The national collection was a great success: nearly one million daler was obtained for endowment. The Danish king, Frederik VI, had definitely not been in favor of the undertaking, but he accepted the overwhelming public mandate with good countenance, donated the estate of Töyen near Oslo as a site for the university, and graciously permitted the new institution to be called "The Royal Frederik's University." Incidentally, the king also let his royal grace shine upon Abel; in 1813 he awarded him the order of Dannebrog. Undoubtedly it was with a great deal of satisfaction that Abel thereafter added the title "Knight" to his signature.

The Napoleonic era was drawing to a close. In Sweden the royal family was dying out and the government deemed it advisable to select a capable military man as successor to the throne. Their choice fell upon one of Napoleon's most able generals, Marshal Jean Baptiste Bernadotte, Prince of Pontecorvo, later to be known as King Carl Johan. His military mind immediately conceived the idea of a conquest of Norway. As a result, when the Napoleonic empire fell apart, Bernadotte deviated from the straight march on Paris and invaded Denmark. In January 1814, Denmark was compelled to sign the peace treaty of Kiel, ceding Norway to its victorious opponent.

In Norway the news was received with consternation and bitterness. Hasty elections were held for representatives to an assembly at Eidsvoll with the mandate of composing a constitution for the country. It proved to be a document formulated in wisdom; it has served the country ever since without great changes. The viceroy, a Danish prince, was elected king, and frantic efforts were made to collect money and equipment for the army and the new volunteer corps. But against an opponent with Bernadotte's military experience and twice the number of seasoned troops that Norway could command, there was no hope of victory. An armistice was arranged with the understanding that while a union with Sweden would be accepted, it should be done in legal form and Norway should not be regarded as a conquered nation. Perhaps there still lingered in Bernadotte's mind some recollections from his own revolutionary days.

An extraordinary session of the parliament, or Storting, was called to effect the necessary changes in the constitution before the election of the Swedish king to the throne of Norway. Abel was a representative to this important session and was not without influence in the deliberations. In one of his speeches he summed up his views: "When by these stipulations we have taken into account our national honor, our liberty, and our rights as citizens, when we have taken due precautions that no subjugation in any form or by any regent is possible, then let us be the first to extend a brother's hand to the Swedish people, then let us as a free nation offer Carl XIII that scepter which he has hitherto not been destined to carry."

Among the constitutional safeguards that were considered was a section intended to prevent the appointment of Swedish officials to Norwegian positions. Abel felt strongly on this point, but several peasant representatives were not inclined to support him. On the eve of the final vote Abel invited them to a punch party and under the influence of generous libations he succeeded in converting enough of them to ensure a favorable vote.

Abel's greatest distinction was now conferred upon him; he was appointed to the deputation which was to go to Stockholm to present the Swedish king with the formal act of union, ratifying his election to the Norwegian throne. But a last-minute leg injury prevented Abel's departure.

In his diary Bishop Pavels, a contemporary observer, passed judgment upon the actions of the various members of this Storting. About Abel he had this to say: "Pastor Abel made beautiful speeches, but the methods he used to enroll votes in the naturalization case cannot be approved. In intercourse one always notices a too ribald student tone."

Pastor Abel had gone far toward gaining national reputation, but his father, the old pastor, would probably have viewed his course with concern and warned: 'For what is a man profited, if he shall gain the whole world, and lose his own soul? or what shall a man give in exchange for his soul?"

2

THE CATHEDRAL SCHOOL

◆§ IN THE FALL OF 1815 it was decided to send the two oldest Abel boys, Hans Mathias and Niels Henrik, to school in Oslo. Niels Henrik was only thirteen years old, younger than usual for a boy to be sent away from home, but there seem to have been special conditions at the vicarage which made it desirable. Until now the father had been in charge of the boys' education, but as they grew older, their lessons required more time than he could spare. He might have followed the custom among higher officials and engaged a tutor for his children, but his economy could not afford such an expense. However, it was not only the Abel finances which were in a miserable condition, there were also indications that the reputation which Pastor Abel had built during many years of assiduous work was beginning to crack.

Sometimes he showed poor judgment in community work. According to an age-old custom the peasant boys were wont to visit in the girls' sleeping houses on Saturday nights. Abel preached against this immoral custom and when no improvement was noticeable he tried to catch the culprits by joining some of the itinerant groups in disguise; it certainly did not add to his prestige to be unmasked during such excursions. Gradually Abel seems to have lost some of his cordial and heart-warming manners, and gave way to authoritarian and even dictatorial habits in his dealings with the congregation. He had always shown a greater inclination to use forceful means than had his peace-loving father, who relied largely upon moral principles to inspire fear of the Lord. To reduce the number of beggars and vagrants Abel engaged deputies to chase them away. More incisive in the life of the community was the formal contract which he concluded with twenty-five peasant representatives on behalf of the congregation. It was, indeed, a document attesting to the power of the minister in the community. Here was pre-

scribed in great detail what luxuries were permitted in dress and enter
tainment for all occasions. For instance, at a wedding no more than four
bushels of malt could be used for brewing beer; only eighteen quarts
of brandy could be consumed, two pounds of coffee, no imported wine
or other beverages. The agreement was a legal document, contraven-
tions were to be punished by fines, enforced by the courts. The contract
was to be perpetual, read from the pulpit twice a year.

There were other difficulties as well. To the parish of Gjerstad was
attached an annex district, Vegaardsheien, located in the uplands a
considerable distance through the mountains. Access to it was difficult
and Pastor Abel's required visits could entail great hardships, particularly in the winter; even his patient father had exclaimed more
than once: "These trips to the highlands will be my death." But it
was not only the inclemencies of the weather and roads which made
the work in the annex so oppressing. The parishioners could at times
be extremely difficult to deal with: they felt slighted because the pastor
spent by far the greater part of his time in the central district; they
magnified or willfully distorted small incidents. One Sunday Abel
missed the services and on the next occasion they closed the church
door in his face. Abel made great efforts to effect a reconciliation; he
collected money for a new church and himself gave 100 daler, as much
as the richest farmer. His dedication speech was so moving that it was
separately published, but all in vain. Abel finally tired of these vexa-
tions. Quietly he arranged with the bishop to have the annex transferred to another parish from which the access was supposedly easier.
But, though eager to rid himself of his troublesome parishioners, he
was not willing to renounce in full the accruing fees. This involved
him in a violent dispute with his neighboring colleague, a conflict
which was not resolved until the bishop stepped in with a dictum.

But still more serious than all these wranglings were the ugly rumors
in circulation about the family life at the vicarage. No one could blame
the pastor, or even his wife, for a few daily drinks, but evident intoxication could not be tolerated in the public opinion. And graver yet
was the common talk that the minister's wife was not the paragon of
virtue that her position demanded; the servants dropped hints that
under the influence of alcohol she could be quite free with her favors.

All in all, Pastor Abel felt that it was high time for the older children
to receive their education elsewhere.

Niels Henrik and his brother entered the Cathedral School in Oslo, a venerable institution founded about 1250 A.D. and long the Latin school for children of government officials. Fortunately for the Abels, it was able to award fellowships to needy students: it still retained some of its medieval wealth and had another source of income in the fees earned by student choirs which the school was obliged to furnish for Sunday services, weddings, and burials. The first year the father paid tuition for Niels Henrik and his brother, later they were supported by the school.

The school's rector, Jacob Rosted, was a sincere humanist who through long years of service had built up the faculty and the facilities of the school in a most capable manner. It was ironical to him that the new institutions which the nation so revered, the Storting and the university, were now threatening to undermine his life's work by stripping the school of both building and personnel.

The school owned an excellent building; its auditorium was the only large hall in the little provincial town which now was to serve as the capital of a nation. And so, while the Storting was in session, it took over the auditorium as well as many of the classrooms, compelling the school to rent rooms in town wherever they could be found. When Niels Henrik entered the school its place of exile was a dance hall which had been partitioned into small classrooms by temporary board walls. The arrangement was highly unsatisfactory: the noises carried from one room to another and the air was "stinking and unhealthy." The rector and the faculty complained bitterly, but without results.

A few years previously the teachers at the school had been among the best in the country, but when the university opened its doors no fewer than four among them were appointed as professors at this institution and others followed shortly after. Even the janitor took advantage of the situation for "scholastic" promotion.

The school's new teachers were insufficiently qualified; in addition, some of them suffered from the most common defect of the times, drunkenness. The Cathedral School carried in its medieval seal the cross-laid insignia of the birch and the ferrule: the symbols that learning should be beaten in. Rector Rosted had succeeded in abolishing all corporal punishment, but with the new teachers discipline again became a prime problem. To assert themselves in class they often resorted

26

ABOVE *The Oslo Cathedral School (1718–1823).* BELOW *The courtyard of the Cathedral School*

to blows and kicks, and a rough-and-tumble fight could develop when the victim retaliated in self-defense.

A great loss to the school was the appointment of Sören Rasmussen to a professorship in mathematics at the university. He was an excellent teacher. One of his former pupils, now astronomer and professor of applied mathematics, Christoffer Hansteen, confessed that it was Rasmussen's classes which first awakened his interest in mathematics and science. "I have never seen anyone with his ability to instill interest in his subject, to lecture clearly and thoroughly, and to keep the strictest discipline with his mien or at most with a sharp word." Sören Rasmussen had, in addition, pronounced administrative talent. He played a prominent role in all the practical problems which had to be solved in the newborn country; he was one of the moving forces in the Society for the Norwegian Weal and one of the principal organizers of the newly created Bank of Norway.

The replacement for Rasmussen as mathematics teacher was Hans Peter Bader, from all evidence a poor bargain. It is true that Bader knew his subject, but the pupils were unanimous in their opinion that in the severity of his punishment he far exceeded all other instructors. He could be brutal in his attacks and the rector frequently heard complaints from the boys that they "had received a bloody nose, a swollen cheek, or an aching head" from being beaten by Bader. Rosted admonished him, but even the rector was forced to admit that the relations between teacher and students had steadily worsened and developed into aversion and hatred, particularly "because of Bader's generally harsh manner and the malicious way in which he laughed and ridiculed those who could not succeed on account of their lack of ability or inclination to study."

The main subject in school was, of course, Latin, with some added instruction in other languages, religion, history, and geography. Niels Henrik had also three hours a week of mathematics. In addition, he studied a good deal of Greek; since he did not intend to study theology he was permitted to substitute English for Hebrew. A quite unusual and temporary innovation was a smattering of natural philosophy.

It appears that Pastor Abel had tutored his sons quite satisfactorily; they began with no difficulties and received high marks. As a prize for

27

diligence Niels Henrik was awarded a book on natural science. He did not receive the prize in mathematics although Bader gave him excellent marks and reported that he was satisfied. Both boys seem to have behaved well; Rector Rosted wrote that Niels Henrik's deportment was "very good, orderly, and modest" and the other teachers acceded. One of them added that he was "a little roguish," a comment which probably indicated that he was fond of a little fun.

For a pupil, life in Oslo did not offer too much diversion. School hours were long, preparation and church singing took considerable time. Pocket money was certainly very scarce so that amusements had to be of the cheapest kind. The greatest events were theatrical performances. During the winter seasons there were presentations once or sometimes twice a week. If he could possibly scrape the money together Niels Henrik would be in the audience. Throughout his life the theater remained among his greatest joys. Occasionally some of the pupils at the Cathedral School had taken part in performances as extras but such a frivolous occupation was considered so improper that it had been criticized in the newspapers.

Besides the theater there were chess and card playing, both pastimes in which Niels Henrik showed unusual skill. But above all, he was dependent upon being part of a circle of friends. In a party he was the gayest among the gay, alone he was sad and depressed. He described himself in one of his later letters: "As it happens, I am so constituted that I absolutely cannot, or at least only with the greatest difficulty, be alone. Then I become quite melancholy and not in the mood for work." He suffered from bashfulness and was deeply perturbed whenever he had committed some *faux pas*.

Among his best friends was his schoolmate Carl Gustav Maschmann, better known by his nickname Basen (the Boss). His father was a leading citizen in town, the owner of the Elephant Pharmacy on the central square. The Maschmanns were acquainted with the Tuxen family; the apothecary in Arendal, Ole Tuxen, the brother of Lieutenant Tuxen, had served as Maschmann's pharmacist. The big house was open to Niels Henrik and he visited almost as a son. Long before any university existed in Oslo old Maschmann had been made titular professor, an honor occasionally bestowed by the Danish king, often without much regard for the intellectual standing of the recipient. Maschmann, however, was a qualified chemist who occasionally lec-

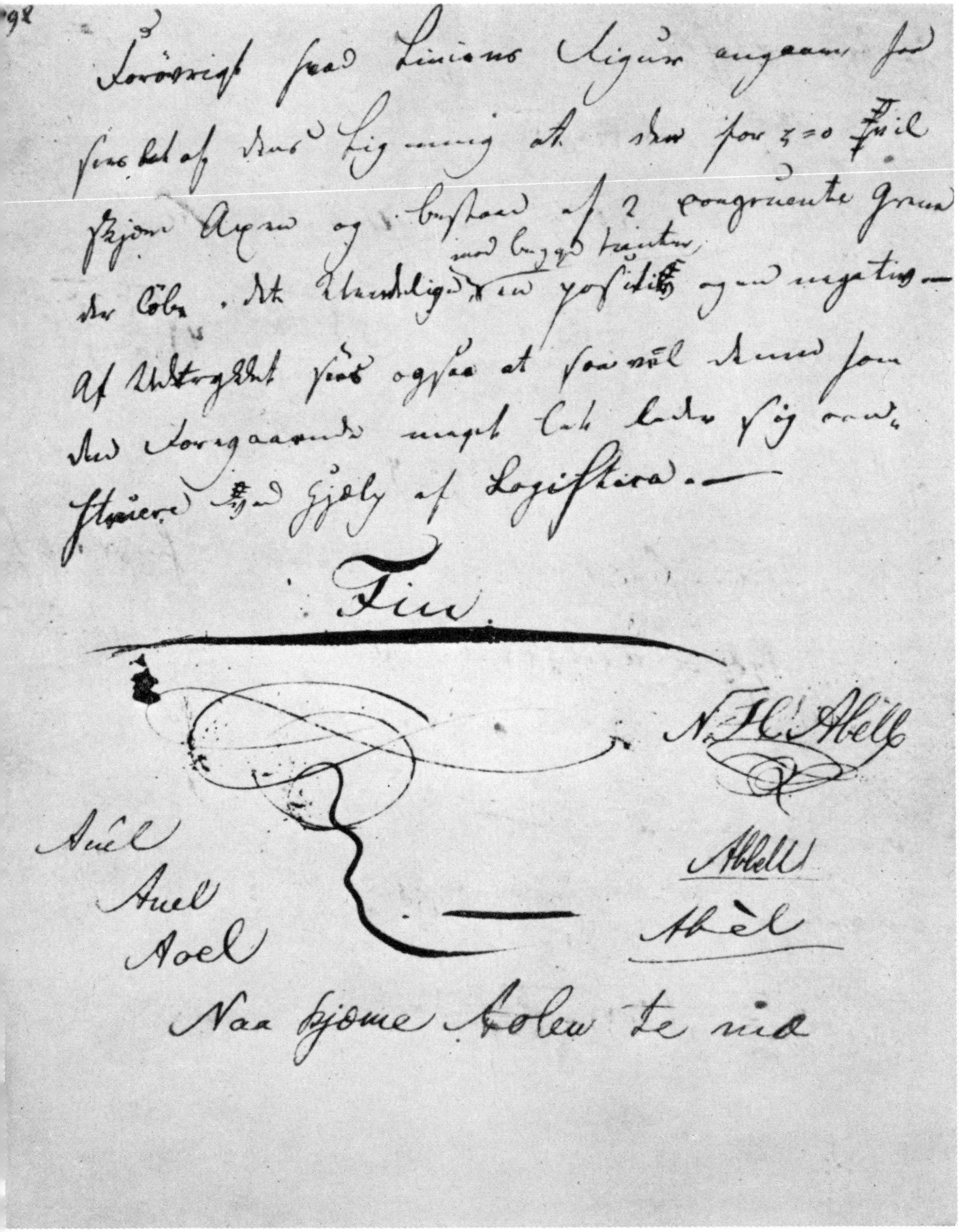
Fin.
N. H. Abel

Facsimile of one of Abel's manuscripts from his school days

tured at the university and always remained a devoted patron of the sciences.

At the age of fifteen Niels Henrik was confirmed in the Church of Our Savior and the pastor reported that his deportment and knowledge were excellent. But in school a decline had set in, his marks deteriorated, and in 1817 and 1818 he was only provisionally advanced. He could not muster much interest for any of his subjects, and several of his teachers were difficult for him to deal with. He did understand his mathematics, but Bader beat him nevertheless; in the fall of 1816 he could no longer stand being tyrannized and quit school for a while.

Even if Niels Henrik did descend to the lower ranks in his class, the activities of his father prevented him from gaining the anonymity of mediocrity. In these years few men could find their name in the newspaper columns as often as did Pastor Abel. There were in particular two public controversies in which he took a prominent role. In both cases the polemics were conducted according to the then accepted principle that the most effective procedure was to insult and ridicule the opponent, rather than to illuminate conflicting views by cogent arguments.

Truthful Account of Denmark's Political Crimes against Norway was the title of a publication which appeared in 1816. It was anonymous, but everyone knew the author to be Nicolai Wergeland, a minister in Christiansand, whose hostile feelings toward Denmark were well known. The book divided the country into two camps. The ensuing public discussion, which lasted for several years, was as unrestrained as the publication itself. In the town of Brevik a copy of the book was placed in the pillory. Abel entered the fray with a bombastic challenge to the author — "the mountain brought forth a mouse," said the opponents — signed pointedly by Abel as "Knight of Dannebrog and Pastor in Gjerstad, near Brevik."

When the question of religious textbooks for the schools was under discussion a new newspaper controversy arose in which Abel's person came still more into the foreground. An anonymous writer published a long analysis of Abel's *Religious Questions* which had just appeared in a new edition. He denounced the book as rationalistic and even heretical and computed with extraordinary ingenuity that it must have been a contributory cause to the eternal perdition of at least 10,000 Norwegian children.

Abel was intensely angered, and in his first response he proceeded to show in fourteen elaborate points that his opponent was insane. He also challenged him, in case he should have any "lucida intervalla," to answer the rather pertinent but difficult question of how many souls he himself and the text he preferred had saved from perdition.

The extensive polemics elicited sharp attacks, but there were also distinguished clerics who stoutly defended Abel. One writer berated the anonymous reviewer for abusing a man "who during many years has held the post of teacher of religion among us and hitherto in this work always has been esteemed and loved, both in his congregation and elsewhere, and never has been blamed for his life or doctrine." But Bishop Pavels, commenting upon current events in his diary, was of the opposite opinion. He found that "Abel has disgraced himself to a far greater extent than his antagonists could do, by his haughty and declamatory reply to the opponents of his text. This response must be the product either of intoxication or of un-Christian arrogance. One ought to place the best interpretation upon everything; thus I willingly accept whichever of these two explanations may be the more charitable."

The discussion reached the level of the ridiculous when one witty contributor began formulating his item in verse, with all the rhymes matching the name of Abel. The idea released a flood of similar attempts and the material was readily available: sabel (sabre), snabel (elephant's trunk), and many others, supplemented by a raft of French adjectives: amiable, admirable, capable, miserable, deplorable, detestable, which in Norwegian rhyme perfectly with Abel. It seemed as if the whole town were rhyming. There still exists in Oslo a popular ditty which may derive from this incident:

> Abel, spandable
> hva koster din sabel?

(Generous Abel, how much costs your saber?)

Niels Henrik read the verses in the newspapers, he heard the ditties in school, and he winced. The history teacher, one of the best in the school, perceived the preoccupation of the young mind and the difficulties the boy was faced with. He reported that Niels Henrik's behavior was "very good; he is a quite singular person and somewhat depressed by the other pupils' having their fun with him."

3

AN INSPIRING TEACHER

&§ BOTH FOR THE sixteen-year-old Niels Henrik and for his father the year 1818 was to be a turning point in life: for Niels Henrik it was to open a new scientific world of ideas where he would soon rise to heights hitherto unscaled by anyone; for his father it was to represent the end of all ambitious plans and hopes, in short, the end of his career.

One day the town became violently excited, when rumors circulated that one of the pupils at the Cathedral School had been killed as the result of punishment administered by a teacher. The unbridled Bader had continued his reign of terror until one morning he went too far, mauling one of the boys to an extent which even for him was excessive. The victim, son of a representative to the Storting, died eight days later. Indignant citizens lodged complaints with the rector and with Bishop Bech, a member of the board of directors of the school, who both appealed to the highest administrative authority, the Department of Church and School Affairs. Bader was immediately suspended.

The students testified before an investigating committee that Bader had treated the victim cruelly. They all agreed that they would refuse to continue in school if the teacher was not dismissed. Bader admitted that he had put the boy in a corner of the room and had hit him repeatedly with his clenched fists, but denied having kicked him while he was on the floor. Bader was discharged, but not brought to court, because the physician who had attended the boy insisted that the cause of death was a nervous fever, not the beating. Evidently the teacher must have had his defenders, for he was not barred from further service in the school system. A statement from the Church Department, which seemed to confuse solemnity with wisdom, ran as follows: "Whereas Bader according to the testimony of the rector and other trustworthy men possesses a capability which ought not be lost to the government or to himself, whereas it may be presumed that he in due time will learn greater prudence in association with youths as well as with elders, the department does not believe that a discharge ought to be conveyed without hope or encouragement to him to make himself worthy of further advancement."

It was now necessary to find a substitute teacher immediately. Rector Rosted had in mind two brothers, Christoffer Andreas Holmboe and Bernt Michael Holmboe, who had graduated from the school a few years earlier. They came from a family of seventeen children; their father was now minister in a district some distance to the southeast of Oslo. Sören Rasmussen had considered them to be among his most promising pupils and both had continued their interest in mathematics at the university. Rosted first offered the position to Christoffer Andreas, the younger of the two, probably because he was interested in classical languages, which in the opinion of the rector were the foundation of all disciplines in the school. But Christoffer Andreas refused the offer and continued his linguistic studies, later to become professor of oriental languages at the university in Oslo.

Thus it was Bernt Michael Holmboe who early in 1818 joined the staff of the Cathedral School as adjoint, or assistant teacher. He was a young and enthusiastic liberal, inflamed by a patriotic spirit which had led him at his graduation in 1814 to join the student volunteer corps. Literature and music were among his interests; as a teacher of mathematics he was probably the best qualified to be found. He had been an assistant to Professor Hansteen, the professor in applied mathematics, and both at school and at the university he had been inculcated with the subtle art of instruction under Sören Rasmussen, the professor of pure mathematics. His knowledge of the subject was excellent, much greater than the schoolwork required. Still he never made any original contribution to mathematics; a few small papers which he produced are strikingly insignificant. His great contribution to science, for which he will always be remembered, was his awakening and guidance of Niels Henrik Abel's mathematical genius.

Holmboe began immediately to make instruction more interesting by letting the pupils work independently and by encouraging them to try their ability at some suitable problems. It did not take long for Niels Henrik to discover not only that this was fun, but also that he could master questions too difficult for the others. Holmboe encour-

ABOVE *Abel's uncle and aunt, Peder Mandrup Tuxen and Elisabeth Marie Tuxen.* BELOW *Abel's teachers, Sören Rasmussen, professor at the university, and Bernt Michael Holmboe,* adjunct *at the Cathedral School*

aged him, gave him special problems, and let him borrow his own textbooks from Rasmussen's course at the university. These were the standard texts of the time: Euler's Latin introductions to the differential and integral calculus. Holmboe wrote later: "From now on Abel devoted himself to mathematics with the most fervent eagerness and progressed in this science with the speed characteristic of a genius. In short order he completed elementary mathematics and then, after his request, I gave him private tutoring in higher mathematics. Subsequently he studied on his own initiative LaCroix, Francoeur, Poisson, Gauss, Garnier, and particularly the works of Lagrange. He already began to treat for himself various parts of mathematics."

It seems that once he had been seized by the enchantment of mathematics, Niels Henrik devoted almost all his time to it. No longer did he borrow novels and light reading from the school library; from now on he was interested exclusively in books in pure and applied mathematics; Newton's Works, Lalande's Astronomy, d'Alembert's Dynamics — truly heavy fare for a boy of sixteen. He recorded some of his mathematical studies in a large, gray notebook which is still preserved; "Compositions in Higher Mathematics by Niels Henrik Abel" one reads in beautiful calligraphy on the title page. The content consists mainly of well-known topics from the texts and some quite formal generalizations without great depth, but one feels strongly the boy's delight in combinations and computations of mathematical formulas. This school journal evidently dates back to the period before Niels Henrik had embarked upon serious original work.

Holmboe was excited over the progress of his pupil and missed no opportunity to praise Niels Henrik to the other teachers and even to the university professors. Already in 1819 he wrote in the report book: "An excellent mathematical genius." The next year his enthusiasm was still greater: "With the most excellent genius he combines an insatiable interest and desire for mathematics so that if he lives he probably will become a great mathematician." The three last words appear somewhat anticlimactic and they occur as a correction in the protocol. The original words have been carefully scratched; they might be construed to read "the world's foremost mathematician." Rector Rosted and his colleagues were not entirely in agreement with this specialization, which they considered harmful to the school's objectives; young Holmboe may have been requested not to use such immoderate expressions.

The rector as a true classicist emphasized the necessity for a harmonious development of the whole man. He elaborated on his point of view in a school program at this time: "Consequently it must be an important rule for the teacher that he, with the correct grasp of what each ability requires, prepares his instruction accordingly and never attempts to bring one talent to a perfection which cannot exist without the others."

Niels Henrik was blissfully ignorant of all pedagogical principles; for him personally it did not matter much what the other teachers thought or believed, provided he could remain in school. He had found his own talent and it provided him with a new understanding of the values which life can give; it filled his soul like music and made him forget all the irritations and adversities that he might encounter. He had also gained an older friend who admired him and faithfully stood at his side in all difficulties. It was a friendship which never cooled, even when fate later made them direct competitors.

During his last two years in school young Abel began in earnest to try his wings, and with the optimism of youth he attacked some of the most profound mathematical problems which still remained unsolved. Among them there was one, in particular, under intense discussion: how to solve the quintic equation, that is, an equation in which the unknown appears to the fifth power, or even equations of higher degree. The formulas, if they existed, would have to be complicated expressions containing root extractions, similar to those for equations of lower degrees. Niels Henrik made many attempts before he discovered a method which he was convinced would prove satisfactory. Neither Holmboe nor Hansteen could find any erroneous calculations or any flaws in the arguments.

In Oslo there were as yet no facilities for scientific publication and so Hansteen proposed that the boy's calculations be sent to the Danish mathematician Ferdinand Degen with a request that he recommend them for printing by the Danish Academy of Science. The students regarded Degen as a most peculiar individual, but as a mathematician he was the best known in Scandinavia and the only one who had made any original, albeit modest, contribution to mathematics. Degen was unable to discover any faults in Abel's method, but having greater experience than his Norwegian colleagues, he regarded the work with considerable skepticism, for there had been many great mathematicians of the past

34

who had made similar attempts and failed. In his response to Hansteen he said of the purported solution: "Even if the goal should not have been attained it shows that [young Abel] possesses an unusual brain and exceptional insight, particularly at his age. However, I must set the condition that Herr Abel send me a more detailed deduction of his result and also a numerical illustration."

Degen had the feeling that it might be difficult to make progress in the topics which Niels Henrik had chosen for his speculations; he advised him to seek new fields, a suggestion which very likely had great significance for the direction of Abel's future studies: "It is difficult for me to suppress a wish that the time and mental exertion which Herr Abel expends on such a topic — to my view somewhat sterile — could better be applied to a topic whose development would have the greatest consequences for analysis and mechanics. I refer to the elliptic transcendentals. A serious investigator with suitable qualifications for research of this kind would by no means be restricted to the many beautiful properties of these most remarkable functions, but could discover a Strait of Magellan leading into wide expanses of a tremendous analytic ocean."

No sooner had Niels Henrik seen Degen's reply than he proceeded to compute special examples, something he would undoubtedly have undertaken previously had he possessed greater experience. It soon appeared, as a result, that his solution could not be correct in all instances. This was a great disappointment to him, but many a young mathematician has shared his fate and grown wiser. However, on this problem Niels Henrik had not by any means said his last word; it represented only a first attempt to break through into new worlds of mathematical discoveries. He methodically revolved the problem in his mind and scrutinized it from every angle during the following years. He had confidence in his own force and, as far as ability and knowledge were concerned, he knew that not even the professors at the university exceeded him.

The episode soon became known in the school and the little town. It produced a reputation for the young pupil at the Cathedral School who had made calculations which neither his teacher nor the professors had been able to fathom and which they had been obliged to send all the way to the Academy in Copenhagen for judgment.

For Hans Mathias, the elder brother, school days were over. He had done very well in the beginning, better than Niels Henrik; after one examination he received a book prize: *Our Duty toward the Animals.* But the light of his mind had begun to flicker. In 1818 he was the last man in his class and in 1820 Rector Rosted was obliged to certify: "At first his natural ability was considered to be good, his industry even very good, both in school and on the homework. This continued until he advanced into the highest class, when his mind seemed to have become so weakened, and with it his interest and effort, that hope was small that he would ever enter the university. When his father, who was then still living, was informed, he found it advisable to take him out of school, the sooner the better, and asked that he be discharged."

4

DEATH OF THE FATHER

At home in gjerstad matters were rapidly getting worse. Old Grandmother Abel died in 1817 and with her disappeared one of the bulwarks against the downward slide of life in the vicarage. Money problems became steadily more pressing. The economic support which old Simonsen had represented also vanished; the financial crisis which followed the Napoleonic wars had swept his house and many other lumber trading firms into bankruptcy. About this time the Storting abolished virtually all restrictions on the distillation of alcoholic spirits, assuming that this would encourage agriculture, reduce imports, and free the farmers from their dependence upon the trade privileges of the cities. As a consequence almost every peasant ran his own distillery. When Pastor Abel found it difficult to pay his farm workers, instead of paying cash he gave his servants the yield of his potato fields. To make money they peddled their potato brandy at the church during the services; drunkenness and gambling around God's house became a common occurrence. In truth, for Pastor Abel it was a long fall from his early days of authority and good will in the community.

The pastoral duties in Gjerstad had become distasteful to Sören Georg, yet the possibility of a transfer was slight. Abel recalled nostalgically his stimulating term of service in the Storting of 1814 when he had been charged with tasks of nation-wide importance. He made great but ineffectual efforts to be re-elected in 1816; in 1818 he succeeded. His political opponent, a prominent ironworks owner, spat out the seeds of his sour grapes: "It suited me quite well that Pastor Abel was so desirous of going to the Storting that he moved heaven and earth to reach his goal. May he depart in peace, only I hope he does not, by the same disorderly life at the Storting as at home, bring shame on the people and district which he represents. Or perhaps such an intoxicated representative as he is better suited for the Storting than is a sober person like myself, who does not share my compatriots' exalted feelings in regard to the wonderful constitution of the country."

At the 1818 session of the Storting Abel was very active, took part in the debates, and served as a member of several committees. Politically he belonged to a group which at the time was considered the radical opposition, working for the progress of the peasants. As a consequence he was not in the good graces of the other public officials, who were irritated by his apparent attempts to impress the gallery. Bishop Pavels, who had never liked him, wrote again in his diary: "Through drinking Abel has despoiled his good natural gifts, and all he brings forth is said to be pitiable nonsense."

This was not an impartial judgment, for Abel did excellent work on the new bills concerning schools and education; in fact, from a modern point of view he was much more farsighted and progressive than the majority of his colleagues. He firmly opposed a new bill regulating the instruction in the high schools, which unquestionably would have represented a backward step. The bill provided that there would be no specialized teachers for the various subjects, each class was to have the same teacher in all topics. The basic subjects were to be Latin and Greek to a still higher degree than before; some even wanted to make Hebrew compulsory. Norwegian had a very modest place in the curriculum, while the natural sciences were to be completely eliminated.

Abel spoke against the proposal at great length and said in part: "It seems very peculiar that it is proposed to exclude absolutely those topics which interest the young the most, namely the sciences or information about nature. It is certain that there cannot be so much study of Latin and Greek that there should not be left a few hours weekly for the natural sciences." Nevertheless, the Storting approved the bill. The government, however, refused sanction, guided by the advice of Minister of Education Treschow, Pastor Abel's old teacher.

A proposal for reform of the public grade schools was deferred, much to Abel's indignation: "Permit me to observe that even if one provides ever so much for the advanced schools and if all wisdom could be taught there, it benefits us little if their effect is not spread to the lower classes by means of improved schools. Otherwise the higher school is like the rainbow: It delights by its colors, but contributes nothing to the fertility of the earth."

38

Abel had one personal triumph in the field of education: his proposal for the establishment of a veterinary school was approved and the first appropriation granted. He also suggested, probably guided by his own experiences, that it might be useful for the ministers to have tutoring in the veterinary art. He had to suffer some ridicule as a result, for it was easy to say, as one mocker did, "he wanted to make the pastors into horse doctors."

If Abel had confined his efforts to matters which he really understood, he might have left the session in good standing; possibly he could have continued to build that political career which now had become his prime ambition. But his nature was not suited to long-term strategy. Through lack of judgment and too impetuous a desire to appear in the political limelight he committed a fateful blunder. At one meeting Abel, without warning, read a statement from a manager of one of the ironworks, charging two representatives, Magistrate and Chamberlain Borchsenius and Solicitor Krogh, with unjust imprisonment of the man and encroachment upon his property.

The statement produced an uproar in the Storting; Abel's action was a personal attack unprecedented in that venerable assembly. The two jurists, as well as other prominent men who were involved, demanded specific proofs and satisfaction from him. Solicitor Krogh furiously stated: "Since Herr Pastor Abel has surreptitiously read in public, before the Storting and the audience in the gallery, without the permission of the chair or the majority of the Storting, the infamous complaint against myself and Chamberlain Borchsenius and has thereby made it his own, it is to be assumed that he must be held responsible for these malicious, shameful, and highly insulting charges and also for the torment, taunts, and mental anguish the presentation of them have produced."

To his sorrow Abel soon found out that the complaining manager was a man of dubious reputation who had been discharged from his position for various malpractices. Abel had not a single proof, and his only salvation would have been to make an unreserved apology. This he was not willing to do; he argued that every man had the right to present his complaints to the Storting. A committee appointed to consider the case recommended to the chair that "Abel be requested to make a statement to the Storting to the effect that he, misled by compassion for a person he did not know, had offended the Storting and

Solicitor Krogh by reading a supplication containing dishonorable attacks, in part against Krogh. Since he had no reason to believe these charges to be justified, he now declared them to be null and void and asked the Storting and Solicitor Krogh to accept the statement as a satisfaction for the insult which had been suffered."

This was a last and well-prepared attempt to give Abel an opportunity to settle the affair in an honorable way, but he stubbornly refused to agree to the proposed apology. As a consequence impeachment proceedings were considered against him. However, by the end of the session tempers had calmed down sufficiently so that the Storting had come to feel that impeachment was a cumbersome machinery, to be set in motion only in more worthy and important cases.

Pastor Abel returned to Gjerstad in the fall of 1818 after having made a last desperate attempt to be transferred to a different district. Sad and disillusioned, Abel no longer could envisage the future with any hope of seeing the fulfillment of his ambitions. In the community work he could find neither peace nor satisfaction; at home love and happiness were denied him. Alcohol became his sole consolation and he drank to such an extent that it soon was evident his health was breaking. It is told in Gjerstad that one day on a sick call Abel was so exhausted that he had to rest his head on the table when he sat down. The deacon brought a pillow and could not help observing, "You will not live long." Abel inquired: "How long do you think I may last?" Reluctantly the deacon observed that it was difficult for him to say. "Do you believe another year?" Abel insisted. "Scarcely," the deacon admitted.

The bishop, concerned for his congregation, dispatched Dean Krog for a visitation in the fall of 1819. It was an ordeal for the pastor. For his sermon Abel fell back upon his favorite topic, education, but even this was difficult to master. The dean reported:

"The congregation in this district is very willing and eager to attend church as one may see from the number of old and young who appeared on this workday during the busiest harvest time. The minister, Herr Abel, Knight of Dannebrog, preached on education, Ephes. 6:4: 'bring them up in the nurture and admonition of the Lord.' This man is no longer what he has been, and can hardly be restored. There was a time when this man labored for the good cause of education in this district as well as in the annex of Vegaardsheien which later was separated from it according to his own wish.

"Now he preached briefly with a voice which hardly could be heard where I sat. False ambition, a miserable home life, and dishonorable habits seem to have made only chaff of the beautiful seed, promising fruition, with which nature had endowed him. What little was said from the pulpit was orderly, but far from complete or satisfactory. Undoubtedly he felt the deficiency in his whole position — he excused himself publicly, in part by his long absence from his position during the last Storting, in part by his debility after his return. All I could reply was that neither from private persons nor from officials had it been requested that he seek assistance in his office. What I deplore most in this district at present is the lack of knowledge in the young people of natural religion in general and Christianity in particular."

Early in 1820 Pastor Abel was taken seriously ill. At the time Captain Tuxen was traveling abroad on a mission for the Danish navy. His wife Elisabeth had been keeping him informed of the news from Copenhagen and the family in Norway, but she was in childbed when word of Abel's sickness arrived and her brother-in-law, Ludvig Tuxen, wrote in her place: "From brother Ole [Tuxen in Arendal] we have received a letter, also for you, but since it is opened and of little content I copy it to save postage. It came by means of his brother-in-law Smith at Froland works. He mentions that Abel is sick, from what illness I do not know; however, I believe it is not serious. I have said nothing to your wife since I fear it might produce unnecessary and harmful concern."

Pastor Abel rapidly grew worse. Elisabeth Tuxen reported his condition without sympathy; she mentioned repeatedly his drunkenness and unreasonableness: "Abel is said to be so miserable that I expect word any day that he is no more. Anne Marie does not grieve, so there seems even less cause for any of us to do so. He has been drinking so heavily recently that he has weakened himself completely; it is a pity."

Captain Tuxen replied from Rochefort: "You say that Abel's illness is serious. Should he recover it might have a beneficial influence on him; it is horrible how he has changed. It is peculiar that this is the first place I have seen the name Abel, and here it is, painted on the wall of my room, the first familiar name since I left. It must have been a Dane who wrote it, for it is no French name. It was one of the first things I observed when I arrived and it struck me as being an omen."

In June 1820 Elisabeth could report: "I recently had a letter from Norway: Abel is dead. I knew it so long in advance that I cannot say it made a great impression upon me. Had he lived he would nevertheless have been lost to the world and to his family, but later on we can talk more easily together about the reasons for the fall of this man, who by nature was endowed with such rich and rare gifts. What decision my sister has made I do not know; in her place I would remain at Lunde and cultivate potatoes, but I do not know whether she can because of the children. I shall let you know as soon as I hear."

Tuxen also received the news without emotion, but he was aware of the conjugal tragedy now concluded: "I was prepared for Abel's death. It is melancholy that a good friend can change to such an extent that one can see him pass without sorrow. He was once a man worthy of respect, and we both loved him. He must have died about the time I saw his name in Rochefort; I arrived June 11, but then he was already dead. . . . I do not know how he felt, but it cannot be said that Anne Marie treated him as she ought. God forgive her if she could have averted any evil."

The burial was an appalling occasion; if in the congregation there still remained shreds of respect for the minister's widow they vanished on this day. In spite of her children and her family, the members of the congregation and the visiting officiating clerics, she consoled herself flagrantly, first with drink and then with her favorite among the servants. The next day she received the condolences of the departing officials in bed with her paramour at her side. The sister in Copenhagen suspected from letters of friends concerning the burial that something was amiss; she wrote to her best friend in Risör and asked for and received an explicit account. It is evident that from this moment she transferred the blame for the marital tragedy from Pastor Abel to her own sister Anne Marie:

"I assure you, I was petrified after the reading: On his deathbed Abel was compelled to recommend his children to the care of others, while their mother was still alive. What I felt by all this, my dear Tuxen, I cannot describe, it is my own sister. I commiserate deeply with her, but I cannot deny it is mingled with bitterness. I have often, even when I was very young, shuddered at the thought of her character and domestic relations; it could not end well, but I would have considered it impossible for a person of the more cultivated class to fall so low. Since she really does not lack intelligence it seems futile to attempt to bring her to reflection and a better life.

42

"I have just written her a letter as if I knew nothing, consoled her upon the loss of her husband, and recommended her to seek happiness in the upbringing of her children. I believe what I wrote on this occasion will impress her more than all reproaches, but alas, it is altogether too late. I assure you, my whole body shakes when I write about this, but I felt that you ought to know."

Afterwards, "I have heard nothing; more than a month has passed since I received that pretty news. I both wish and do not wish to hear something again. It would be best, I believe, if I could forget I ever had an older sister. Hans [Mathias Abel] is the same helpless creature on whom neither sorrow nor joy makes the least impression. God knows what will happen to the others. They mourn their father deeply. You have known my sister and all of them just as well as I, so I shall not make any other comments. But when you have time write me a few words in the matter and let that conclude it."

Tuxen in his next letter is reluctant to touch this "beastly subject" but a little later he cannot avoid giving expression to his feelings:

"I often recall Anne Marie's strange character. I had always considered her to be phlegmatic and had not in the least ascribed to her such base passions. From Finnöy I recollect plainly that there was a good-looking peasant lad she liked well, but to me she appeared so cold that I could not consider it to be anything but simple kindness. However, I recall vaguely having heard something more about such an inclination. At that time in my green youth I loved Abel and Anne Marie with a sort of childlike passion. I shall never forget the walk from the vicarage to the shore when I left them. We all wept and I continued to cry a whole hour after I had embarked. They were a couple of blessed persons, at least in my view then.

"But nothing corrupts more than idleness; it is, in truth, as one says, the headrest of the devil. Anne Marie was never mistress in her own house; Abel also soon realized what he had missed in his wife. She never worked, he secluded himself in his tasks while she associated only with peasants. When he came to town he found cheer and gaiety, perhaps he found compensation for what was denied him at home. And that wretched passion — drinking — never decreases, always increases. The desire for work abated and at home he had no sympathy.

"Probably he has never treated his wife as he ought to. Crossness followed upon indifference; she lacked a sensible adviser who could

43

show her how to fulfill the duties of a housewife. It was not want of intelligence, but indifference and lack of better company which gave her inclinations a direction which she would have despised under other circumstances. But one is inclined to excuse oneself and she did not encounter soon enough anyone who attempted to turn her to a better path.

"So I forgive them both. My once so respected friend, who degenerated so terribly, has ended his joyless career; peace with his dust!

"Unfortunately it is now too late to ponder what he could have become with a capable wife or she with her good natural ability under better instruction and more careful guidance from her husband. She is still young, but her future does not appear in any pleasing perspective. She can never enjoy her children since they must be estranged from her. The poor little Elisabeth has no model worthy of imitation; the poor boys must comfort themselves on being in God's hand. Their best fate would probably be to become sailors or peasants; to be poor students is not enviable. She would probably fare best in the country if someone is willing to provide for the boys. To move to town with them would augur little good for her or for them.

"But this teaches us, dear wife, to appreciate good education as the highest enjoyment in life; God give us the strength to bring up our own flock in such a manner that we shall be able to depart from this earthly residence in the firm hope that we have formed our little ones into useful citizens, and, above all, active persons. Then they will never be unhappy, because if one finds inner satisfaction and has the strength and inclination to perform one's duty in this world, all difficulties fade away and all sorrows are smoothed out."

Fru Tuxen was also worried over the future of the children: "It really gives me many dark moments; my heart bleeds for the poor children. I have so often carried them in my arms without dreaming in the least of the miserable fate which lay in store for them. To me as well as to you this family was so infinitely dear. But what good is speculating about it? Perhaps her eyes might still be opened. The children may well become peasants as long as they are not always compelled to have this bad example before their eyes. Lately I have had no letters and I am ashamed to inquire about my family from anyone who I believe might know, for fear that they might have heard gossip about my sister. I would be really ashamed if anyone of our family here in Copenhagen should come to know about it."

44

The next fall Apothecary Tuxen in Arendal invited his sister-in-law to visit him while awaiting the arrival of her husband on his return trip from England. Fru Tuxen was unwilling to accept — Gjerstad had no attraction for her. Her father was dead. Her own family, like most of her Norwegian friends, had become impoverished in the crises following the Napoleonic wars. The wealthy days of Risör were gone; the joyful life had been stilled. But shortly afterward she could report: "A young man by the name of Aas has been appointed to the Gjerstad congregation, so that very soon all will have changed at this, our favorite place, where the foundation was laid for all my happiness in life."

The new minister, John Aas, came to Gjerstad a few months later and won the affection of the community. He was a gifted man who belonged to the first entering class of the university. Since he received the highest marks at the entrance examination of 1813 he was placed first on the list; as a result he has occasionally been called the first student at the new Norwegian university.

There were no public acknowledgments of the death of Pastor Abel, except for an impersonal memorial poem in the Christiansand newspaper by a friend. Bishop Pavels wrote finally in his diary: "The infamous representative to the Storting, author of the text 'Religious Questions,' Pastor Abel, is dead, only 48 years of age."

Sören Georg Abel was buried at the side of his parents in the cemetery at Gjerstad. John Aas prepared an inscription for the tombstone:

"Halt, wanderer, whoever you may be,
    let this grave remind you,
that often fortune's smile to tears turned.
Life may rise in joy as sunshine,
yet sighs and tears be its decline."

Fru Abel decide to live on the farm at Lunde and received a small pension from the parish. The youngest child was only six years of age. The family had no easy position in the community; economically the widow and her children were poorly situated, for evidently they had no ability to handle their own affairs. They may have hoped for an inheritance from old Simonsen, but at his death, a few weeks after Abel's, they received nothing; his estate was insufficient even to support his own widow. However, Pastor Aas faithfully looked after the family through many years and shielded them against the most serious wants.

For Niels Henrik a new period in life had begun; childhood and adolescence had passed. No longer was the home in Gjerstad a refuge; on the contrary, from this time until the end of his days it was he who bore the burden of responsibility for his family, even in times when his own difficulties appeared to be a weight heavy enough.

Niels Henrik faithfully made every effort to assist his brothers and sisters. By loving care and sacrifice he succeeded in saving those two who were closest to his heart, his sister Elisabeth, and the fourth of the brothers, Peder Mandrup Tuxen Abel. In the frivolous and irresponsible family there was no one to share his task. Hans Mathias by now showed strong symptoms of insanity and remained with his mother, helpless until his death. The third brother, Thomas, was still quite young, but possessed neither ability nor strength of character. Peder was the only one who showed promise. Niels Henrik still had only the scholarship from the Cathedral School for his support, but he had begun making his plans. His aunt, Fru Tuxen, wrote to her husband as early as September 1820, the summer of Pastor Abel's death: "I have had a letter from Niels Henrik Abel which in all respects was well written. In a year he will be a student at the university and he hopes then to earn something by tutoring other young people so that he may help his brother Peder who has a good head and wants to study. The poor boys, I feel awfully sorry for them."

At the University

5

THE FIRST UNIVERSITY YEARS

⋙ In July 1821 Niels Henrik Abel graduated from the Cathedral School, highly recommended by Rector Rosted. The entrance examinations to the university, the Examen Artium, were held the following month; he passed with mediocre marks in all subjects except mathematics. In arithmetic and geometry he was awarded a rare distinction — the highest mark, written in the peculiarly ornate way used to indicate exceptional excellence.

Niels Henrik was delighted to have reached the freer atmosphere of the university and eagerly looked forward to specialized work according to his own desire. To this there still remained one obstacle: the university at this time did not yet have any organized science degree. For all faculties there was a common introductory program leading to the Examen Philosophicum, usually requiring a year or at most two, and Niels Henrik was expected to take this examination.

The new university had practically no funds for fellowships, but did assist some needy students by providing free room, light, and firewood in Regensen, the university dormitory. Abel applied for this aid to the Collegium Academicum, the executive committee of the university:

"The undersigned who in the month of August passed the Examen Artium applies to the high Collegium to obtain one of the vacant places at the university dormitory. This request I base upon the fact that my father is dead and that my mother, who besides myself has five unsupported children, is not in such circumstances that she can give me any assistance."

For Niels Henrik, who had absolutely no resources, a free room was clearly insufficient aid; he therefore also applied for a cash grant. Some of the university professors, acquainted with the genuine promise of the young student, took an exceptional step; they personally contributed money for a fellowship, in order, as Holmboe later put it, "to preserve this rare talent for the sciences, a care to which he made himself more than worthy by his unceasing diligence and good behavior." Among his supporters were Professors Hansteen and Rasmussen as well as the rector of the university, Niels Treschow, who remembered Pastor Abel from the time when he was a pupil at the Latin school in Elsinore, and who always retained a kindly interest in the affairs of young Niels Henrik.

The university, in contrast to the itinerant Cathedral School, had just succeeded in finding a satisfactory permanent solution to its building problem. Originally it had been planned, somewhat romantically, that the university should be located at Töyen, the suburban estate presented to it by the Danish king, Frederik VI. A spacious park for the benefit of the students and townspeople was to surround the main building; each professor would live on his separate little farm with a couple of cows for his milk supply. However, the project was abandoned when by a fortunate coincidence the university was able to buy very reasonably one of the largest private town houses; in 1819 it moved into the renovated building, leaving Töyen as a residence for its rector. One of the wings of the new building was reserved for the dormitory, with accommodations for about twenty students. This then was Niels Henrik's home for four years. A pair of students usually shared a study and a bedroom; however, during the last two years Niels Henrik was honored by being granted the only single room available.

Niels Henrik had promised his brother Peder aid in completing his education, and during his first year at the university petitioned the Collegium to allow Peder to share his quarters. "I have a brother who intends to study, but the support he can obtain is not sufficient for his subsistence in Oslo, and so I venture to request permission from the high Collegium for my brother to stay with me in the university dormitory." It was considered highly irregular to let a fourteen-year-old boy live in Regensen — he was too young for the life of the gay blades — but after Abel's roommate had certified that he had no objection to the arrangement, permission was granted.

In January 1822 Niels Henrik wrote to John Aas informing him that the matter had been favorably settled:

"S. T. [Salvo titulo] Herr Pastor Aas: I have received your very honored letter of the 8th of this month and I am happy to hear that my brother is safely recovered from his illness and able to come to Oslo. I

ABOVE *The main buildings of the Oslo University (1820–1852).*
BELOW *The inn Noah's Ark, meeting place of the students*

cannot, my dear friend, thank you enough for your trouble, as well those gentlemen who are willing to assist my brother; my foremost wish is that I may be able to repay you. It was well that Peder did not arrive at Christmas time, because I went with Holmboe to his parents' home in Eidsberg, from where I returned only a couple of days ago.

"Let me say in regard to his journey hither that I can receive him at any moment, but since I have not been home for such a long time it is possible that I may come home in about a week and Peder can then accompany me on the way back. However, this I do not know for certain; I shall let you have word next mail day. Otherwise it will be best, as your Reverend observes, to find someone to drive him here overland. Kindly remember me to my mother, my sister, and brothers, saying that I am in good health and spirits. Obligedly yours, Niels Henrik Abel."

The letter was sealed with his signet: "N.H.A. Deus et virtus."

In his next letter Abel informed Pastor Aas that he would not come to Gjerstad, for classes were soon to begin and he had heard that the snow on the roads had been melting, making sledding difficult. "However, may I ask you to provide my brother with one pair, preferably with two pairs, of bedsheets for a double bed. Furthermore, I have a receipt for my mother's pension which cannot be paid unless I have an attestation that she is alive and unmarried; perhaps you would be good enough to write such a statement and send it to me with my brother." Peder did not get the sheets, they were to be sent later; whether they ever came is questionable because one of Abel's comrades related that the two brothers had only one set of sheets and when they were being washed, probably on rare occasions, the boys managed without. Peder arrived by ship shortly afterward and was duly impressed by the great town: "I met my brother in the best condition and he accompanied me to the market place where I saw much. I like the city of Oslo since it is a jolly place. Today for the first time I heard the military band which was very beautiful. So I don't know more to write this time, except that I am well and lack nothing."

In his next letter to Pastor Aas Peder sounded equally content — he was being tutored in Latin and French by some students and had the best of intentions: "I shall be as diligent and orderly as it is possible. All goes well. You may believe, I find Oslo a wonderful place, I could not have come to anything better. God reward you for all you have done for me. . . . It would be very good if also Thomas could be on his way, because to stay at home leads to nothing. . . . I have been to comedy a couple of times and enjoyed myself greatly. I don't know more to write this time except that I live well and lack nothing."

Money and clothes were scarce commodities for the two brothers. Niels Henrik's modest stipend had to be stretched to include Peder, although he did obtain a little support from Pastor Aas and some old friends of the family in Risör. In addition, Niels Henrik tutored in mathematics, but the income was presumably not great.

Niels Henrik felt at ease in university life and had many friends among the students. He was known to be gay and the closely knit group at the Regensen accepted him as a good sport. After their studies the students spent the evenings playing chess or cards, preferably Whist or Boston. If money was available they went for a midnight snack to Madam Mikkelsen's shop, also known as "Noah's Ark." This was an inn much frequented by peasants bringing their wares to town — hence it was still better known as "The Peasant Cheese." Some evenings they would spend in loud and lively conversation at the "Asylum"; this was a simply furnished back room in one of the town's modest eating places. The refreshments were equally spare — a glass of beer and a cornet of tobacco for the pipe served on a saucer. The variegated discussion was the main enjoyment.

One of the duties incumbent upon the members of Regensen was to write an annual report, in Norwegian or preferably in Latin, on some topic from their field of study. It was a bother to write such a composition, and shortly after Abel entered, they concertedly applied to be relieved of the task, justifying their request by the argument that they were so little advanced in their studies that what they said would have scant value. The Collegium was of a different opinion and felt that aside from the pedagogical value of expressing one's thoughts the students should be delighted to have such an opportunity to express their gratitude. The letter of refusal was circulated and everyone had to indicate by his signature that the content had been noted.

Lest someone be led to the erroneous conclusion that laziness in any way may have inspired this application from Regensen let us quote another request to the Collegium from the same body. It must have cheered all interested in the activities of the university except possibly the janitor and his wife:

"According to experience the morning is the part of the day best suited for studies, and thus we, the undersigned incumbents at the university dormitory, have become accustomed to rise at about 5 o'clock. Since, we, as most people, from childhood have been wont to enjoy a cup of tea immediately after getting out of bed, and also since it is harmful for the health to be about too long without nourishment, we take the liberty to apply to the most esteemed Collegium to obtain a modification of that rule for the university dormitory which gives us the right to receive hot water at 6 o'clock, to read that we in the future may obtain the same at 5 o'clock in the morning."

The university had several hundred students, most of them living in private rooms around town; but the little group at the dormitory served as a focus for all student actions and discontents, and their names usually headed the list of signatures on the addresses to the Collegium Academicum.

In the spring of 1824 the city received a state visit by the crown prince, Oscar, and the crown princess, Josephine, after their nuptials. An elaborate ceremonial took place. The students paid their respects before the royal residence by singing a pompous cantata in the evening. But the solemnity of the occasion was marred when disturbances broke out the same night among the public gathered at the central square. In town the students were blamed for the riot, and to clear their reputation a writ was presented to the Collegium demanding that an investigation committee be appointed. The Collegium replied wisely that it considered such action superfluous; the innocence of the students was taken for granted.

At times the relations between town and gown were marked by a good deal of tension. The students occasionally drank and celebrated, as most students do. Parents were worried, also not an unknown phenomenon. It was even proposed in the newspapers that the university be moved to a smaller town to avoid the temptations and dangers of metropolitan Oslo, which was rapidly soaring toward a population of 10,000. The town's nightly revel sometimes led to street fights and other disorders, all of which the citizens were inclined to ascribe to the students. The sons of Athene, on the other hand, felt they were being unjustly accused. This led to the hotly debated proposal that the students be permitted to wear a special uniform. The proponents of the idea argued, first, that it would give the student corps a more distinctive appearance on solemn occasions; secondly, that it would improve the relations with the burghers of the town.

The Collegium was opposed to the project and a minority of the students were unwilling to sell anonymity for a touch of military splendor. However, the proposal may have appealed to the military spirit of Bernadotte, for it was passed by royal decree. The student uniform consisted of a long military coat with embroidered lapels, broadly striped trousers, and a three-cornered hat with a cockade in red, blue, and white, the national colors. It was never commonly used and disappeared a few years later.

Aside from a little portrait by Johan Görbitz we know little about Niels Henrik's appearance. The descriptions in his two passports are at such variance that one can conclude with certainty only that he was able to read and write. The drawing was made in Paris and gives the impression of a face of unusual beauty and spirit. The resemblance to the subject is undoubtedly great as in all portraits done by Görbitz, but he had the fashionable painter's penchant for flattery and embellishment. None of his contemporaries mentions Abel as being strikingly good looking. One report says that he was of medium height, had ash-blond hair, and during his last student years looked pale and haggard. Life at Regensen was not particularly healthy and when the spirit of mathematical discovery moved him he probably often made night into day. He was noticeably slovenly in dress, rather from indifference than poverty; a few years later when he returned from abroad, his attire was quite à la mode.

Around the university and in town it was well known that Abel was a genius, supported by professors who expected great things from him. But he was a modest genius and did not dominate his circle of friends, or boast of his talents. He was immature in some respects, but certainly not impractical or detached from the world. He willingly and competently helped his friends, and when required, tended to his family's needs with understanding and thoughtfulness. But above all he was a friendly soul, himself deeply craving sympathy. Almost without exception those with whom he associated were drawn in friendship to him. It is remarkable how willing his friends were to speak for him and to assist him whenever it was required.

At home he was usually called Niels; among the students, who pos-

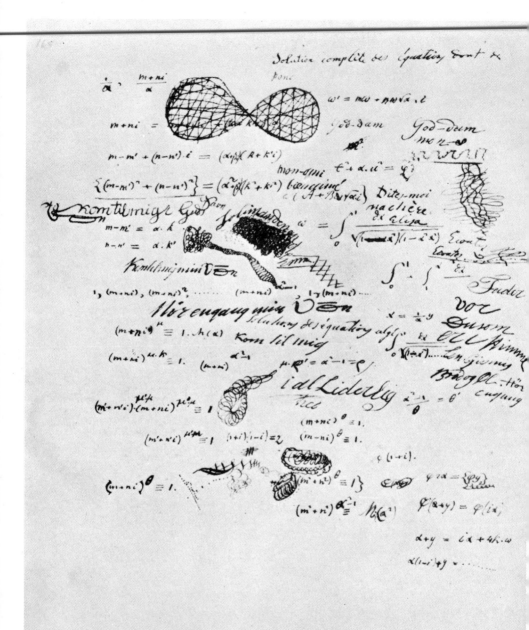

Mathematical doodling from one of Abel's manuscripts

sibly alluded to his pale countenance, he was known as "Tailor-Niels." Among certain special friends he was occasionally dubbed "Megaro," the man from Megara, probably an academic joke for the initiated denoting the "Second Euclid." (During the Renaissance the famous geometer in Alexandria was often confused with the philosopher Euclid from Megara.)

Niels Henrik doodled assiduously while engulfed in his mathematical studies and scribbled nonsensical words and sentences, not all fit for print. The name "Soleiman" (the great Turkish sultan) he wrote in so many variations that one almost feels that it indicates himself. A favorite phrase runs as follows: "Soleiman the Second, is a hell of a guy, so I say quite lewdly. Amen. Niels Henrik Abel."

The patronage of the university professors opened for Niels Henrik the doors to many prominent families in Oslo. With the unmarried Holmboe and his many brothers he associated on comradely terms; at young Maschmann's home he was very welcome. His visits to Sören Rasmussen's house were more formal, but the professor was filled with good will for the young man. It is true that his understanding of Abel's mathematical problems diminished: Rasmussen had become the financial expert of the government and his work for the Bank of Norway took too much of his time. The quality of his lectures deteriorated and attendance dropped correspondingly.

Christoffer Hansteen was the great light in the natural sciences at the new university, and Abel selected him as his faculty adviser. His distinguished studies of the magnetism of the earth made him famous throughout Europe. He had a practical bent, and his administrative ability was put to use in innumerable public commissions and projects. He created the university observatory and edited the Norwegian almanac for fifty years. He was director of the Geodetic Survey, supervised the mapping of the country, and was the expert member of the Commission for Weight and Measure.

Hansteen was a man of influence in the administration of the university, and it was principally he who laid the plans for Abel's education and scientific training. He also tried to interest Niels Henrik in his own research, though the attempt was not entirely successful. But while Hansteen guided Niels Henrik's career Fru Hansteen much more profoundly guided his soul and sentiments. He called her his second mother and never tired of praising her goodness toward him.

55

Johanne Catherine Andrea Hansteen, nee Borch, was the daughter of a Norwegian professor at Sorö Academy, outside Copenhagen, originally a school for boys of noble families. Hansteen had met her while serving as a teacher in Denmark before his appointment to the university in Oslo. Her father was dead; the family was large, six daughters and three sons. Her mother presided over a hospitable home in Sorö, where her beautiful daughters attracted some of the most prominent men in Denmark to her gatherings. The old lady enjoyed seeing happy people around her and even on her burial day she entertained in a way which preserved her memory for a long time in the little village of Sorö; in her will she had stipulated that on the day of her interment free beer should be served to all the needy.

Abel soon made the acquaintance of two of Fru Hansteen's sisters. The older, Fru Henriette Fridrichsen, invited him to Sorö on his first visit to Copenhagen. The other, Charité Borch, was the youngest of the sisters, and about Niels Henrik's age. She later married her cousin, a well-known Danish author, Paludan-Müller, who like Abel was greatly charmed by the sisters. He once described to Fru Hansteen the inspiration they had been for his writing: "How much I owe the Borch family, and in particular you and your two sisters Henriette and Charité no one can feel more than myself. It was a turning point in my life when I came to know you. How your singularly deep and varied nature — forgive me the expression — affected me, and still does, can never be erased from my soul; I consider it the richest gift ever granted me from heaven that my life on earth coincided with yours."

Abel had similar feelings although he could not express them in the same elegiac manner. Fru Hansteen was fifteen years older than Niels Henrik, old enough to be his "most beloved motherly admonisher" and at the same time young enough to feel his need for understanding and sympathy. The Hansteens lived in a large house, surrounded by an orchard, on the outskirts of town. As often as he dared Abel would wander out to make a call. Nowhere did he feel so at home as in this house. He would often fetch a footstool and sit at Fru Hansteen's feet, listening and talking. She gave him advice, encouraged him when he was downcast, checked his clothing so that it was not too disorderly, tried to help him over his bashfulness, and instructed him in the social graces.

Fru Hansteen carried her attempts at understanding the scientific

ABOVE *Professor Christoffer Hansteen, Abel's faculty adviser, and Niels Treschow, rector of the university.* BELOW *The home of the Hansteen family*

circle around her so far that she, with a group of prominent young ladies, attended popular lectures on physics and other scientific topics, an unheard-of innovation in town. It has been told that Hansteen, at that time without a laboratory, used her kitchen to compare the various standard measures with the prototypes for the country, which he kept at home. Fru Hansteen was an earnest assistant, but once she happened to file away too much from the weight she was working on. In her eagerness to restore balance she gave the precious prototype a couple of heavy strokes with the file. This may be true, at least it has been reported that later when the Norwegian pound was compared with the Danish standard it was a couple of grams underweight.

To Niels Henrik the visits to the Hansteen home were so precious that he was concerned that he might trouble her by coming too frequently. While on his return trip from abroad he wrote to Fru Hansteen that he expected to visit her often when he came home: "That will, indeed, be one of my greatest pleasures. My Lord, how many times haven't I wanted to call on you, but not dared? Many a time I have come as far as the entrance and then turned back for fear of inconveniencing you, for the worst thing that could happen would be that you should tire of me. It is well that I know that this will not occur."

The young Paludan-Müller again mirrors Niels Henrik's feelings; he saw her often while she lived in Copenhagen during Professor Hansteen's long expedition to Siberia: "You dear Andrea. Every morning when I pass Vestergade on business I look up to your windows. But you are not present, yet your spirit lingers up there, your image within my soul waves to me. I recall all of the past summer, your life here, my visits to you, our talks, disputes, small quarrels, your exhortations, your mild moralities — I never heard them from such dear lips — your friendliness toward me, so alive, so instructive and still so pleasant, the whole house takes on a sweet meaning to me, becomes so dear and sacred and I always recall the words of Goethe: 'Die Stelle, die ein guter Mensch betrat, ist eingeweiht.' I don't know how it is, but in my thoughts I often confuse you with my mother, she must have been like you, so mild, so loving."

In another letter Paludan-Müller develops the same theme in a different vein: "I have an intuitive picture of you all, and especially of you, the amiable observatress of the Norwegian observatory. Please mount the stairs to the large telescope once in a while and look down toward Copenhagen. There at the customs house you will see a young man in a tremendously long overcoat with a shaggy collar who eagerly looks for the Norwegian skippers, and when he encounters one he pulls out of his breast large packages full of longing and affections which he asks him to convey against a suitable reward to the address: S. T. Fru Hansteen, The Observatory, Oslo."

During Niels Henrik's student years Charité Borch came to Oslo for a prolonged visit with the Hansteens. For him as well as for many other young people in the capital she was an inspiration from the great world. One lady writes in her memoirs: "It must have been toward the middle of the twenties that Charité Borch came from Copenhagen to visit her sister, Fru Hansteen. When I now see a homely picture of Fru Paludan-Müller in a literary work I cannot reconcile it with the clear recollection I have of the refined youthful being I met at that time. In all her appearance she carried a message from a higher cultural sphere, a richer and deeper intellectual life than we were accustomed to. However, it was not by these characteristics that she unwittingly produced a revolution among us. The first time I saw her she had a red cotton print dress; it did not have a tight bodice, but waist and skirt were ruffled in front. This was called a blouse dress, extravagant and extremely daring, but well worth copying. But what should one do with all the tight dresses? There was not material enough for a single wrinkle except for the little queue in back."

Charité was charming and took an interest in the awkward mathematician who was losing his heart to her; his genius impressed her, but not to the extent that she was willing to share his romantic inclinations.

6

A TRIP TO COPENHAGEN

⚛§ In June 1822 Abel completed his preparatory examinations and was entitled to use the imposing title Candidatus Philosophiae. His marks on the whole were again mediocre; however, he was rewarded with the highest mark in theoretical physics and the same, with the special ornation, in mathematics. Now at last he was free to pursue his studies as he desired. During his school days and first university year, he had devoured practically the whole collection of advanced mathematical works in the libraries. From this time his passion for reading abated and his productive period began. Very early he had attempted original investigations, but the results had not been of any particular importance. Now he had passed from pupil to journeyman in a science of which he soon was to become a master. He felt that some of his new results were worthy of publication, but the great question was: Where?

This was a problem which confronted several of the budding scientists. Before the founding of the university, the scientific milieu in Oslo had been practically nonexistent. The new group of professors had brought about a rapid change and now a generation of gifted students was eager to embark upon the fascinating explorations of the natural sciences. Even during his years at the Cathedral School the precocious Niels Henrik had been deemed worthy to take part in the small gatherings of a group of science students. Gradually the meetings became more organized and finally a science society was established. Among the youthful leaders of this movement were two of Niels Henrik's intimate friends, who both had graduated from the Cathedral School a few years before him.

Christian Peter Boeck was the more dynamic of the two. His family was prominent: his father was manager of the large forests belonging to the silver mines at Kongsberg; his uncle, Jonas Collett, the minister of finance, was one of the best known men in the country. Young Boeck studied medicine, but he was equally interested in zoology and paleontology, and was continually devising new plans, new expeditions and travels. Immediately upon completing his Artium he had become teacher of natural philosophy at the War Academy and a little later military surgeon although his medical degree had not as yet been earned. "Herr Company Surgeon" his friends addressed him — perhaps a little ironically.

Baltazar Mathias Keilhau was of a quite different temperament. He had but one single, overpowering passion — geology. He had been the first to complete mineralogical study at the university and had then proceeded to the practical problems at the School of Mines at Kongsberg. He had written excellent papers and was generally regarded as the coming man in geology.

Mining had long been an important industry in Norway — proceeds from the silver mines at Kongsberg, the copper mines at Röraas and the many lesser ironworks were essential in the Norwegian economy. Norwegian nationalistic thought in this period was dominated by the idea that the vast expanses of the mountains could, by suitable exploration, yield riches which would in due time promote the country, now poor in population and wealth, to its rightful position among the cultured nations.

Keilhau was a strong believer in this idea, and he and Boeck had already made an initial effort by traversing some of the wildest unexplored mountain ranges in southern Norway. They scaled a number of the highest peaks — one of them still carries Keilhau's name — and the two are often considered the discoverers of Jotunheimen, the highest complex in Norway. An account of the expedition appeared in the newspapers and the two young students acquired a country-wide reputation. They also shared an ideal for which they continually worked, namely, the creation of a scientific society for the purpose of a systematic exploration of the country, preparatory to an evaluation of its natural resources.

It was recognized that the existence of a periodical for scientific publication was a prime necessity for scientific progress. During the fall of 1822 prospective patrons throughout Norway were asked to support such an undertaking, and nearly 200 subscribers were found; by reason

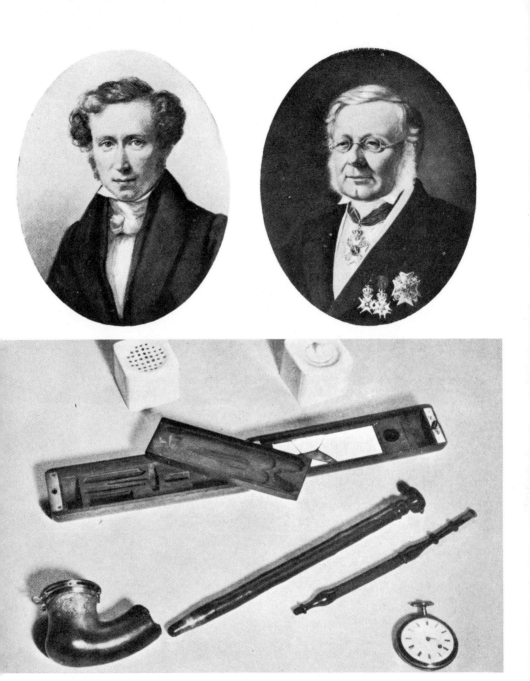

Friends of Abel's student years, Baltazar Mathias Keilhau and Christian Peter Boeck. BELOW *Abel's ink pot and sand case, his travel shaving case with mirror, his pipe, and his watch*

of the alphabet Niels Henrik headed the printed list. Early in 1823, the first number of the new "Magazine for the Natural Sciences" (*Magazin for Naturvidenskaben*) appeared under the joint editorship of Professors Hansteen, Lundh, and Maschmann. There is reason to believe that the latter carried the lion's share of the expenses.

The editors were eager to explain the purpose of the *Magazin* and the role of the subscribers: "We dare to consider the subscription as a small voluntary tax, which we have wheedled away from some of our compatriots, for the advance of this undertaking, and hope that only a few of our subscribers will regret having rendered a mite to it, although to them many articles may seem useless and uninteresting. It seems to us that it is most important to further the good and the useful by clearing obstacles out of the way and creating opportunities. If this does not help, it shows that no germinating ability exists, the soil is barren, and all further encouragement will be in vain. . . . Every new idea should be regarded as a treasure which may prove productive in the future. The principal goal of the *Magazin* is therefore to collect the grains of gold and make the yield available to all."

The number opened with a long article by Hansteen in which he reviewed the known measurements of the magnetism of the earth, its force and direction. He then advanced his favorite conjecture — based on the directions of the force in the southern and northern hemispheres — that the earth probably had two magnetic axes, and correspondingly four magnetic poles. On the northern hemisphere one pole coincided with the accepted one north of Canada; the other, he conjectured, was located off the coast of Siberia. At present such a theory, first promulgated by the astronomer Halley, may appear fantastic, but to Hansteen's credit let us add that at the time very few measurements had been made, particularly in such remote areas, and some of these involved systematic errors which actually made them point to another center. Hansteen added a note containing the rather sensational news that His Gracious Majesty, the king, had granted him permission to undertake a journey of observation, two or three years hence, through Siberia to the Bering Strait.

In the next number of the *Magazin* Studiosus N. H. Abel had the exhilarating experience of seeing his own work in print for the first time. It was a paper on the so-called functional equations, indigestible fare for the many subscribers who expected popular science. To soften the blow Hansteen had provided the article with an explanatory introduction:

"It may seem that in a periodical intended for the natural sciences, a memoir in pure mathematics is not in its right place. But mathematics is nature's doctrine of pure form. For the scientist it is similar to the dissecting knife of the anatomist, an absolutely necessary tool without whose aid one cannot penetrate the surface. Over the curtain which hides the entrance to the inner sanctum, the master builder of nature has placed the same motto as the Greek philosopher above the entrance to his lecture hall:

μηδεὶς ἀγεωμέτρητος εἰσίτω
[Let no one ignorant of geometry enter.]

"Most of those who attempt to enter without this provision will be turned away in the forecourt. But with it, Galilei, Huygens, and above all Newton, penetrated more profoundly than any of their predecessors, and handed their successors a guiding thread by means of which they may safely venture into the labyrinth. In this respect, present-day French physicists form for their contemporaries a model worthy of imitation; in their hands, therefore, every new discovery progresses much more quickly and definitely toward its perfection than in other countries.

"Thus I believe that the *Magazin* in addition to scientific materials, should also preserve the tools serving for their analysis. It will be reckoned to our credit that we have given the learned public an opportunity to become acquainted with a work from the pen of this talented and skillful author."

One newspaper reviewed the *Magazin* in detail and commented about Abel's paper: "A memoir which justifies the greatest expectation for the young mathematician." Encouraged by Hansteen, Abel composed some further small mathematical papers which appeared in subsequent issues. In spite of the praise they received, it must be admitted that for the most part these contributions were not of great importance, but were the smart calculations of a beginner. They were printed in Norwegian, but Abel's later reputation did not suffer because these works were not available to mathematicians abroad. However, the lion had begun to show its claws. One of the papers contained the solution of a so-called integral equation, a topic which only much later would develop into a very important field of mathematics.

The Norwegian readers of the *Magazin* cannot have enjoyed particularly this kind of article, for when the second volume appeared in 1824, Hansteen again attempted to defend the position of a research scientist:

"We have realized perfectly that many of our readers will have been disappointed in their expectations. Many looked for popular expositions, for few are interested in abstract investigations. To this we can only reply: Every research scientist works his way forward on a cumbersome and, in part, untrodden path. He cannot without great personal sacrifice abandon the position he has gained: he would lose more than others would gain. He can only inform us of his discoveries during his progress. For him to deviate from the direction he has decided upon to reach his goal would be contrary to his duty.

"But for those who for their own benefit write for the enjoyment of the public, the matter stands differently. They must accommodate themselves to the taste of the reader, as a firm to its market. We therefore repeat what we have stated from the beginning: We consider the support of our subscribers a small sacrifice which they voluntarily donate to elicit serious research and spiritual activity in their native country."

The first papers Abel published may not have been important, but during the winter of 1822–23 he created a work which in all likelihood would have been reckoned among his greater ones. Unfortunately we have not been able to determine its fate. In the minutes of the Collegium for March 22, 1823, this item may be found: "Professor Hansteen appeared before the Collegium, and presented a manuscript by Student Abel constituting a memoir with the purpose of giving a general method to decide the integrability of any kind of differential formula. He inquired whether the university would find it appropriate to assist in the publication of this work. It was decided to turn the manuscript over to Professors Hansteen and Rasmussen to make a joint report on the value of the paper, and in case it was found worthy, to propose the manner in which it most suitably could be supported."

For the first time Niels Henrik addressed himself to the international world of science: the paper was written in French. His fellow students at the dormitory were a little curious about how he had accomplished this, being well aware that in school he had in no way distinguished himself in languages. However, Abel countered with a joke — the article was so full of formulas that he only needed a French word here and there.

Shortly after this meeting of the Collegium Abel received a friendly letter from Professor Rasmussen, who enclosed 100 daler which he proposed be used for a trip to Copenhagen, so that Abel could make the acquaintance of the Danish mathematicians and their works. Niels Henrik was delighted.

According to the university rules, each student was expected to keep the Collegium informed of his whereabouts. On June 2, 1823, he reported: "The undersigned takes the liberty to report to the high Collegium that during the summer vacation he intends to undertake a voyage to Copenhagen. My purpose is in part to visit my family there, in part to extend my mathematical knowledge as far as time and conditions will permit. The journey will take approximately two months, so that I expect to return in the middle of August."

Before his departure Niels Henrik, together with Professor Hansteen, paid a visit to Rector Treschow at Töyen, presumably to carry fresh greetings to the rector's colleagues at the university in Copenhagen. Hansteen also took him to his tailor — probably upon the suggestion of Fru Hansteen — and Abel departed with two new suits, more elegant than ever before in his life.

It was the most wonderful vacation he had ever had. Overwhelmed he described his adventure in letters to Holmboe. The voyage began when he embarked upon a little passenger sloop sailing irregularly between Oslo and Copenhagen: "The first day we only made a few miles, the second we came to Dröbak where we stayed two days. I was invited to a party at Zwilgmeyer's [a former teacher at the Cathedral School] who has three pretty daughters. The next day the wind was favorable, so that we came out of the Oslo fjord, and the next few days we sailed swiftly. I arrived in Copenhagen on Friday, and proceeded immediately to the sister of Fru Hansteen, Fru Fridrichsen, where I was exceedingly well received. She is a very agreeable woman, is very beautiful, and has four stepchildren, but none of her own. Her husband left for the West Indies a short time ago. In a week she leaves to see her mother at Sorö and she has asked me to visit them there. I believe I shall accept the invitation."

While Niels Henrik was in Copenhagen he stayed with the Tuxens whom he could still remember from their visits to Gjerstad. "I am extremely well situated here in town. I live at the house of my uncle, Captain Tuxen, who has offered me free keep as long as I care to remain.

His family is very large and interesting, so I think it will be quite entertaining. He has eight children." This number was increased considerably in the following years. There can be no doubt that Niels Henrik had an amusing time: "On July 1, Regensen celebrated its jubilee, and I participated. We courageously drank 800 bottles of wine. There has twice been comedy. I was there both times; the last play was booed."

To fulfill his official obligations, Abel tried to meet everybody who was interested in mathematics. About some of his acquaintances he stated his opinion in no uncertain terms. On the other hand, the Danish ideas about Norwegian science were not very flattering. "Scientists here believe that in Norway sheer barbarism reigns, and I make every effort to convince them of the opposite." The two leading mathematicians were von Schmidten and the old Degen, who seemed particularly to have been to Abel's liking. "Today I saw Professor Degen, the most peculiar man you can imagine. He paid me many compliments, among other things saying that he could learn many things from me. This, as you may believe, made me very bashful. Degen is married, which I had not expected. He has a pretty wife, but no children."

In his next letter Abel played a little mathematical joke on Holmboe in dating his letter:

$$\text{"Copenhagen } \sqrt[3]{6\ \overline{064\ 321\ 219}}$$
$$\text{(Take the decimals into account.)"}$$

The calculation gives August 4, 1823. Here he wrote almost exclusively about mathematics and mathematicians: "I shall now report to you the observations I have made. Mathematics does not exactly flourish here. I have still not been able to ferret out among the students anyone who shows any promise, still less anybody who cultivates mathematics *ex professo* — The only one who knows mathematics is Degen, but in return he is devilishly clever. He has shown me several of his smaller papers and they have great subtlety. I have also shown him some of my own; he liked them and was particularly enthused over one on the factors of a number — he could not understand how I had found it. You remember the little paper which treated the inverse functions of the elliptic transcendentals; I asked him to read it; but he could not discover any erroneous conclusions or where the mistake may be hidden. God knows how I can pull out of it!"

Abel continued to note the new discoveries with which he became acquainted as well as the novel results he had himself obtained. It is most interesting to observe that besides the equation of fifth degree, he had made an attack upon another of the most famous unsolved problems, Fermat's theorem. Since the seventeenth century, when Fermat marked this theorem in the margin of a book, and stated that the space was too narrow for the proof, mathematicians have exerted themselves greatly to discover a demonstration. Abel wrote: "So I have tried to prove the impossibility of the equation

$$a^n = b^n + c^n$$

in integral numbers when $n > 2$, but I am at the end of my tether. I have not succeeded in going any further than the enclosed theorems, which are curious enough." The solutions which Abel included in his letter have since been called Abel's formulas. Even if it cannot be decided by means of them whether Fermat's problem is impossible, they do at least show that if solutions exist, they must be of colossal size.

As suits a novice traveler, Abel expressed himself quite critically about Copenhagen: "Everything is poorer here than in Oslo. — There are many windbags here. — The ladies are extremely plain, but neat." This last judgment Niels Henrik probably revised somewhat. He kept it a secret from Holmboe, but before he left Copenhagen he had fallen in love. He met the young lady for the first time at a ball, and quite optimistically engaged her to dance. After a few fruitless attempts they halted, looked at each other and burst into laughter: neither of them knew how to dance.

Christine Kemp, the lady of Niels Henrik's heart, was known by the nickname Crelly. She was penniless, but of good family, the daughter of War Commissar Christian Kemp. The father, long dead, had been head of the accounting department in the Admiralty. Captain Tuxen had had a great deal of business with him, particularly in regard to his prize money during the war. Although she could not be called a beauty, Crelly was very charming, fresh, and lively. Abel wrote to his friend Keilhau quite openheartedly: "She is not beautiful, has red hair and freckles, but she is a wonderful girl." She must have been independent and enterprising, for she decided to make her own living — a quite natural desire but unusual for young ladies of the period. She was well educated and once, in advertising for a new position, described herself as "a female from Copenhagen of kind, moral character, who gives in-

66

Christine Kemp (1835)

struction in French, German, drawing, the usual school sciences, and all kinds of needlework."

The return trip from Copenhagen took ten days. Abel came back in excellent spirits, eager to harvest many mathematical ideas which had ripened in his mind. Hansteen and Rasmussen procrastinated; the report on his memoir concerning the integration of differential expressions had still not been made. Abel began work on the two topics which had become his main interest: the elliptic functions and the theory of equations. Without using the most technical mathematical formulas and language, neither can be described in a satisfactory manner. Let us restrict ourselves to a few general observations, mainly on their history.

After the calculus had been discovered and it was possible to integrate the simplest types of functions, mathematicians discovered that certain kinds of integrals of square roots of expressions of third and fourth degree played an important role in many problems, in both pure and applied mathematics. One of the simplest of such problems was the calculation of the lengths of arcs of ellipses, and so they were called elliptic integrals. No one had found any expression for these integrals in terms of other, known functions; nevertheless, many interesting properties of such integrals had been discovered, particularly by the overwhelmingly productive Swiss mathematician Euler. At this time the greatest expert on the theory of elliptic integrals was the eminent French mathematician Adrien Marie Legendre, whose works were the point of departure for Abel's studies.

From the information which Abel gave to Holmboe in his letters from Copenhagen, it is evident that he had passed through the Strait of Magellan, which Degen had talked about, into a new ocean of mathematical discovery. He had arrived at an idea which would revolutionize the whole theory of elliptic integrals. Instead of investigating these integrals themselves, he turned to the inverse functions, the elliptic functions. By this device everything took on a different aspect. The theory of elliptic functions became an immense generalization of trigonometry. Many of the properties of elliptic functions became analogues of well-known laws for sine, cosine, and other trigonometric functions. Guided by this analogy Abel discovered a great number of important results, and at the same time, he revealed quite new, surprising properties which had no prototype in trigonometry.

Few fields of mathematics have as ancient a history as equation theory, the second principal field for Abel's research after his return from Copenhagen. The Babylonians and the Greeks knew how to solve quadratic equations in much the same way as is being taught in the high schools today. The Babylonians tackled in vain the cubic equation as did the Greeks, from whom the Arabs inherited the problem. When the great scholar Omar Khayyám tired of writing poetry, he turned to the mysteries of mathematics. The cubic equation was one of his favorite studies.

Not until the late Renaissance did the mathematical school in northern Italy succeed in reaching the goal for which classical and medieval mathematicians had striven without success. About the year 1500 A.D. the solution to the cubic equation was found by Scipione del Ferro, professor at the University of Bologna. Typical of the scientific outlook of the period, he found it advantageous to keep the discovery secret. Professors could be challenged publicly for their positions, and in such situations a secret weapon, a novel scientific method, was a most valuable asset. These learned rivalries, to obtain university positions or simply for the sake of reputation, often took on the aspect of a tournament at arms: bombastic challenges, public disputes over problems proposed by the participants, considerable money prizes, prominent referees, and a clamorous public which gambled on the outcome and cheered its favorites.

When del Ferro died, his secret was inherited by his son-in-law, Anibale della Nave, and by one of his pupils, Antonio Marie Fiore. The latter could not resist the temptation to capitalize on his knowledge, and in the year 1535 made the error of challenging the well-known *abacista*, master of reckoning, Niccolò Tartaglia of Venice. A few days before the expiration of the time limit for the deposition of the solutions, Tartaglia found the rule, and Fiore suffered an ignominious defeat. Neither did Tartaglia have any thought of surrendering such a valuable treasure, although it was well known that he possessed the rule. This brought him into contact with Gerolamo Cardano, physician and public lecturer in Milan, one of the many universal geniuses of the Rinascimento. He had prepared the manuscript for a text on mathematics; before it went to press he sent an emissary to Tartaglia to ask his permission to include in the book, as its crowning glory, the solution of the cubic equation. He was willing to give Tartaglia all possible credit. If he so desired, Tartaglia could write his own supplement to the book. Tartaglia was adamant; the rule belonged to him and if it were ever published it should be in a book of his own. Finally Tartaglia made a visit to Milan, and in a weak moment agreed to divulge the method to Cardano, provided he would swear never to publish the secret, or communicate it to anyone. Cardano swore by his Christian faith to fulfill these conditions.

The years passed, and in 1545, ten years after Tartaglia had rediscovered the solution, Cardano published his *Ars Magna*, the great art of algebra, a fundamental work initiating the study of the theory of equations in modern times.

Here is to be found among many discoveries the solution of the cubic equation, with the information that it had been originally discovered by del Ferro and found a second time by Tartaglia.

The *Ars Magna* contained another great discovery: the solution of the equation of fourth degree. A few years earlier Cardano had taken into his house a bright servant lad, Lodovico Ferrari, whom he had educated. The young man had a phenomenal mathematical aptitude and it was he who had mastered the quartic equation.

Tartaglia, quite naturally, was incensed at the publication of the *Ars Magna*. He wrote a book of his own to unmask Cardano as a dishonest scientist who stole the ideas of others and was capable of breaking the most solemn oaths. But Ferrari was a hot-tempered young man, and to clear the name of his master, he composed a wrathful cartel, challenging Tartaglia, which was sent to all prominent scholars and patrons of the sciences in Italy. Ferrari pointed out that the solution of the cubic equation only apparently belonged to Tartaglia; in reality it was the solution of del Ferro which he and Cardano had been permitted to see by della Nave among the posthumous papers of del Ferro.

Tartaglia countered with another cartel — no fewer than six cartels and counter cartels were exchanged in the dispute. All Italy excitedly followed the controversy, one of the liveliest in the history of science. Charges, insinuations, abuses, insults, and ridicule were exchanged, yet the altercation is historically of importance as the first discussion of a crucial question: Is it ethically justifiable to keep scientific discoveries secret? Tartaglia held the medieval view — the solution was personal property of which he had been deprived. Ferrari maintained that in reality Tartaglia never had intended to publish his solution, and emphasized that it was morally objectionable to possess such a treasure without sharing it with humanity. If the corollaries following from Tartaglia's method were to be considered private property, it would soon be impossible for Cardano, or anyone else, to teach or study mathematics. The climax of the controversy was a public disputation in Milan over a series of mathematical problems proposed by the two opponents, a solemn occasion presided over by the Spanish viceroy. There can be no doubt that the victory belonged to Ferrari; although Tartaglia later claimed that he had been prevented from developing his arguments because of disturbances created by enthusiastic Ferrari supporters.

The next natural step was to seek the solution of equations of fifth and higher degrees. The great systematic importance of this problem was evident, and interest in it had been stimulated by the dramatic events which followed in the wake of the solution of the cubic and quartic equations. Through the intervening centuries the skill of many famous mathematicians had been measured by this problem. The greatest efforts had been made by the French mathematician Lagrange; Holmboe relates that his works were those which Niels Henrik had studied most intensively at the Cathedral School.

From this time the quintic equation never left Abel's mind; he examined it repeatedly, and finally came to the conclusion, shared by many others, that no solution of the desired kind with radical expressions could be found. Thus after his return from Copenhagen, rather than continuing to seek a solution, he attempted to demonstrate that such a solution could not exist. He examined what properties such expressions must have to be a solution, and around Christmas 1823 convincingly demonstrated that a solution was not possible. Thus he had reached his first great goal which for years had appeared inaccessible.

7

GOVERNMENT FELLOWSHIP

~§ SHORTLY BEFORE CHRISTMAS, after nine months' delay, Hansteen and Rasmussen submitted their recommendation on Abel's memoir to the Collegium. Originally they had been appointed to consider the desirability of publishing the paper at university expense. However, a different question was now in the foreground. For two and a half years Abel's studies had been financed by the professors and it was evident that they could no longer personally continue to support him. It was high time that some more satisfactory arrangement be found, and an appeal was made to the Collegium to consider the matter.

In their recommendation Hansteen and Rasmussen wrote: "Instead of proposing a grant for the printing of this work by Student Abel, we feel particularly obliged to recommend this young man, whose moral character is above reproach, for a subvention so that he may continue to cultivate a science in which only few at his age have given proof of such excellent progress. The Collegium is familiar with the fact that he is without means, and only through monthly contributions of several men has been able to subsist at the university under straitened circumstances.

"Now he needs greater support in order to become that ornament for his country which one can expect him to be according to his ability and progress. We assume that a stay abroad in those localities where the most distinguished mathematicians can be found will contribute greatly to his scientific training. In Paris it seems likely that he will find an opportunity to have his work on integration included in the memoirs of the French Institute which will circulate it in suitable form.

"In regard to the amount of support for which we so warmly recommend him we shall respectfully make the following proposal: (a) 20 daler monthly from January 1, 1824, until he begins his foreign travel;

(b) 150 daler for equipment one month before his departure; (c) 50 daler monthly during his stay abroad which should last not more than 18 months; (d) 30 daler a month during the first six months after his return, provided he does not before this time obtain a position yielding greater income.

"If the honored Collegium recognizes as the duty of those in charge of the university — as it undoubtedly does — that whenever they discover rare natural gifts, so to speak created for some particular science, these should be supported to ensure their most fertile development, then we are convinced that the Collegium will recommend Student Niels Henrik Abel for the public subvention which we know the university cannot grant him from its own funds."

This was a well-reasoned plan with quite liberal conditions for the young candidate. Even the twenty daler a month in the preliminary period, together with a free room at Regensen, was, according to the standard salaries, sufficient for a modest but comfortable student life. The ordinary teachers in Oslo did not receive as much, and the amount was comparable with the lowest salaries at the Cathedral School.

The plan was probably formulated after conference with Abel, but even so, it must have been a proud moment when he heard that it had been presented to the Collegium. With the support of two men like Hansteen and Rasmussen, both influential in the Collegium and in government circles, there could be little doubt that in the main the plan would be accepted. The Collegium considered it shortly after Christmas and, with one important exception, approved the proposal. The last point, providing for continued assistance after his return, was deleted. This was unquestionably a shortsighted omission. Had it been retained it would have saved Abel many economic worries, and the university many serious reproaches. The Collegium in its recommendation to the Church Department added these flattering words:

"If the Royal department should regard this proposal favorably, and by its forceful and influential support grant Student Abel this most humbly suggested Royal favor, then the Academic Collegium is convinced that we will have gained an excellent man for the sciences, a victory for the country, and a citizen who by his unusual ability in his field will one day repay in rich measure the assistance now granted him." The university evidently perceived the genius with which fate had endowed it.

The Collegium recommended that the journey begin in late spring, and Abel immediately began to make scientific preparations. He was aware that in order to impress the famous mathematicians abroad, particularly the French, it would be necessary to have his finest work ready for presentation. The papers in the *Magazin* were written in Norwegian, and were of relatively little importance. However, his new result on the quintic equation should cause a sensation. The paper was composed in French: *Mémoire sur les équations algébriques où on démontre l'impossibilité de la résolution de l'équation générale du cinquiéme degré*. Eager to have it printed immediately, and knowing it was impossible to serve such indigestible fare to the readers of the *Magazin*, Abel decided to have it printed at his own expense, by Gröndahl, the publisher of the *Magazin*. In the newspaper list of new publications the title was corrupted somewhat. In particular "équation" had become "épurations" (purifications), which his fellow students probably considered a good joke.

To save on expenses Abel had reduced the whole pamphlet to a half-sheet. The scant six pages of actual print is a publication now considered one of the greatest rarities in mathematical literature. But this unavoidable parsimony resulted in a brevity of style which made it difficult to follow his arguments. In places Abel restricted himself simply to indications. In an introductory passage he explained:

"Mathematicians have been greatly occupied by the problem of finding a general method for solving algebraic equations, and several have made attempts to prove the impossibility of it. I dare to hope, therefore, that mathematicians will receive favorably this article which has for its purpose to fill this lacuna in the theory of algebraic equations."

This pious wish was not fulfilled; the paper long remained an unrecognized masterpiece. None of the foreign mathematicians seem to have received their copies of it with any interest; even the incomparable Gauss in Göttingen, who often was and still is referred to as the uncrowned king of mathematicians, filed the leaflet away among his papers, where it was found uncut after his death. Some copies Abel presented to his Norwegian and Danish colleagues, but the greater part he retained to be used as a sort of introduction when he called on the famous foreign mathematicians in person. On the copy dedicated to Hansteen he wrote: "I venture to offer you this, my first work, as a feeble sign of my gratitude."

At the time Abel composed his paper he was unaware of one fact. A relatively unknown Italian mathematician, Paolo Ruffini, had twenty-five years earlier published a proof for the same result. It is true that Ruffini's analysis was deficient in certain respects, but even Abel's proof in its first, abbreviated form cannot be said to be entirely satisfactory. Abel himself tacitly admitted this by later publishing two more elaborate proofs, in which all requirements of stringency are fulfilled; then he also indicated his awareness of the existence of a precursor:

"In this paper I shall treat the question of the solution of algebraic equations in all its generality. If I am not mistaken, the first to attempt a proof of the impossibility of an algebraic solution of the general equation was the mathematician Ruffini; but his memoir is so complicated that it is difficult to judge the correctness of his argument. It appears to me that his reasoning is not always satisfactory."

Many of the most important conquests in mathematics have been reached in a similar fashion, the perfectly valid form of a proof has only been found after a series of increasingly incisive attacks upon the the problem. Historians of mathematics have taken this into account by naming the result on the insolubility of the quintic equation by radicals the theorem of Abel-Ruffini.

At the university there was no one who fully understood Niels Henrik's ideas, but the institution was happy to harbor him and was proud of his progress. Almost all students followed the regular courses and passed the standard examinations; independent research such as Abel's was a rare occurrence. In the university's annual reports Abel is mentioned several times; for instance, for the year 1824 one finds this passage: "Among those who eminently pursue the study of mathematics should be mentioned particularly Candidatus Philosophiae N. H. Abel; having completed the work for his academic degree he continues with uninterrupted diligence to make unusual advances in this study for which he shows such promise."

The proposal for a stipend for Abel had to pass through the regular channels. From the Collegium it was sent to the Church Department and then in turn to the Department of Finance. The latter quite surprisingly departed from its routine replies of yes and, mostly, no, and turned up with a proposal of its own, composed in the best of departmental style:

"It appears most correct to this department that Student Abel, before he is recommended to receive that grant for a journey abroad for which the Collegium Academicum on account of his rare ability for mathematical study has nominated him, is granted a suitable subvention of perhaps 200 daler a year for a couple of years so that he will be enabled to further educate himself during a continued stay at the university in those languages and auxiliary sciences which it seems plausible, in view of his young age, to assume that he does not possess to the desirable extent in order that he should be able to take full advantage in his principal science of the suggested sojourn at foreign universities, assuming that the proposed subvention for this purpose in due time may gracefully be awarded him."

How the Department of Finance arrived at this new view is difficult to say, but one may conjecture that Rasmussen had exerted his influence. The Collegium approved the proposal, and the stipend was granted shortly afterward by the government. Abel had no choice but to accept, although in certain respects he was annoyed. He would have preferred to depart at this time, since two of his best friends would have given him good company. Young Maschmann was leaving for Berlin to study pharmacology; he had decided to become an apothecary and eventually take over his father's lucrative business. Furthermore, Keilhau had received a government grant for foreign study, expedited by the praise which foreign geologists had lately heaped upon him. In Leipzig, Professor Karl Friedrich Naumann was translating Keilhau's papers into German. Naumann had recently spent two years studying Norwegian mountain formations and his own book on the subject had just appeared. The native Norwegian philosopher Henrik Steffens extolled the achievements of Keilhau more directly to the Norwegian public. Steffens was a professor in Breslau and represented the romantic movement in natural philosophy. During an excursion, he had ceremoniously from a mountain peak bequeathed to Keilhau the Norwegian mountains as his distinct geological realm. In his lectures in Oslo, Steffens singled out Keilhau for special praise. A letter by a contemporary author, Maurits Hansen, runs as follows: "If I could only have been in Oslo and listened to Steffens. I suppose you have heard how highly he esteems Keilhau. He has declared that at present all geologists must lay down their pens and await the consequences of Keilhau's ideas. My heart jumps in my chest when I hear such statements. One hears nothing about Abel, but he too should be worth watching."

The authorities were hurried along by Steffens' enthusiasm. Shortly after, Keilhau received his fellowship and left Oslo for the venerable geological seminary in Freiburg, Saxony. He described his bliss in a letter to Boeck: "Now I have finally got it. The money, I mean, 600 daler for a year's travel. Hurrah! I have only applied for one year; the second, I believe, comes easier when I have the first. It is all because of Steffens. I am now on good terms with Treschow. He told me that Steffens had threatened the worthy cabinet members to scandalize them, and that quite completely before all of Europe, if they did not let me travel."

Abel did not particularly relish the prospect of spending another year, perhaps more, at the university, studying languages and auxiliary sciences, as the terms of his fellowship required. However, the extra year in Oslo proved to be no drawback for him. On the contrary, he was already far beyond the stage when lectures at any foreign university could yield him any substantial profit. Now he was quite well provided for, and even if he had to sacrifice some of his time to study languages, there was abundant opportunity for mathematical speculations. When he did undertake his great journey, Abel seemed to have a cornucopia of eminent works, and there can be no doubt that a large part of these results were drawn from the reserve fund he created during his year of waiting.

Abel continued to be anxious about the publication of his large memoir on integration, for which he originally had requested university support. The manuscript circulated with the documents concerning his fellowship, until it disappeared without a trace in some public archive. In a letter to Degen dated March 1824 Abel wrote:

"Since the time when I enjoyed the instructive association with the Herr Professor, I have occupied myself especially with the integral calculus, and I may venture to say, not without success. I have reviewed the first part of integration which I had developed before I came to Copenhagen, and have been fortunate enough to give it a very systematic form. I had hoped to get it printed here in Oslo at university expense, but nothing came out of it, since I was at the same time proposed for a travel grant and the Collegium was of the opinion that the publications of some academy of science would be a more suitable place for my memoir. God knows where I can get it printed! I wished it so dearly, for I believe that my own papers will be my best recommendation during my foreign travel, which I have reason to believe will occur in a year or thereabout."

In the same letter, Abel gave a résumé of some of his new discoveries, and mentioned especially that he had followed Degen's good advice and studied the elliptic functions. But most interesting from a mathematical point of view are the few lines in which he discussed integrals of so-called general algebraic functions. The formula he indicated is not quite intelligible as it stands, but there can be no doubt that it contains the idea for the result which later was called the great Abelian theorem, his *momentum aere perennius*, a monument more lasting than bronze. He was fully aware of its importance, and intended to use it to gain a foothold among the French mathematicians. "This theorem, and an article about it, I expect to send to the French Institute, for I believe it will throw light over the whole theory of transcendental functions."

Abel concluded this imposing scientific letter with a few words of the greatest modesty: "Finally, I must ask the Herr Professor to forgive my audacity in inconveniencing you with this letter. If it should contain expressions which appear unbecoming to a disciple and fledgling mathematician, then I have erred out of ignorance, and dare to count on your goodness in this respect, for nothing should be more displeasing to me than to abuse it."

While Abel reaped a great harvest in abstract mathematics, his attempts in applied mathematics were less successful. Hansteen, continually preoccupied by his studies of the terrestrial magnetism, had ambitiously proposed to map the intensity and direction of the magnetic force all over the globe. This was not the work of a single man, and so he gathered material wherever he could find collaborators. On the whole Hansteen was quite adept at getting people to work for him. He had constructed a small magnetic oscillation apparatus which made it relatively simple to perform the measurements.

He felt that the oscillations of the pendulum might be influenced not only by magnetism and the gravity of the earth, but also by the attraction of the moon, which might be the cause of some of the variations in the observations which he had found. Hansteen suggested to Abel that he perform the necessary calculations. The problem was not particularly difficult and Abel concluded that the moon really had an

77

influence which would appear in accurate measurements. He wrote a little paper, *On the Influence of the Moon on the Movement of the Pendulum*, which Hansteen printed in the summer of 1824.

To Hansteen the problem seemed so important that he sent the article to a colleague, the astronomer Heinrich Christian Schumacher in Altona. Hansteen had made his acquaintance while Schumacher was professor of astronomy in Copenhagen. Schumacher had later been put in charge of the Danish Geodetic Survey, and as director of the observatory in Altona, he had made this the center for geodetic measurements in Europe. Schumacher had greatly assisted Hansteen by obtaining for him the instruments for the new Norwegian observatory. At this time he had just founded a new periodical, *Astronomische Nachrichten*, and it was Hansteen's hope that he would print Abel's article, translated into French or German.

Schumacher's reply came promptly, in August 1824, and was quite blunt: "I do not want to print Abel's paper. He has forgotten that the moon also attracts the center of the earth, so that it is not a question of the absolute attraction on the pendulum or the plumb line, but only of the difference between this attraction and the attraction at the center of the earth. Thus the effects he has calculated become 60^3 times less, or quite insignificant. According to his formulas, the sun should give a deviation of several minutes of arc on the plumb line. So for his own sake, let us not discuss it any more."

Abel was immediately obliged to write a correction for the *Magazin* and he must have regretted that he had ventured into a field in which he was not thoroughly familiar. Strangely enough, a few years later an English astronomer committed exactly the same error. Schumacher, writing his colleague Gauss about it, remarked, "Anyone who would have judged Abel on the basis of this article would have received a very erroneous impression."

Abel was not only occupied by mathematical questions of high importance after his return from Copenhagen. There were also personal problems which required his attention. In particular, he could not put the pretty little Crelly Kemp out of his mind. During the years 1823 and 1824, Abel and his roommate tutored the young son of a customs official in the little village of Son at the Oslo fjord for the entrance examination to the university. From the boy he learned that some families in Son were looking for a suitable governess to instruct their young children. Niels Henrik, realizing that this might be an excellent opportunity for bringing Crelly closer, wrote to her in Copenhagen. Not long afterward, Christine Kemp arrived as schoolmistress in Son.

Son was only a short day's travel from Oslo, so the two could meet from time to time. At Christmas 1824, Abel was invited to spend the holidays with the parents of his pupil in Son, and on this occasion Crelly and Niels Henrik publicly declared their engagement. The young fellowship holder returned happily to Oslo and informed his friends of the betrothal. At the "Asylum" he was cheered as the first to reach this great station in life.

Journey to the Continent

8

WINTER IN BERLIN

&⸞ TOWARD SUMMER IN 1825 Niels Henrik felt that it was time to set out on his scientific journey. He had begun to tire of studying auxiliary sciences and he wanted to start the tour since his marriage would have to be delayed until his return. Furthermore, another opportunity for excellent company had arisen. In 1818 the Storting had approved the plan proposed by Pastor Abel that a veterinary school be created, but here the matter had since rested. Recently the plans had been resurrected and a fellowship granted for the education of some suitable instructor and eventual director for the school. The candidate selected was Niels Henrik's good friend Boeck, who was to visit similar institutions abroad preparatory to his appointment. In addition, there were two other friends, both geologists, who wanted to join the "great Norse trek" to the south.

One was Nicolai Benjamin Möller, about the same age as Abel, who also had taken his first step in science by publishing an article in the *Magazin*. He intended to study mineralogy in Berlin. Later he held positions at various Norwegian mines, and finally was put in charge of the mining operations at Kongsberg.

The second young scientist, Nils Otto Tank, was the son of a wealthy businessman who owned huge forests and operated sawmills at Halden, on the coast near the Swedish border. Old Tank had played an important role as a member of the government in the fateful year 1814. Otto Tank was in a period of *Sturm und Drang*; he had been completely charmed by Steffens' romanticism in science and radicalism in religion. When Steffens departed after his visit to Norway, Tank and Keilhau accompanied him a considerable distance on the sloop to prolong the precious hours of association.

Thus the new university was sending out into the world its first crop of young scientists. Hansteen devoted a little column in the *Magazin* to reports of their activities abroad under the heading "Our Traveling Young Scholars." He stated with evident pride: "These young men represent the hope of our future."

Abel's traveling fellowship had not been granted formally. On July 1, 1825, the day before a meeting of the Collegium, he submitted an application, addressed, as was customary, to the king, in which he requested "most humbly, a travel grant for 600 daler a year for two years, to study the mathematical sciences at the universities of Paris and Göttingen." Hansteen and Rasmussen voiced their warm support: "Few young students promise as much as Student Abel, who most likely one day will make himself favorably known in Europe through his investigations in theoretical mathematics."

The Collegium forwarded the proposal expeditiously but the Church Department would have violated its traditions had it not found an occasion to demur: "Before the department will be in a position to humbly present this application, it must, since neither this nor the previous depositions contain anything about it, request a further declaration from the Collegium whether the university cannot itself disburse such a travel grant, and also whether the Collegium does not feel that the stipend can be moderated somewhat in view of the fact that the studies of the suppliant do not require extensive travel, but only his sojourn at two definite localities."

The Collegium replied without hesitation that, as the department well knew, the university budget was so meagerly allotted that it was impossible to pay the sum from this source. Furthermore, there were precedents for the amount. Holmboe's brother had had the same sum while studying oriental languages, so that the Collegium "did not believe it should propose a smaller stipend for Student Abel, since it knows his absolute lack of fortune and private support would make it impossible for him to manage with a smaller amount. He not only has to subsist in foreign places, but also needs to purchase equipment and several expensive works which are indispensable for his studies."

After this exchange of letters the difficulties were surmounted, except for the minister's request that Abel send a detailed itinerary to the department. This seems a little strange, since in his application Abel had specified Paris and Göttingen as the only places he would visit — but perhaps there were rumors that he had also considered alternative plans.

The fellowship was granted a couple of months later. There was no longer any question of 150 daler for equipment as originally proposed, but Abel was no doubt very well satisfied. He could contemplate the future with great expectations. For two years he would be his own master, travel with his best friends, work on his own multitudinous and fascinating ideas, write about what he pleased, and personally present his works to the most eminent mathematicians in the world. He hoped that when this period was up he, like his friends Boeck and Keilhau, would have a scientific position awaiting him so that he might marry his Crelly and become an esteemed member of the university in his native land.

During the summer of 1825, Abel was preoccupied with the preparations for his journey. His fiancée was independent and could manage her own affairs, but his family presented more difficult problems. He felt himself to be the only adult and responsible person among them, and as far as it lay within his power he was obliged to make plans and arrangements for them before he left. Peder, his best friend among the brothers, barely scraped through his Artium the same year, and now intended to study theology. But Niels Henrik was gravely concerned about him, for it could not remain unnoticed that Peder showed signs of succumbing to the family weakness for alcohol. Niels Henrik had been able to act as his brother's keeper while they lived together at Regensen; but now, when Peder must stand alone, the outcome might be tragic. Abel implored Fru Hansteen to take care of him and left 50 daler with her which she could dole out whenever necessary.

At home at Gjerstad conditions had become more and more deplorable. Fru Abel was increasingly indifferent in regard to herself and her surroundings. On special occasions, Pastor Aas would invite his predecessor's widow to the vicarage, dispatching a maid beforehand to make certain that she was suitably dressed. Niels Henrik probably shared some of his newly acquired wealth with his mother. The oldest brother, Hans Mathias, was so feeble-minded that he was beyond help. Thomas was now twenty years of age and showed no inclination for book learning; the Tuxens found a job for him as an apprentice in Copenhagen.

Niels Henrik's favorite, his sister Elisabeth, was confirmed the same summer and ranked highest at the ceremony. Pastor Aas praised her "excellence in knowledge, continual diligence and good deportment." She was fifteen years of age and Niels Henrik saw only too clearly that home was no place for her. Once again Fru Hansteen graciously intervened and took the beautiful and very gifted girl into her house. Half a year later she found an excellent home for her with Rector Treschow at Töyen.

On September 6, the Church Department informed Abel that his fellowship for foreign travel had been granted and became payable the day of departure. The next day he was off with Boeck and Möller. The fourth member of the expedition, Otto Tank, had suggested that they travel overland through Sweden to Copenhagen, and had invited them to spend a few days at his father's estate as his guests. They preferred, however, to take the packet directly to Copenhagen and meet Tank there. Abel wanted to have a last meeting with Crelly before the long separation and took the coach to Son; Boeck too had a sweet and sorrowful adieu to say in Oslo — he had just become engaged to his cousin Elisabeth Collett, daughter of the finance minister.

Hansteen could not, of course, let such an opportunity go wasted. He had provided them with several instruments to measure terrestrial magnetism, giving them strict orders to observe wherever their journey might take them and let him know the results at their earliest convenience. He himself traveled along the shores of the Gulf of Bothnia all summer for the same purpose, and did not return until the middle of October. The most important piece of apparatus was the oscillation instrument, and for the moment Hansteen had none available for the travelers. He had, however, entrusted one such instrument to his friend Hans Christian Oersted, the Danish physicist famous for his electromagnetic discoveries. Abel was instructed to pick up the piece of apparatus when passing through Copenhagen. His letter of introduction ran as follows:

"If you, my dear friend, still are in possession of the little oscillation apparatus which traveled with you to England, oblige me by surrendering it to the bearer of this letter, Herr Studiosus N. H. Abel, our rising mathematical sun. As you know, I let these instruments travel around the globe as far as my own and my friends' arms and legs will reach, and thus I rarely have one on hand. Schumacher has promised to circulate one among the German astronomers; another soon will leave for St. Helena, the East Indies, and China; a third I take with me this summer to Torneå to examine the whole shore of the Gulf of Bothnia; finally, one goes to Brest with the cadet ship."

86

The trip by packet to Copenhagen was never comfortable, but usually safe, although the passengers at times may have doubted it. This
time the passage was extremely rough, and the young men may have
regretted not having accepted Tank's offer. Boeck and Möller boarded
the crowded vessel in Oslo, and late at night picked up Abel on the
pier at Son. The first day the wind was favorable, the second they lay
becalmed off the Swedish coast and later a stiff gale blew up. Neither
Abel nor Möller were heroes at sea, and had to creep below deck with
the rest of the frightened and seasick passengers. One of the passengers
had repeated fits of panic, wrote his testament several times, and threatened the captain's life to make him turn back. Boeck on the other hand,
at least according to his own description, was in full vigor, and as a
good samaritan exercised his medical art wherever he thought it might
be of any use.

Early in the morning of the fifth day they sighted Kronborg castle
near Elsinore, and waves and winds rapidly subsided. Abel and Boeck
had been on deck since early dawn watching the passage through the
Sound, the numerous sailing vessels, and the white straw-covered cot-
tages along the shores of Seeland, until they glided in under the towers
and castles of Copenhagen. Otto Tank awaited them in town. It had
been agreed that the others would continue almost immediately, while
Abel stayed a week in Copenhagen to visit family and friends. Later,
they would all meet in Hamburg.

Abel stayed with his uncle and aunt Tuxen, and also found time to
drive out to Sorö to visit Fru Hansteen's mother and sisters. He called
on the Danish mathematicians and was saddened by the news that his
old friend and adviser, Professor Degen, had died a short time before.
His large library, which had been so useful to Abel during his first stay
in Copenhagen, was scheduled to be sold at auction in a few weeks. Abel
hurriedly wrote a note to Holmboe, asking him to distribute the catalogues, hoping, perhaps, that the university library in Oslo would take
advantage of this exceptional occasion.

Abel had applied for a fellowship to Paris and Göttingen, and it was
assumed that he would first go to Paris. Hansteen was particularly
anxious that Niels Henrik become acquainted with the French mathematical school — the most distinguished in the world — and that he submit his paper on integration to the French Institute. But Niels Henrik
long had had other thoughts; he was much too dependent on his friends

to relish the idea of working alone in Paris. Boeck, Möller, and Maschmann were all spending the winter in Berlin, and Tank and Keilhau were within visiting distance. A detour to Berlin, even it if were of only short duration, would be a delightful experience. In Copenhagen Abel took his first independent and somewhat highhanded action and decided to stay in Berlin for a while. Hansteen, who felt a strong responsibility to the department for his protégé, did not like it at all. But as time revealed, this step proved to be one of the most fortunate decisions the young mathematician ever made.

The mathematicians in Berlin had no great distinction, but Abel's detour could be justified only by visiting them. Thus Abel turned for recommendations to his Danish colleagues, who encouraged him in his purpose. Professor von Schmidten wrote several letters of introduction for him, particularly to Privy Councilor Crelle, well known for his warm interest in mathematics, his ability in technical problems, and his influence with the Prussian authorities.

On the voyage from Copenhagen Abel, for the first time, made use of that wonder of modern technology, the steamship, which carried him over the Baltic to Lübeck. But the last part of his journey to Hamburg brought him back to the accustomed conditions. The diligence swayed forward in the sea of water and mud which covered the roads, at times on the verge of capsizing and sinking. In the inn, "Zum grossen wilden Mann," he found his friends who had also had an enervating journey. Hansteen's precious oscillation instrument had been so shaken that it was necessary to have it repaired by an instrument maker in Hamburg. Without delay, as ordered by Hansteen, they proceeded together to the observatory in Altona to visit Schumacher. The councilor of state received them benevolently, seeming to have attached no importance to Abel's little blunder in regard to the motion of the pendulum. A few years later Schumacher wrote to his friend Gauss: "As a man Abel was just as amiable as he was excellent as a mathematician."

The company remained only a few days in Hamburg, and the journey to Berlin was uneventful. But in town there was a joyful reunion with Maschmann who had rented rooms for them "Am Kupfergraben 4." Boeck wrote to his dear Elisabeth Collett: "We arrived here on October 11 and are completely settled. Nothing is missing except the beginning of the lectures and letters for me — Möller has received several letters, Abel's arrived a couple of days ago, Tank's while we were in

Hamburg, but I still have none." His comrades teased Boeck occasionally for having captured the golden bird: "I notice that my compatriots here seem to feel that I have jumped pretty high in catching the daughter of the minister of finance."

Abel immediately made use of his letters of introduction by calling on August Leopold Crelle. Geheimer Oberbaurat Crelle was not a professor of mathematics, but a construction engineer who had directed large public works. A great number of the highways built in Prussia during the years 1820–30 were laid according to his plans. Later he directed the construction of the railroad between Berlin and Potsdam. Mathematics was Crelle's great passion; in all his spare hours he wrote and studied mathematical articles. He was entirely self-educated in the subject, however, and in spite of his many capable publications he never became a mathematician of first rank.

Abel spoke German only haltingly, and Crelle found it difficult to understand what the purpose of the young foreigner's visit was. He later related that he first was under the impression that this was a student who wanted to pass the entrance examination to one of the trade schools in town, until Abel broke out in despair: "Nix examination, only mathematics." Abel's own version of the interview appeared in his first letter to Hansteen, which he wrote a couple of months after his arrival. He evidently felt reluctant to explain the detour to Berlin before he could send good news:

"I could well have written to you before, Herr Professor, and I ought to have done so; but I wanted first to bring various things in order, so that I could let you know how I benefit, and will benefit, from my stay here. You may have wondered why I first went to Germany. I did so, for one thing, to be among my friends; secondly, because I ran a lesser risk of not using my time to advantage, since I can leave Germany at any moment to go to Paris, which of course remains the most important locality for me.

"Here in Berlin I have made an insignificant catch in regard to public libraries. In mathematics they are extremely poor; almost nothing of the newer things, and what there is, is very incomplete. If you will permit me to say so, our library is far better provided. However, in another respect I am exceedingly satisfied with my sojourn in Berlin. I have made the acquaintance of a couple of excellent mathematicians, namely Geheimrat Crelle and Professor Dirksen.

"The former had been described to me by Professor von Schmidten as an excellent man in all respects, and so when I came to Berlin I repaired to his house as quickly as possible. A considerable time elapsed before I could make clear to him what the purpose of my visit was, and it all appeared to be heading for a melancholy end when he asked me what I had already read in mathematics. I took courage, and mentioned to him the works of a couple of the foremost mathematicians. He then became very amiable and, as it appeared, really happy. He began an extensive conversation with me about various difficult problems which were still not resolved. When we came to the solution of the quintic equation, and I told him that I had demonstrated the impossibility of giving a general algebraic solution, he would not believe it and said he would dispute it. I therefore gave him a copy, but he said he could not see the reason for several of my conclusions. Others have said the same, and I consequently have made a revision of it.

"Next he talked about the poor state of mathematics in Germany, and said that the knowledge of most mathematicians was restricted only to a little geometry and something which they called analysis, which is nothing but a little combinatorial calculus. However, he was of the opinion that a more fortunate period for mathematics in Germany had been initiated.

"When I expressed surprise over the fact that there existed no mathematical journal, as in France, he said that he had long intended to edit one, and would presently bring his plan to execution. This project is now organized, and that to my great joy, for I shall have a place where I can get some of my articles printed. I have already prepared four of them, which will appear in the first number. Since they are written in French, Crelle will oblige me by translating them. In this manner my little French serves me in good stead.

"About the form of my papers Crelle stated that they were very clear and well written, and this pleases me greatly, because I have always feared that I should have difficulties in developing my thoughts in an orderly fashion. But he advised me to be a little more elaborate, particularly here in Germany. He also offered me an honorarium for my articles. This I had not counted on, and I refused it, although I felt that he had preferred to see me accept it. Crelle has an excellent mathematical library which I may use as my own; it is particularly profitable because it contains all the newest material, which he obtains as soon as it is available. Among other things he subscribes to the *Bulletin universel des sciences et de l'industrie,* which appears in France under the editorship of Baron Ferrusac; this is especially useful for me since it announces all new books and discoveries in mathematics.

"I have a standing invitation to Crelle's house every Monday evening. He then holds a kind of assembly where the main entertainment is music, for which I have no understanding. Nevertheless, I enjoy myself, for there are always a couple of young mathematicians I can talk to. Thus I gain some much-needed experience in speaking German, which does not go too well. Formerly Crelle also held a meeting of mathematicians once a week. He was compelled to discontinue these sessions on account of a man named Ohm [a brother of the physicist] with whom nobody could get along because of his terrible arrogance. It is really tragic that a single man can obstruct science in this manner.

"The young mathematicians in Berlin and, as I hear, all over Germany almost worship Gauss; he is the epitome of all mathematical excellence. But even if he is a great genius, it is also certain that he has a bad presentation. Crelle says that all Gauss writes is *Gräuel* since it is so obscure that it is almost impossible to understand. Gauss is now preparing a large work on physical astronomy. The first three parts are ready for print, as one of his pupils here told me. It is supposed to contain many new things. . . . In Hamburg I visited Schumacher, but he was not too well at the time.

"My winter quarters will be here in Berlin. I have not quite made up my mind when I shall leave. For the sake of Crelle and the *Journal,* I would like to stay here as long as possible. According to what I hear, there is probably no place in Germany which would be more profitable. It is true that Göttingen has a good library, but that is all, since Gauss, who is the only one who knows anything, is absolutely unapproachable. However, I shall, of course, have to go to Göttingen. On the whole, it is my plan to visit as many universities as possible, for I shall be able to reap a little at each place.

"I ask the Herr Professor to remember me to Professor Rasmussen and B. Holmboe, and to tell the latter that I shall soon write him a long mathematical letter. I hope with all heart that you are well, and that you will continue to treat me with the same goodness you have always shown me. I shall endeavor to make myself worthy of it."

Such is the story, told in simple words, of the foundation of the

Journal für die reine und angewandte Mathematik, or Crelle's *Journal* as it is often called. All during the nineteenth century it was the leading mathematical periodical in Germany, even in the world. In two short months Abel had written four articles for it, and a few weeks later he reports to Holmboe that he has six papers ready to be printed in the first volume. Six papers in three months, some pre-eminent in the history of mathematics, were truly an admirable achievement for the twenty-three-year-old mathematician.

Christmas was approaching, and in the midst of his great scientific adventures, Niels Henrik was homesick and concerned about his family. In his letter to Professor Hansteen he included a note to Fru Hansteen:

"From my letter to the professor you will see what happens to me. But to you I also have a prayer. You have always been so good to me, God bless you. Please do not forget my brother. I am so afraid he will go wrong. If he should need more money than he already has received, may I ask you to give him still a little more. When the 50 daler have been used up, I shall make arrangements for you to receive more, provided you will continue to show me the kindness of keeping the money in custody and give it to him as it may seem appropriate to you. I hope that with God's help he will endeavor to behave decently. When you see him, please remember me to him and tell him to write. He can send the letter to my fiancée to be forwarded, or better still, mail it unpaid.

"I sent you a small package from Hamburg with merchant Bisgaard, which you presumably have received. My fiancée has written me that she has not yet received the enclosed letter, but since Fröken Collett has obtained the letter from Boeck sent on the same occasion, I presume that it only has been delayed.

"Otherwise I live quietly and I am very industrious, but from time to time I am awfully homesick, and it is aggravated by the fact that I only rarely hear anything. My dear sister lives well, I presume; greet her profusely. And the sweet and kind Charité I wish well with all my heart. Good-bye, dear Fru Hansteen, I cannot write any more, I am really melancholy. Adieu, and do not be angry with me, I must appear a little peculiar to you."

Brother Peder continued to feed on Niels Henrik's limited means. A little later when Abel offered to buy books for Holmboe, he added: "You need not send me money, pay Fru Hansteen because I owe it to

her." There was really serious cause for concern over Peder's development. He had been unable to bear the newly won liberty of student
life. The police files record that during the fall Student Peder Abel
and another student with whom he shared private rooms had been
called in for investigation "owing to the fact that they very often have
parties where there are drunken fights and rows to the extent that the
public peace is disturbed during the night." Peder promised that he
would mend his ways: "The accused admitted that the complaints were
justified and solemnly assured us that such incidents should no more
occur."

9

A SHATTERED HOPE

◦§ IN CRELLE, Niels Henrik had won a fatherly friend and a warm admirer. The elderly mathematician well understood Abel's modest way, humane feelings, and, above all, his deep craving for friendship. Crelle was a sufficiently good mathematician to comprehend the wide range of Abel's ideas and the profoundness of his genius, even if he could not always grasp the details in Abel's articles. Abel continually praised Crelle from the bottom of his heart. During January 1826, he wrote to Holmboe: "I am exceedingly well satisfied that I came to Germany, and particularly to Berlin, before I went to Paris; for as you perhaps already have heard from my letter to Hansteen, I have made the acquaintance of Geheimrat Crelle. You cannot imagine what an excellent man he is, just to my taste, not filled with this terrible politeness that so many otherwise honorable people serve you with. I associate with him as straightforwardly as I do with you and some of my best friends. Mathematically, he is extremely active, which is so much the more praiseworthy since he, as a public official, has many affairs to attend to. During the last few years he has published several mathematical books, which seem very good. He has presented me with most of them. . . .

"I go to Crelle's home every Monday evening. Furthermore, we take a walk together for a couple of hours every Friday noon. Then, believe me, we really attack mathematical problems as fast and furious as my rebellious tongue will permit. However, I manage in a way. He cannot get it into his head that I can understand everything that is being said, and still am not quite able to speak myself.

"The Berlin dialect is not the best; in some ways it is quite hard, in others extremely soft and vapid. So, for instance, one sounds 'j' for words beginning with 'g' and this sounds damned funny. For example: O

Jott, which one hears every moment. There is the following expression with which to poke fun at the Berliners in this respect: 'Eine jute, jebratene Jans ist eine jute Jabe Jottes.' Another of their peculiarities which produces a strange effect is their confusion of 'mir' and 'mich,' 'dir' and 'dich,' and 'sind' and 'sein.' My attendant always says: 'Wollen Sie so jut sind mich Jeld zu jeben, ich werde jleich hier sind.'

"As Hansteen perhaps told you, a new mathematical journal will be making its appearance at the beginning of the year, which pleases me greatly. Probably it will contain very few things which are bad, but inevitably some, since I presume many will write for it. You may be certain that it will contain a couple of my articles in every issue, and believe me, I shall produce the best things I am capable of. I have already prepared six. Of these, either one or four will appear in the first number, which is due shortly, in about a month. One of the articles is the proof of the impossibility of resolving equations in general. This I have presented more elaborately than I did in the paper published in Oslo. In regard to this article, Crelle said it was honorable, but he could still not quite understand it. It is difficult to express myself intelligibly in these matters, which have been explored so little in my manner.

"Since I came to Berlin I have also tried to solve the following general problem: To find all equations which can be solved algebraically [by radicals]. It is not yet finished, but as far as I can see, it will work out. As long as the degree of the equation is a prime there is no great difficulty; but when it is a composite number, then the devil is on the loose. I have made applications to the equations of fifth degree; and luckily solved the problem in this case. In addition to the equations which were previously known I have found a large number of others which may be solved. I flatter myself that the article will be good when I have completed it in the way I want. What appears to me to be most important, it contains something general, and there will really be method to it."

Abel was not Crelle's only protégé. Another young man he encouraged was Jacob Steiner, a Swiss mathematician, who after many vicissitudes finally had obtained a minor teaching position at one of the trade schools in Berlin. His father was an innkeeper who saw no reason to educate his children, and the boy only learned to write when he was fourteen years of age. Later he attended Pestalozzi's Institute, where his exceptional mathematical ability was discovered. In particular, the boy had a geometric intuition which made it possible for him to visualize the most complicated relationships. He became one of the leading geometers of the nineteenth century and the founder of the so-called synthetic geometry. In 1834, a special professorship was created for him in Berlin.

Neither Abel nor Crelle had a special geometric aptitude; thus, when Steiner accompanied them on their Friday walks, as he very often did, he could supplement their knowledge and arguments in many ways. A witty student once commented, as the three passed by in eager conversation: "There goes Adam with Cain and Abel." This would have been a better joke had Crelle's first name been Adam; however, with two so entirely different "mathematical sons" he needed to have no concern about material for his *Journal* — in the first volume besides Abel's six articles Steiner had five.

At the time in Berlin there was a considerable group of active students, and Abel, for the first time, entered a real mathematical milieu. Many problems were under eager discussion, but one particular development held the center of interest: the new demands for greater logical stringency in the mathematical methods. The leaders of this new school of thought were two of Europe's most eminent mathematicians, Gauss in Göttingen and Cauchy in Paris. Less well known, but equally incisive in his analyses, was the Czech cleric, philosopher, and mathematician Bernard Bolzano, whom Abel evidently admired. "Bolzano is a clever man," he once scribbled in his notebooks.

Abel's own training had been entirely in the old, formal tradition of which Euler was a typical representative. By its methods, one computed without concern or limitations, hoping that the result would prove correct. When, in some instances, the outcome was obviously unacceptable, it was disregarded as far as possible. Under the new critical standards, it was imperative that each single step in the deductions be logically justified. For instance, if one operated with limit values, it must be established that they exist; by infinite series it had to be verified that they had a sum, that is, were convergent and not divergent. In the latter field particularly, many sins of omission had been committed. Abel's own first papers in the *Magazin* were not free from blemishes in these respects, and the need for reform was now evident to him. He wrote to Holmboe about the modern points of view — he had been newly converted, and showed the glowing enthusiasm of a neophyte:

96

"On the whole, divergent series are a deviltry, and it is a shame to base any demonstration upon them. By using them one can produce any result one wishes, and they are the cause of many calamities and paradoxes. Can you imagine anything more horrible than to write

$$0 = 1 - 2^n + 3^n - 4^n + \cdots$$

when n is a positive integer? *Risum teneatis, amici* [quotation from Horace: Friends, can you keep from laughter?]. My eyes have been opened in the most surprising manner. If you disregard the very simplest cases, there is in all of mathematics not a single infinite series whose sum has been stringently determined. In other words, the most important parts of mathematics stand without a foundation. It is true that most of it is valid, but that is extremely surprising. I struggle to find the reason for it, an exceedingly interesting problem. — I don't believe you can propose many theorems to me in which infinite series appear, where I cannot make justified objections against the proof. Try it, and I shall reply. — Even the binomial formula is not proved satisfactorily."

He was writing an article on this topic, he told Holmboe, but it embraced much more than the binomial series; it gave in reality a prototype for the treatment of infinite series. "It progresses quite well, and it interests me intensely," he could write of it with secure conviction. It became one of the classical memoirs in mathematics.

For the young scientists life in Berlin was pleasant, almost fashionable. They had good lodgings near the Spree, and an attendant — a luxury they had never experienced before. In their spare time, usually on Sundays, they visited the churches, palaces, and museums of the town and its surroundings. They saw the royal family at church services and were not particularly impressed. Once the Duke of Wellington visited and was honored by a great military parade.

Occasionally they would go to balls, and not rarely was there a little celebration at night as one would expect from gay young blades. They lived in the same house as the philosopher Hegel, and at times disrupted his studies. It is told that he tried to find out from the landlord who these youths were who disturbed the quiet of his nights. Upon hearing that they were Norwegian students, he exclaimed: "They must be Russian bears."

The theater was their favorite diversion, and they saw almost all the

97

plays of the season. They discussed the pros and cons of all actresses, knew the most recent gossip about them; in short, they had all the interests of young men. During the carnival time they went to balls and masquerades. Boeck explained his expenses to his father in the familiar manner: "It is true that we spend some money, but we have to see something while we are abroad." To Hansteen the description of their daily routine was somewhat more subdued: "We live in the student manner: attend lectures, learn songs, sleep, and once in a while go to comedy. Thus the time passes, one day like the other. Eternal rain and mud do not tempt us to go outside any more than we are compelled to."

Tank departed early for Breslau "to flutter a little with Steffens" as Boeck said; the latter was no admirer of the romantic direction in natural philosophy. As Christmas approached they agreed to gather in Berlin for the holidays. Boeck related: "Tank comes here to eat his Christmas porridge in the Norse manner. We had also expected Keilhau, but he dare not come due to his scant supply of cash." On December 20, 1825, Boeck wrote to Hansteen: "Tank arrived today from Breslau and stays till after Christmas; we expected Keilhau, but he probably will not come. The whole Norwegian colony manages very well, particularly Abel, who now, in addition to his regular Monday concerts, also has one on Saturdays at the home of a rich lady, Madame Levi — or something like it. We are longing for winter, but in vain for a Norwegian one. Tonight they play *The Snow* at Königstädtisches Theater, but it looks like rain outside and we are tired of it. I suppose it is better in Oslo. I hear we can expect to cry Hurrah for a new prince? So at Christmas time: Skaal for him, for Norway, and all that is Norwegian."

Christmas was celebrated in style and high spirits. Abel attended a ball at Crelle's house. He was in full dress, and felt that he was well on his way to becoming a man of the world.

All three friends, Abel, Boeck, and Keilhau, lived in a somewhat uncertain expectation of being appointed to a scientific position upon the completion of their foreign studies. Keilhau had strong hopes of becoming a kind of state geologist whose duties, at least in part, should consist in the exploration of the hidden wealth of Norway. Boeck prepared himself for a position in the veterinary sciences, and wrote repeatedly to his father about his prospects. For Abel, too, an enticing possibility had appeared.

The government's financial problems took so much of Professor Rasmussen's time that he had little to spare for his university lectures, which finally became bothersome for him and unprofitable for the students. He had repeatedly indicated that he might resign, but not until shortly after Abel's departure had he finally made up his mind and accepted a leading position in the Bank of Norway. The group received the news shortly after their arrival in Berlin. On October 25, 1825, Boeck while reporting the latest magnetic observations to Hansteen, cautiously tried to put in a good word for Abel: "My cousin Johan Collett writes me about Rasmussen's bank appointment. What will then happen to his position? Is there any hope that Abel might obtain it upon his return, or perhaps Holmboe is ahead of him? However reasonable the latter may be in certain respects, it does not appear quite just, since Abel presumably ranks a head above Holmboe."

Abel was aware that the university authorities were considering how to fill the vacancy, and he must have lived under a certain tension all fall. Under such circumstances it was not easy to correspond unconcernedly with Holmboe, and so Abel, in spite of all promises, did not write to his friend for nearly four months, aside from the little note about the book catalogues from Copenhagen. When he finally wrote on January 16, 1826, his apologies did not sound very convincing:

"Dear Friend: Because of my promise when departing from Oslo, you have probably long been expecting a letter from me, and I must therefore ask your forgiveness for not having written until now. I wanted to relate to you not only what happened to me during the first part of my tour, but also the outlook for the whole journey. Furthermore, I wanted to tell you something about the investigations which have kept me busy."

He continues by describing the inimitable Crelle, the *Journal,* and his own studies on infinite series. At this point he breaks off with a dash — as it turned out, a stop sign indicating entrance into a new and more serious period in his life. From now on there is always a background of anxiety in his mind:

"This is as far as I had come when Maschmann walked in through the door. He is our mail carrier, and since I have long had no letter from home I stopped him to inquire about anything for me. There was nothing. However, he himself had received a letter and among other news he told me that you, my friend, had been recommended to be lecturer

99

to take the place of Rasmussen. Receive my most sincere congratulations and be assured that none of your friends are as pleased over it as I. Believe me, I have often wished for a change in your position, for teaching in a school must be terrible for someone like you, who is so interested in his science — It is about time for you to look for a sweetheart, isn't it? I hear your brother, the dean, has found one. Remember me to him and congratulate him *am meisten.* — Now back to my example."

He continued his arguments on the weak foundations of mathematics, and concluded by reporting his plans: "I shall probably stay here in Berlin until the end of February or March, and then travel by the way of Leipzig and Halle to Göttingen — not for the sake of Gauss, because he is said to be extremely haughty — but for the library which is excellent. Toward the end of summer I shall go to Paris. I wish I were back home again. I am so terribly homesick. Please write me a long letter about all sorts of things. Really do it as soon as you receive my letter — Tomorrow I shall see a comedy: *Die schöne Müllerin.* Good-bye and remember me to all I know. Your friend N. H. Abel."

The documents in the case show clearly what had happened at the university in Oslo. On November 19, 1825, the Collegium officially informed the Church Department that Rasmussen had resigned and would discontinue his lectures at the end of the fall term. It was necessary, therefore, to appoint a new instructor as soon as possible, to enable him to take over the classes on January 15, the beginning of the spring term. There was also a vacancy in the law faculty, and for the young university this was a situation without precedent. Rector Treschow asked the Church Department what should be done under such circumstances: Should a permanent appointment be made immediately or a temporary substitute found? "In the present case I do not doubt that the Royal Department, as well as the Collegium, if its opinion is requested, will obtain the best information from Professors Rasmussen and Hansteen, who both, I believe, are perfectly familiar with the scholarship and ability of those persons who should be especially considered upon this occasion."

It was decided to change the professorship into a lectureship, and as early as December 16 the faculty had approved a recommendation, later endorsed by the Collegium and Rector Treschow: "In regard to the honored request of the Collegium that a capable man be proposed for appointment to the vacant university post as teacher of mathematics, we take the liberty to state that we are acquainted with two men whose proficiency make them completely qualified to fill this position, namely Teacher at Oslo Latin School, Bernt M. Holmboe, and Student Niels Henrik Abel.

"The former has shown excellent ability during eight years as teacher at the Latin School and also by his writings demonstrated publicly that he possesses wide and profound knowledge in mathematics. In addition, during ten years as amanuensis to Professor Hansteen he is known to the university as a particularly suitable and worthy man for the position.

"We have also had an opportunity to become familiar with Student Abel's rare talents for mathematics and his great progress in this science through his four years of study at the university and through his published articles. We must point out, however, that he at present is abroad on a journey which only began last summer and from which he cannot be recalled without detriment to his studies. We also believe that he cannot as easily adjust himself to the comprehension of the younger students as a more experienced teacher, and thus would not be able to present so fruitfully the elementary parts of mathematics, which is the principal object of the above mentioned position. On the other hand, we consider him excellently qualified to hold a position in higher mathematics which it is hoped will, in time, be created at the university.

"For these reasons we believe that Teacher Holmboe should be recommended in first place for this appointment. We also consider it a duty to point out how important it is for science in general and our university in particular that Student Abel not be lost from sight."

It was easy to criticize the decision of the faculty, and the friends in Berlin undoubtedly did so many times in the following weeks. Boeck and Keilhau strongly felt that an injustice had been committed, and later on in no way hid their opinion.

Had not Abel already produced an unusually high number of mathematical works? In a brief time he had become known as one of the most promising mathematicians in Berlin. If the university had only requested the opinion of a single foreign authority it would have been impossible to overlook Abel's total superiority as a mathematician. Had the decision not been forced through in a couple of weeks Abel would have been known as one of the most productive and original collaborators in one of the leading international mathematical journals.

Was it not contrary to the idea of a university for the faculty to declare — in regard to one of the most important subjects — that its principal object was to find someone who could teach the elementary parts of mathematics? Everybody agreed that Holmboe was an excellent teacher, but how could the faculty so definitely pronounce Abel unable to adjust himself to the understanding of the young students? True, the mathematicians in Oslo had had difficulties in understanding Abel's articles, but was that a deficiency to be ascribed entirely to the author? And in regard to his journey abroad no one would have returned home with greater satisfaction than the constantly homesick Niels Henrik. Nor was it unusual in the brief history of the university that a position remain vacant or be filled by a substitute for a term or two, in case Abel should have preferred to complete his journey.

The reverse side of the medal was undoubtedly more difficult for the little group to see. Abel was only twenty-three years of age; he was promising, but untried; his qualifications were not fully established, and it could not be denied that there was an error in his paper on the pendulum.

Abel wrote immediately to Hansteen expressing his concern and asking for a more definite statement on the chances for his future. It is not unlikely that in his anxiety he may have used expressions which seemed to indicate that he felt somewhat betrayed by his protector. Hansteen faithfully collected all the letters he received from Abel, and later published them in articles about the life of the young mathematician. Strangely enough this reproachful letter is never mentioned. Niels Henrik may have regretted a bit the form of his letter for he included an epistle to the wise Fru Hansteen, trying to mitigate the impression. Probably, as it not rarely happens, the letter was written mainly to have an opportunity to add the postscript:

"Kind Fru Hansteen: I am so fond of you, dear Fru Hansteen, that I must send a few lines to you. You are so good to me. I was worried that this no longer should be so, for I have still heard nothing from you. It would make me awfully happy. But I have the best of hopes, for my fiancée wrote me that you had the intention of honoring me with a little letter. I have also another reason for being hopeful, for I dreamed last night that I had received a letter from you, and I cannot but believe that my dream must come true. I remember feeling so extremely delighted. Yesterday I saw your husband's favorite Madame Seidler play in *Die schöne Müllerin*, and she was very sweet.

"I am anxious to hear something from Norway. Imagine, I have received no reply from my fiancée to my two last letters and today I write a third; I am worried, but I still blame the mail.

"At Christmas time I was invited to a ball at Geheimrat Crelle's. I did not dare to dance, although I was dressed more smartly than ever before in my life. Think of it, new clothes from top to toe, waistcoat and starched cravat, and spectacles. You see I have begun to follow your sister's admonitions. I hope to be perfect when I reach Paris. I wish I had been there and was back home again. It is so odd to be among strangers. God knows how I shall suffer it when I separate from my compatriots some time early in spring.

"Please extend my greetings to Charité, my sister, and brother. I wrote to him three weeks ago through my fiancée. I exhorted him as much as I could. I suppose that at heart he is really a quite good boy, but he is ashamed. I have been somewhat like him, but not so stiff.

"Adieu, good Fru Hansteen. Send me a few words, otherwise I dare not write you any more. Your N. Abel.

"God knows it was against my intentions, but in my letter to the professor I may have used expressions which are not to his liking. Kindly be my spokesman in this respect and excuse me as well as you can. Live well and remember me to Charité.

Hansteen undoubtedly carried the greater share of the responsibility for the decision of the faculty. On the other hand, he had always actively promoted Abel's welfare; in spite of all his youthful immaturity Niels Henrik was more of a friend than a pupil. Hansteen candidly admired his mathematical genius, and although he could not always comprehend Abel's flight into the spheres of abstract thinking, he was proud to be the fatherly protector of the youthful scientist. Most of the faculty were men who knew Abel personally; some of them had contributed to his fellowship. How then, one asks, could they have arrived at a decision which made Abel so anxious and his future so uncertain? It would evidently have been much more provident had the faculty definitely proposed a position for Abel when they appointed Holmboe to the lectureship. A reference to the fact that the professorship voluntarily had been reduced to a lectureship would have provided them with an excellent economic argument. The desirability of such an arrangement was mentioned, but nothing decided, probably in view of the plans which Hansteen had in mind.

Hansteen felt that the responsibility for the future of the two candidates rested in his hands, and that scientific careers should be made possible for both of them. Perhaps he could discern that Holmboe was not a first-class scientist and that his mathematical contributions had scant value. However, for many years Holmboe had been an able and faithful assistant to Hansteen in his studies of terrestrial magnetism; he had devoted all his spare time to conscientious labor which had little distinction. Should Abel now be awarded the only scientific position in mathematics in the country, a similar opportunity would most likely never appear for Holmboe. A personal motive may also have influenced Hansteen; the relations with his amanuensis might have become very strained were Holmboe to be disregarded upon this occasion.

Hansteen, before the faculty, may have used the humanly so understandable and scientifically so unjustifiable argument that because of Abel's youth and talents, it would be easier to find extraordinary expediencies for him. And in this respect Hansteen could outline a definite path. His plans for an expedition to Siberia to study the gravity and magnetism of the earth, and in particular to prove or disprove the existence of the conjectural new magnetic pole, were now taking more definite form. Royal approval of his project made him confident that economic support would be forthcoming from the government. Hansteen had begun a correspondence with scientists interested in participating in the exploration of these inaccessible parts of the globe. He counted on being ready for departure about the time Abel was scheduled to return, and expected the young man to replace him in his position during the two years the tour would last. Later it would be time for Hansteen and the other members of the faculty to use all their influence to make the government accede to the creation of a new university post for Abel.

Abel carefully hid his disappointment in the letters to Holmboe. The bitterness which he undoubtedly felt was in no way directed against his former teacher, and the friendship continued as warmly as ever. His great concern was that there might be no possibility for him to continue his scientific work when he went back; for that reason the idea of teaching in some school was repulsive to him. His requirements were not great; had the faculty brought forth some proposal whereby the position had been divided, leaving Holmboe in charge of the most elementary instruction, he would have been heartily content. As matters now stood there were reasons for concern. The only two posts in mathematics beyond the schools were held by Hansteen and Holmboe, and it would most likely be very difficult to influence the government into granting a third, apparently somewhat superfluous, position in this field. The government was in no way opposed to research, but its members were guided by the practical man's utilitarian ideas of what fields should be promoted. Meanwhile, there was not much Niels Henrik could do except to wait for some hopeful reply from Hansteen, and to fulfill the sad duty of writing to Crelly to tell her that their marriage would have to be postponed indefinitely.

10

A JOURNEY WITH KEILHAU

◆§ WHILE HIS FRIENDS lived opulently in Berlin, Keilhau barely subsisted in Freiberg, and had not been able to visit them during the autumn. His stipend was almost exhausted and it was uncertain whether it would be renewed. "It depends entirely upon Finance Minister Collett, who probably does not regard me too favorably." As a consolation he let his thoughts dwell upon the fascinating excursion he was planning with his two fellow geologists, Möller and Tank, to study Central Europe both above and below the surface. "In these vexing days I have found my greatest pleasure in meditating upon our common journey, and I have made such wonderful plans," he wrote to Boeck on Christmas Day. They intended to examine the formations in some of Europe's most beautiful mountain districts, Bohemia, Tyrol, and Switzerland. They would also travel through the magnificent cities of Prague, Vienna, Trieste, Venice, and later Basel, Lyons, and Paris. "Fate would deal me a blow from which I would recover only with difficulty, should I be prevented from taking part."

Keilhau was anxious that Boeck, his comrade of many strenuous marches in the Norwegian mountains, should accompany him. "I am so very reluctant to give you up. Would it not be possible to modify our plans somewhat so that they might be brought into agreement? Let me hear from you whether you cannot force your route into some form which is less devastating for me, and you shall have a hurried reply."

It was also a grave disappointment to Keilhau that he could not be present at the great wassail in Berlin; he even mentioned the possibility of selling one of his most precious treasures, the Norwegian mineral collection. Shortly afterward Keilhau decided upon a very brief visit to Berlin, which actually lasted a month. His friend, the geologist Naumann in nearby Leipzig, had completed the translation of Keil-

106

hau's works, found a publisher for them, and *mirabile dictu,* been promised a small honorarium for them. Keilhau drove from Freiberg to Berlin in the mail sled, and wrote to his mother about the trip and his experiences among his friends:

"Upon my arrival in the morning I hurried to my compatriots, who long had been awaiting me. The meeting was dear to me, as they are some of my very best friends, Boeck from Kragerö and Möller from Porsgrunn, with whom I have been together at the university, at Kongsberg, and in our mountains, and also Student Abel who already is so great a mathematician that within a few years he will be an honor to Norway.

"I have stayed with them now for three weeks; at Easter time we shall all gather in Freiberg, and if I receive more money for travel we shall journey together to Vienna, Venice, Switzerland, and to Paris where we are expected to arrive in August." He assured his mother that he spent most of his time at the mineralogical museum, but clearly there was also a little time for diversion. On the name day of the king they were all invited to the Swedish embassy. In hired silk dominoes they went together to the masquerade at the opera. "Most of the ladies were of the doubtful kind. I had had greater expectations." From his letters about art and the theaters, it is evident that he was the member of the company with the most profound understanding of the *beaux-arts.*

Boeck was finally persuaded to take part in the excursion, and the details in the plan were eagerly debated. One interested auditor was a young Dane, Rudolph Rothe, who had joined the colony and was considering following it at least some distance on the way. He had a small government stipend to learn the art of park gardening, and was now working at the Sans Souci gardens at Potsdam. He later wandered afoot through large parts of Central Europe, earned his living wherever he went, and became an expert in gardening and park management in his home country.

Only Niels Henrik listened to all these proposals and detailed plans with envy in his heart; his official track was fixed to pass over Göttingen to Paris, but Crelle's promise to accompany him to Göttingen and perhaps all the way to Paris — in order to promote the *Journal* — made the impending separation a little easier to bear.

Keilhau, obliged to return to Freiberg to arrange his affairs before the departure, tempted Abel to take the little trip: After all, there were no fixed obligations holding him in Berlin, and he could write mathematics wherever he wanted; furthermore he would not be without mathematical associations in Freiberg. The mineralogical seminary had an excellent professor in mathematics, August Naumann, the brother of Keilhau's geologist friend; in addition there was a gifted Dane, Jürgensen, studying mathematics. Abel was not difficult to persuade, in spite of the fact that Hansteen was certain to dislike such an unnecessary detour. But in any case Hansteen would have to be informed of his whereabouts; furthermore he had received no response to his important letter. Thus toward the end of January 1826 Abel wrote:

"I suppose that you have received the letter which I wrote you some time ago; I am longing for a reply since I shall leave Berlin in about three weeks and go over Leipzig to Freiberg with Keilhau. Later on I shall return to Berlin and, together with Crelle, take the trip to Göttingen and the Rhine districts. In Göttingen I shall dwell only briefly, for there will be little to detain me. Gauss is inaccessible, and it is impossible that the library is better than those in Paris. It is likely that Crelle also will travel to Paris. I will be exceedingly glad to have his company; he is an excellent man. The *Journal* progresses satisfactorily; you will receive the first issue in April. As you see, I work as hard as I can."

Abel also informed Hansteen that he had been looking for a publisher for some of his studies on integrals, mainly his memoir submitted earlier to the Collegium in Oslo. He had not been successful, for as the publisher had explained, the demand for such special publications was very small. Crelle was of the opinion that it would be easier later when some of his articles had appeared in the *Journal*.

The two friends departed as planned, and on February 27, Keilhau reported to Boeck from Freiberg: "Here I am and also Abel. As you probably saw when we departed, the trip to Leipzig was not comfortable, for the carriage was crowded and our companions were boasting merchants and *Geschäftsleute*. After our separation, we arrived in Leipzig at a quarter past seven in the evening. We found lodgings in the Stadt Berlin, right across from the post office and this presumably will also be most convenient for you. The waiters commented: These must be peculiar people. *Der eine Herr hat vor schlafengehen ein Glas Punsch getrunken und den Nachttopf zusammengeschmissen.* That, namely, was Abel's unfortunate fate. Naumann [the geologist], his wife, daughter, and mother are all well; they are looking forward to your arrival."

In Leipzig Keilhau called on his publisher, but the printing of his book had not yet been completed. He charged Boeck with collecting the royalty and the complimentary copies when he passed through town.

"We stayed in Leipzig a day and a half, for the mail coach for Freiberg left Friday noon. During the first 20 miles we had only one fellow traveler, probably a shoemaker; the next 25 miles we were all alone; then for 15–20 miles a very obscure person, and during the last 12 miles we had to suffer a blind passenger. We arrived very tired at half past nine in the morning; that same evening we played cards with Jürgensen and drank punch. Today Abel has had his first conference with Naumann; he finds that he is a very capable fellow. I should say many nice things to you in regard to my stay in Berlin. Receive my thanks. Greetings to Maschmann and Rothe. Abel wants to be remembered." Niels Henrik added the postscript: "The trunk has not arrived, but I suppose it will. Please do not forget to bring my cravat pin, my ambiguous girl's head, and my clothes."

Abel stayed in Freiberg a whole month, working energetically. He completed a large memoir, and was inordinately proud because he had written it in German without help. He reported his new results to Crelle, and was greatly perturbed when Crelle was compelled to inform him that, due to the pressure of official business, he was unable to take the necessary time off to accompany Abel to Göttingen. Abel was again in a dilemma. Should he travel to Göttingen and face the formidable Gauss alone, or should he once more follow his heart's desire, give all official travel plans a wide berth, and accompany his friends on their southward trek?

Carl Friedrich Gauss, "princeps mathematicorum" as he sometimes has been named, was by his contemporaries almost unanimously considered the first among mathematicians. His father, a stone mason, had shown no enthusiasm for his son's higher education; but the talents of the young Gauss overwhelmed his teachers. He was introduced at the court of the Duke of Braunschweig, who became his protector. During the greater part of his life he was director of the observatory in Göttingen. Here he lived, lonely and reserved, but the center of a wide circle of correspondence with the scientists of his day. He cared little for students and pupils, was indifferent in regard to honors, but from time to time he brought forth works which were mathematical masterpieces. One of the first was his book on number theory, *Disquisitiones Arithmeticae*, which Abel had studied in detail during his first year at the university. He was deeply impressed, as were all other mathematicians, by Gauss' solution of a problem which had remained unanswered since the classical period of Greek mathematics: Which regular polygons can be constructed by the use of compass and ruler?

Abel suffered a peculiar aversion against going to Göttingen. Possibly it was only his resistance to a separation from his friends. But Crelle was evidently not anxious to see him visit Gauss, nor did the mathematics students in Berlin seem to have given him any particular encouragement. It is interesting to speculate on the exchange of ideas which might have taken place at such a meeting of giants of mathematics, but it is not unlikely that Abel's own evaluation would have been correct: Gauss was no longer active in the fields which particularly interested Abel; a formal call might have been the only result of the journey.

The great Norse expedition to the south was to congregate in Dresden; Möller arrived in Freiberg in advance of the others. Keilhau left word for Boeck and Tank with his friend Professor Naumann in Leipzig: "Möller arrived here yesterday evening at nine o'clock in fine condition. According to the council held, it has been decided that we shall leave here Wednesday, March 22, and stay in Stadt Berlin in Dresden. Should it prove impossible to obtain rooms, then Im Deutschen Hause in Schleffelsgasse. We three should like to make the stay in Dresden as brief as possible, and it will depend on you whether we depart for Prague on the second or third day of Easter. I must request you to bring the copies of my book to Dresden, and also the money which I believe Naumann will extort from Barth [the publisher]. If I do not receive the money here I do not know when and where; we are all having money difficulties." The company gathered in Dresden as agreed; Boeck probably carried financial reinforcements to Keilhau and, in addition, a true surprise, a letter from Hansteen, the first they had received on the whole journey:

"You have the best reason, my dear Boeck, to be angry with me, since I reply only after having received five comprehensive letters from you. The case stands as follows: Since I returned from the Gulf of Bothnia I have been loaded down with courses and examinations, both ordinary and extraordinary, for graduates and non-graduates, for myself and for the retired Professor Rasmussen, the almanac, etc. Since the new university law has gone into effect, the university post seems like one of the city commissions, the Collegium room a stock market, my study a trade bureau. One has no time to think of anything but the meetings of the faculty and the Collegium, discharge of current matters, declarations, study plans, regulations, registrations, etc., etc.

"There is such life and action at the university *dass Gott sich erbarme!* In this misery, no one can complain that the professors and lecturers do not write enough, but whether they gain any laurels by it is doubtful. In addition to all this, let me point out that I was eager to analyze my travel observations, that I have been sickly for a quarter of a year, and then as usual there has been delaying and restlessness. However, it is certain that I have received your letters with the greatest interest and wanted to thank you sincerely for them."

Hansteen's list of his troubles was long, but far from complete. To others he complained vociferously about his economic difficulties and the insufficiency of his salary. He was also in a quandary in regard to the financing of the *Magazin* and had run into a violent controversy with one of its contributors, Dean Hertzberg in Hardanger. The quarrelsome dean had filled the *Magazin* with weather observations and popular sayings about the weather, and now urged Hansteen to include weather predictions in the almanac. Hansteen expressed himself in very derogatory terms about this kind of science, and would print no more of it; the dean responded with threats of legal action.

After discussing at length the magnetic measurements undertaken by the company, Hansteen continued: "In the last issue of the *Magazin*, I included a little column entitled 'Our Traveling Young Scholars,' in which I gave information in regard to the whereabout of Keilhau, Boeck, Abel, Möller, and Tank, and also what they were doing as far as I could see from various letters, and this article seems to have interested the public."

To Abel there were a few reassuring words: "My most friendly greetings to the good Abel and tell him that I shall write him by next mail. In regard to his future he may set his mind at ease. Part of the content of his letter I have used in the miscellaneous article. I have asked Fröken Kemp to tranquilize him for the moment."

Hansteen was satisfied with the travel route proposed by Boeck and

Keilhau, and found it "excellent in regard to magnetism." He had as yet no inkling that Abel was considering accompanying them still further; as Abel had foreseen he objected even to the trip to Freiberg. "But why that young god Thor, searching for his hammer, wants to swing to Leipzig and surroundings I do not know, presumably on account of the company; but he may flutter his own irregular course as a butterfly with more wings than body.

"However, I hope that you and he realize that I only speak jokingly. It is necessary to let everyone walk on his own feet, even if his boot heels may be askew. If you believe that he might be sensitive to my jest, then don't let him read these lines; I do not have the heart to cause him a single unpleasant moment. He always arrives where he is supposed to, even if he does not move straight to it. Remember me to Keilhau and the other Norwegian friends; I dearly wish to hear from them."

They stayed in Dresden longer than they had anticipated, saw the theater presentations and went sight-seeing. Here as everywhere else they passed through, the government fellowship holders paid a formal call upon the diplomatic representatives of their country and were usually invited to dinner. On the whole they traveled in such style as beseems a group of important and relatively well-to-do young men.

For the sake of conscience Abel had to inform Hansteen of his latest caprice, and wrote him a long letter. He also made an attempt to explain his ideas on the need to create a better foundation for mathematics. Hansteen may have had difficulties in grasping these concepts; he was a practical computer who accepted figures as he found them. Abel also had to tell him about the flattering offer which Crelle had made:

"Highly honored Herr Professor: Many thanks, Herr Professor, for your friendly regards to me in the letter to Boeck. I was afraid that in my last letter to you I had expressed myself strangely, and probably I did so. I must ask you to be lenient with me, particularly in regard to formalities. You have relieved my mind perfectly as to my future, and this was a true benefaction, because I was frightened, but perhaps too much so.

"I am longing infinitely to return home again, and to work undisturbed. I believe it will go very well; there will be no lack of ideas for several years. I shall probably gather more on my travels, for just at present there are many thoughts circulating in my head.

"My work in the future must be devoted entirely to pure mathematics in its abstract meaning. I shall apply all my strength to bring more light into the tremendous obscurity which one unquestionably finds in analysis. It lacks so completely all plan and system that it is peculiar that so many can have studied it. The worst of it is, it has never been treated stringently. There are very few theorems in advanced analysis which have been demonstrated in a logically tenable manner. Everywhere one finds this miserable way of concluding from the special to the general, and it is extremely peculiar that such a procedure has led to so few of the so-called paradoxes. It is really interesting to seek the cause.

"To my mind it lies in the fact that in analysis, one is largely occupied with functions which can be expressed by powers. As soon as other functions enter — this, however, is not often the case — then it does not work any more and a number of connected, incorrect theorems arise from the false conclusions. I have examined several of them, and been so fortunate as to make this clear. It works out satisfactorily as long as one proceeds generally, but I have had to be extremely cautious, for the presumed theorems without strict proof — i.e., without proof — had taken such a stronghold in me, that I was continually in danger of using them without detailed verification. These small articles will appear in the *Journal*, which Crelle edits.

"This man Crelle is certainly a most admirable acquaintance. I cannot praise my lucky star enough for having brought me to Berlin. In reality, when I think of it, I am really a quite fortunate man. It is true that there are few who are interested in me, but these few are infinitely precious to me, for they have shown me such great kindness. May I only approximately live up to the expectations they have for me, for it would be grievous if they should see their well-intended concern wasted upon me.

"I must tell you about an offer which Crelle made me before I left Berlin. He wanted absolutely to persuade me to remain in Berlin forever; and described to me all the advantages which would accrue from it. He offered me the editorship of the *Journal*, if I wanted it. It will probably do well financially also. It really appeared very urgent to him, but of course I refused. However, I had to soften my refusal by saying that I would accept it if I could find nothing to live on at home, as I actually would. Finally, he said that he was willing to reiterate his offer at any time. I cannot deny that this flattered me greatly. Wasn't it nice?

"One thing I promised him quite definitely, namely to return to Berlin before I concluded my foreign travel. This may be of the greatest advantage to me. He has promised quite certainly that he will find a publisher for my larger memoirs, and — think of it — for good pay. We first intended to publish together, from time to time, a collection of more extensive works. However, after more thought and a conference with a book dealer to whom we offered the publication, we decided that it would be more propitious to wait until the *Journal* was well established. I hope our plan can be realized when I return to Berlin.

"Isn't it wonderful? And do I not have cause to rejoice over my journey to Berlin? True, I have not learned anything from others on this trip, but I did not consider that its real purpose. For the sake of the future, the object ought to be to make acquaintances. Are you not of the same opinion?

"I stayed one month in Freiberg with Keilhau, and met an eager young mathematician, a brother of Naumann who was in Norway. He was a very agreeable man and we associated harmoniously.

"You wondered, in your letter to Boeck, what I might seek in Leipzig and the Rhine districts, but I should like to know what you will say when I now inform you that I am going to Vienna and Switzerland. I had first planned to travel directly from Berlin to Paris, hoping to be accompanied by Crelle. But then he was prevented from leaving, and I would have been obliged to travel alone. As it happens, I am so constituted that I absolutely cannot, or at least only with the greatest difficulty, be alone. Then I become quite melancholy and not in the mood for work. Then I thought: It will be best to travel with Boeck and the others to Vienna, and that, it seems to me, I can defend, for in Vienna are Littrow, Burg, and others. They are really excellent mathematicians.

"Furthermore, I shall probably travel only once in my life. Can you blame me for wishing to see a little of the life and ways of the south? I can work quite well on my journey. The road from Vienna to Paris passes almost directly through Switzerland. Why shouldn't I see also a little of it. My Lord! I am not entirely without feeling for the beauty of nature. The whole trip will delay my arrival in Paris by two months, and that does not matter; I shall recover the lost ground. Do you not believe that such a journey will do me good?

"From Vienna to Paris I shall probably travel with Möller, and then

spend the winter with Keilhau. We intend to exert ourselves strenu-
ously. I think it will work out quite well.

"I have received letters of recommendation from Crelle to Littrow
and Burg in Vienna. My vanity compels me to quote a few passages
from the letter to Littrow. After having talked about the *Journal*, he
continues: 'Herr Abel from Oslo in Norway, who presents this letter
to you, is also an active contributor to the *Journal*, and not one of
its least ornaments. I esteem this young man most highly, and I recommend him to your Lordship's goodness and benevolence. The high degree of mathematical distinction he has already achieved gives cause
for the most gratifying expectations for science.'

"We shall stay in Vienna about a month, and probably will then
divide into two parties, one — Boeck, Keilhau — going over Trieste,
Venice, through Tyrol, Switzerland; the other — Möller and I — to Paris.
I have received letters of recommendation from Professor Dirksen in
Berlin to Alexander von Humboldt and others in Paris. I hope to be
only half as fortunate in Paris as I was in Berlin; then everything
would be lovely.

"Keihau and Boeck have been out since early this morning, taking
observations with the oscillation instrument; while we — Möller, Tank,
and I — slept. You will receive a considerable series of observations.
They all want to be remembered.

"We paid our respects to Herr Irgens-Bergh [the chargé d'affaires].
Yesterday he gallantly sent us tickets to the casino of the nobles, *ou l'on
ne danse qu'en escarpins* [patent leather boots]. So for one night we
were members of the nobility: M. de Keilhau, M. d'Abel, etc. There
we saw all the *incroyables* of Dresden in their elegance." They were also
invited to dinner at the legation together with two already famous men,
the Norwegian painter Johan Christian Dahl and the Danish poet Jens
Baggesen, who was then rapidly drinking himself to death.

"You have been so kind, Herr Professor, to promise me an early
letter. I have still not received it, but the reason is probably that it
passes through various detours. I made arrangements with Maschmann
to have it forwarded to Vienna. I look forward with pleasure to hearing
something from you and my second mother. From time to time I shall
take the liberty of writing to you, not because I dare flatter myself that
you will find anything of particular interest, but because I find great
enjoyment in it myself. From me you cannot expect any diverting ob-

servations, coupled with esthetic descriptions; that I must leave to my more gifted travel companions, in particular Keilhau.

"Good-bye, Herr Professor, may you always live as well as I hope. Yours obligedly, N. H. Abel.

"Perhaps you will show me the kindness to give my sister the enclosed note. My most respectful greetings to Professor Rasmussen, but before all, to Fru Hansteen and Charité."

11

TO ITALY IN THE SPRING

◄§ DURING THE LAST FEW DAYS in Dresden, an incident occurred which, for Niels Henrik, furnished an excuse to throw all scruples overboard and travel to Vienna, regardless of the criticisms which almost certainly would be forthcoming from Hansteen. A brief, intense intellectual spring-storm broke out in the midst of the little group, and brought on its separation. Boeck made a most diplomatic use of the situation to explain to Hansteen how his dearest concern, the magnetic measurements, would have suffered if Abel had not unselfishly decided on the trip to Vienna.

"It was a blessing for our magnetisms that Abel decided to continue with us. Tank's practical-aesthetic-spiritual-religious-nature-philosophic ideas were tested so sharply and consistently by us and by our plan of travel that it was impossible to think of a continuation of the fellowship. Furthermore, Möller could not suffer Keilhau's plain speech which actually was designed to plane away some of his absurdities. The company, therefore, was dissolved in Dresden, where the two at present live a pleasant life together. Thus Keilhau and I would have remained alone if Abel had not agreed to come with us. Now that he assists Keilhau we can much more often observe on both instruments. I feel that this trip cannot be extraneous to the purpose of Abel's foreign journey. If he had traveled directly from Dresden to Paris his sojourn there would have been too extended." Boeck confessed that in his own field there was little opportunity for thoroughness while traveling: "I listen to lectures, speak with various people, inspect institutions, and remain about as wise as when I left. There is no time for orderly study if, at the same time, I wish to see and learn the things which are here but not at home. Abel could not easily have traveled alone, for he would have been bored and in low spirits."

On March 31, Abel, Boeck, and Keilhau left Dresden for Prague, where the young gentlemen went sight-seeing for about a week. Their next long stay was in Vienna, which they enjoyed for all of six weeks. The drive from Dresden was an adventure which they described enthusiastically. Austria seemed a strange country to them, particularly its bureaucracy. They were surprised by the official interrogations they underwent in the inns on the road: name, country, place of birth, religion, passport office, and much more, which we now have lost the ability to consider strange. A Viennese tried to console them by the information that if it seemed difficult for foreigners to enter the country, it was many times more complicated for an Austrian to leave.

"The day of our arrival," Keilhau wrote to Hansteen early in May 1826, "the first order of business was to obtain permissions of sojourn and money. I took charge of the former, Abel of the latter. One step outside the hotel door showed me that now, for the first time, I was in a great and hustling city, for Berlin appeared quite insignificant in comparison to Vienna in regard to traffic and population. Only with difficulty could I follow my hired guide through the narrow streets across the Graben Square to the Fremdenbureau. Here there were about 100–150 persons of the craftsman class, waiting in the entrance hall to obtain passports, being kept in order by gendarmes. I forced my way through, and was admitted to a solemn young man who discharged me abruptly with the observation that, first of all, we had to be certified as having the necessary means for the sojourn in Vienna." They were compelled to visit the banker and fill out forms before they were admitted to a prolonged examination at the police station. Keilhau, suffering from the illusion that bureaucracy belonged to the past, was extremely vexed: "Such useless, illiberal regulations, long considered antiquated by less wry and pessimistic governments, here belong to the order of the day."

A few days later Boeck received a sharply worded summons to reappear at the police bureau, because his papers had not been in satisfactory condition. But when Boeck turned up with his diploma from the University of Oslo, written in Latin and with an imposing red seal affixed to it, he was bowed out of the office amidst assurances that the city of Vienna would be proud to have a man of his rank visit within its boundaries:

"After these police matters had been discharged, the next pressing

118

business was to look for private rooms, and this mostly fell on my part. I marched around in town and read the notices at the house entrances, which proclaimed that apartments, rooms, parlors, beds, etc., were for rent, and I made an extensive circle of acquaintances consisting of janitors, landlords, and landladies. We finally found two suitable rooms in a house where there are no fewer than 220 families. Our host is an adjunct at the court chambers. The Herr Adjunct I have not had the honor to behold after a three weeks' stay, but the madam and daughter so much the more often. On account of our morning and evening tea, our laundry, and other domestic matters, they are more busy around us than we desire; the damsel seems to have fallen in love with Abel. By taking various security measures and a strict control of the bill, my relations with the madam are rather strained, but I hope it will work out until the last."

In Vienna they pursued their customary program of sight-seeing and theater-going. "We write, eat, sleep, drink, and trot around so the days pass quickly. We were hardly aware that we had been here a week already." One of their first goals was the tower of St. Stephan's Cathedral, at the time one of the tallest buildings in the world. Keilhau was nearly the victim of an accident when he stuck his head up into the bell chamber; only by quickly withdrawing it did he avoid being hit by the big clapper. They went to the horseraces, where the son of Napoleon was also present. They found that he resembled his father: "he wore a plain black suit and seemed to be cheerful and full of fun."

"Furthermore, we hurried to present ourself to our envoy, Baron Croneburg, who appeared to be very kindly disposed and perhaps more straightforward then most Swedes usually are," wrote Keilhau. "We were later invited for dinner, and I was delegated to converse with Her Grace, who is a very rich, baronized daughter of a Vienna banker."

Not many days after their arrival in Vienna, Boeck received a letter from the sulking dissidents in Dresden. Rothe had come from Berlin, but would not proceed immediately to Vienna. He brought letters, forgotten items from Berlin, and greetings from Maschmann, who was indescribably lonesome and homesick after the departure of his friends. He sent his best wishes to Megaro and the four others, hoping wholeheartedly that they would have a pleasant and enjoyable journey. According to the letter, Tank and Möller had a wonderful time in Dresden, but it was evident that they could now contemplate more calmly the episode with their friends. "Tank does not talk about Steffens any more, since he has tired of preaching to deaf ears; otherwise he is kind and fair as always. The events of the last days before you left for Vienna linger most disagreeably in my memory. I had hoped that all would have been forgotten after the serious drinking session we had the night before your departure. If Keilhau had known how fond I am of him, he would not have treated me in the manner he did. This I maintain quite definitely. Although I do not remember him with the least bitterness, my confidence in him is gone. *Wir sind geschieden auf immer geworden.* By this I intend to say that I have lost him. I rely fully on you not to mention the content of this letter to anyone.

"If you remain faithful to your plan of staying one month in Vienna, then we shall undoubtedly meet there; otherwise we shall perhaps run into you at Fassa or elsewhere, and I look forward to it. Remember Tank and me to Abel and Keilhau. If Abel remains until I arrive, we may make arrangements to go to Paris together." A couple of days later the pair was on its way to Vienna, and the great Norse trek continued without further disharmonies.

In Vienna Abel received his first letter from Holmboe, which he answered at once, on April 16; he was evidently relieved that the ties of friendship between them had not suffered. He described the overwhelming swarm of impressions from his travel, all in his youthful informal manner, outspokenly as was his wont. He had a good sense of humor and the many grotesque little incidents along the road particularly caught his fancy:

"Finally a letter from you! I almost believed you had turned me down for good, but so much more dear was it for me to hear from you. I arrived in Vienna on the evening of the 14th and on the 16th I received your letter forwarded from Berlin by Maschmann.

"I don't suppose you expected me to come to Vienna, but it seemed to me that I should not let such an excellent opportunity to travel with Boeck and Keilhau pass; I have actually decided to proceed still further, namely, by way of Trieste, Venice, Verona, and Turin — to visit the mathematician Plana — to Paris. We shall make a detour of approximately 300 miles on the trip, into Tyrol, Switzerland, etc. However, the itinerary has not been fixed definitely; I, at least, will probably make it a little shorter.

"It may seem terrible to you that I waste so much money on travel, although I do not believe it can be called a waste. One learns so many peculiar things on such a journey, things which are more useful to me than if I should continually study mathematics. You know also that occasionally I must have lazy periods so that I may go to work again with renewed energy. In July or August, when I arrive in Paris, I shall labor terribly, read, and write. I shall prepare my integral stuff, *théorie des fonctions elliptiques*, etc.; with Crelle's help, I have good reason to expect to get it printed in Berlin when I return there. I intend to do this if my money lasts, which I hope it will.

"We use a horrendous heap of money. We have to live in hotels and that adds up terribly. In addition, here in Vienna there is such a hell of an opportunity to live in luxury. The Viennese is a particularly sensual type, especially in regard to food and drink. The customs official examined us while eating; in short, everybody always eats. The other day I noticed a man who began his meal by unbuttoning his trousers; he stuffed himself horribly.

"Vienna is a large city and Berlin is trifling by comparison; that is, in regard to city buildings. There are interminable series of streets, in part narrow with tall houses of 5, 6, 7 stories, and an infinite number of shops, churches, etc. St. Stephan's tower is the highest I have ever seen; we live nearby. The interior of the church is very beautiful and here they carry on with their Catholicism all the time. The Divine Service has really a very solemn aspect, no wonder it appeals to the multitude.

"There are five theaters in Vienna, two in the center and three in the suburbs, and I intend to see them all. There is one in Leopoldstadt which distinguishes itself by affording an excellent occasion to study the Viennese. It is unusually popular, and the plays which are performed deal almost exclusively with Vienna and its inhabitants of the lower classes. The theater is called beym Casperl, after the traditional comic figure, a *Schildknappe* called Casperl. At present the scapegoat is more often the umbrella-maker Staberl, the personified artisan class in Vienna, an infinitely comic type. I was there once, and enjoyed myself greatly. The public was extremely boisterous, applauding and crying aloud all the time. Most plays are a terrible medley of impossible things and outrageous caricatures, but the actors are excellent.

"I have also been to another theater, the Imperial and Royal Court Theater, which is huge. The play was very good, and well acted as one could expect. A good theater is a distinct pleasure. That is something which we lack entirely at home and probably never shall have.

"The theater is very beneficial in respect to language also; there one hears the best and the purest. I must confess that the German I know I have learned in the theaters in Berlin, because elsewhere I have had scant opportunity to hear it. Conversation goes quite well, and I can get along everywhere without trouble. I am more afraid of French, but I suppose I shall manage when I arrive where it is needed.

"The Viennese officials are wary of strangers; one is examined to an extent which seems peculiar to us. Keilhau was asked who his father was and had to tell the story of his life. To be permitted to stay in Vienna one must procure a guaranty that one has enough to live on . . . "

The trip from Berlin to Freiberg and Dresden was described in some detail. "The three of us, Boeck, Keilhau, and I, then proceeded further southward. After a coach ride of two and one half days we came to Prague. Once over the Bohemian border everything changed: people, landscape, etc. It snowed when we passed Erzgebirge, but in the valley below the weather was delightful and the countryside particularly beautiful and fertile.

"When one passes into Bohemia images of saints appear everywhere along the road. We saw many of them; Nepomuk seemed to be very popular. But next to these images were large numbers of beggars, many of them blind, lying along the roadside all day.

"The first day we reached Töplitz, famous for its warm springs. A large number of rich people, sick and healthy, visit during the summer months. After Töplitz one comes to the Mittelgebirge, which afford a tremendously wide view of Bohemia. It is almost like an infinite, fertile plain.

"After traveling across this plain for more than a day, we arrived at Prague. We had planned to stay two or three days, but remained for eight, since Boeck found much of scientific interest there. Meanwhile, I walked around in town and went to the theater, one of the better ones. There I saw an actor from Munich, Ferdinand Esslair, considered the greatest in Germany. I saw him as Wilhelm Tell in Schiller's *Tell*, that was some acting!

"In Prague I called on David, an old professor of astronomy. He appeared to be an old curmudgeon who was afraid of strangers. From this I concluded that his knowledge was quite thin. In Prague there is also another mathematician, Gerstner, who was said to be very good, but I thought differently when I heard that he was called a veteran, for this is a designation often given men who once have achieved something, but now no longer amount to anything. It was well that I decided not to go, for I heard later that he could neither see nor hear.

"Prague is not a bad-looking town, and it is quite beautifully located. A very elevated section is called Hradzin. Here from a tower, one has a terrific view: Mittelgebirge, Erzgebirge, and Riesengebirge when the weather is clear. I went up, but could see nothing since the weather was unfavorable. Behind the Hradzin lies the observatory of Tycho Brahe. The building is now used for military purposes. The grave of Tycho Brahe may be seen in one of the innumerable churches in town.

"The manners in Prague appear to be quite uncouth, the public keep their hats on in the theater; nor are the eating places pretty: one sees one awful hoodlum after the other, and women with great beer mugs in front of them. Beer drinking is particularly prevalent in the Austrian provinces we have passed through — the first demand in a public place is: *Schaaffens Bier, Gnaaden!* But we always stick to the wines which, to my taste, are very good and not particularly expensive.

"From Prague we traveled in a hired coach which brought us to Vienna for about 24 daler, which is not expensive considering that the distance is about 250 miles. We drove very comfortably in a glass-enclosed carriage. Some distance from Prague we passed close to the Elbe, and at the same time we could see Riesengebirge covered with snow. The heat was nearly 20° R [77° Fahrenheit], and it bothered us particularly when we made our magnetic observations at noon and night.

"On the road from Prague to Vienna we passed through a large number of towns, some of which at home would be regarded as important, but scarcely noted here. The inns we stayed in were good and reasonable, but by far not as clean as those in northern Germany. South of Prague the country is not as flat as in the northern part, but very fertile. Mähren is quite barren, and looks like many districts in Norway. The whole picture changes when one reaches Austria. It is the most fertile land I have ever seen and so very well cultivated. There is not a single patch which is not used as a vineyard or a grain field. Often we could see nothing around us but grain fields; meadow land one finds only rarely.

123

"After four days' drive we arrived in Vienna shortly before sundown. From afar we could see the spire of St. Stephan's Cathedral, which is exceedingly tall. A few hours later, the city passed in review before us when we crossed a branch of the Donau. After having been subjected to a lenient customs examination, we drove through Leopoldstadt over the Ferdinandsbrücke into town, and registered at the most expensive hotel, Zum wilden Mann. We are still here but shall move today. We have rented private rooms for which we shall pay 30 Fl. a month, about 15 daler, which is very dear. On the whole, Vienna is very expensive, particularly so for strangers. Our dinner costs us at least one-half daler a person, and still we don't live in abundance in comparison with the Viennese, who eat tremendously."

They visited Möller's uncle, who had lived so long in Vienna that he had forgotten how to speak Norwegian; and as mentioned, they dined at the legation: "Yesterday we dined with the Swedish envoy, Baron Croneburg. There were only we three, three ladies, and the Baron and his wife. All ate enormously, especially the mother-in-law of the Baron, *eine geborene Wienerin*: I did not miss my share, but I should not like to do it over again."

Abel faithfully fulfilled the obligations of his fellowship by acquainting himself with all the mathematicians in town. In spite of his words of praise to Hansteen, none of them were outstanding, and they were far below the level of the Parisian scientists, to whom Abel should long ago have made himself favorably known. But he felt that he had gained in one respect: "I am no longer afraid to approach people. When one travels one has to produce the necessary amount of impertinence to assert oneself."

The only mathematician in Vienna whom Abel mentions as being helpful to him was Joseph von Littrow, the director of the observatory and one of Crelle's friends: "Yesterday, I finally found out where Littrow is. I visited him at seven o'clock in the morning, for he stays almost all day at the observatory. He received me well, discussed various things with me, asked me to visit him frequently, and invited me to dinner next Sunday. I hope to gain great satisfaction from this acquaintance. He is a very active man, of the same nature as Hansteen, whom he resembles a good deal. He is supposed to be a hot-tempered fellow who is readily enraged by opposition."

Littrow had just published a popular astronomy text which Abel liked and was now in the process of completing a larger scientific work in the same field. In a letter to Hansteen, Abel further described Littrow and his peculiar household: "In Vienna I often visited Littrow, and found in him a very excellent man. He has given me a letter of recommendation to Bouvard, director of the observatory in Paris, which I hope will be of great benefit to me. Littrow has asked me for some contribution to the *Annals of the Vienna Observatory*, and I shall, of course, make use of this good opportunity to show myself a little. Littrow has a very pleasant wife by whom he has 12 children, although she is no more than 34 years of age. She is Polish, and greatly devoted to the use of snuff; in her young days she also smoked the pipe 'like a Turk' as her husband expressed it. She retaliated by telling delicate stories about him."

Abel must have associated with mathematicians other than Littrow in Vienna, and it is probable that his discussions with them left a little trace in mathematical literature. About the time of Abel's arrival there appeared the first issue of a new mathematical periodical: *Zeitschrift für Physik und Mathematik*, edited by two professors at the University of Vienna. The next number was published shortly afterward, and contained an anonymous article giving the main lines of Ruffini's proof for the impossibility of solving the quintic equation, provoked, as the author said, by Abel's ingenious paper in Crelle's *Journal*, and the desire to view an important topic in several ways. The proof, however, suffered from the same weakness as the previous one by Ruffini.

The urgent question about the prospects for a position at home still remained unanswered. Abel attempted in all possible ways to make Hansteen reply to his query. Toward the end of his letter to Holmboe he implored again: "Be certain to remember me particularly to Hansteen and Fru Hansteen, and inform them that I have still not received any letter. I wrote to Hansteen from Dresden. Please ask Fru Hansteen to enclose a few lines in your letter. She must absolutely do it."

The original plan of the geologists had been to walk southward through the mountains between Vienna and Graz, but the mountain passes were still nearly impassable due to snow. Only the two really tough members of the group, Boeck and Keilhau, trained by their Norwegian mountain tours, remained set in their purpose. The others decided to take the mail coach to Graz. Abel's thought of dutifully setting out for Paris had again evaporated.

The two walkers were accompanied one day's travel on their way by the rest of the company, all taking a charabanc to Baden. The others returned the next day, after agreeing on a rendezvous in Graz. The excursion was long and strenuous, but highly interesting according to the descriptions of Boeck and Keilhau. The climax was a great celebration at the church in Maria Zell, where they happened to arrive on the day of its anniversary mass. Precious images of the Virgin and saints were carried under baldachins by long processions of pilgrims winding toward the sanctuary, and the cathedral was filled with a praying multitude. The solemn services made an impression on the two tourists, but did not prevent them from observing a few comic incidents. They tried to slip through the kneeling throng, "and there stood a choir boy occupied in melting the wax from small candles which had been presented," wrote Boeck. "I thought this was one of his duties, and that the small balls he made were for some sacred use, but what does the youngster do: when he had prepared a sufficient number he went out in the archway and amused himself by throwing them at some old crones who had completed their assignment of prayers and were looking around."

There was a happy reunion in Graz; they did some sight-seeing again and wrote letters before the departure for Trieste. Abel wrote another little letter without much content to Hansteen, reiterating his fervent desire for a few words: "Möller and I will arrive in Paris in about six weeks. There I hope I can expect a few words from you or your wife, for until now I have not had that good fortune. It would be a considerable encouragement for me, and I cannot say how dear. Once in Paris I shall send you a few lines about my reception, and about another important matter which I dare not bother you with now."

From Graz, the company continued to Trieste, a city which appealed to them: "It was truly refreshing to be in a coastal town again, and particularly in a lively city like Trieste. Here one sees representatives of almost all trading nations. The Exchange Building and the Contrado del Corso where we stayed were particularly interesting. In the milling crowd were the industrious, deliberate German, the active, dramatic Italian, the serious Turk, the sly Greek, the brown, gargling Arab, the free, daring Dalmatian, the broad-cheeked, witty Croat," wrote Keilhau.

They celebrated their arrival by a swim in the ocean, and boarded

Norwegian vessels, getting acquainted with the skippers. They were served home food, which tasted doubly good, since their weekend in Trieste was very meager. There they had been compelled to wait several days for the steamship for Venice. On Saturday noon Boeck forgot to go to the banker to obtain money. Boeck and Keilhau chose to alleviate their hunger by a long walk in the countryside, while Abel and Möller spent their remaining pennies on a bowl of soup. However, they made up for it on their last evening by throwing a party: "For the last dinner we had invited two countrymen; one had been vice consul and now lived in Verona, the other was a skipper from Bergen. We drank Vino d'Istria and the excellent Prosecco. The skipper believed that this should be a real Norwegian feast, and thought it was necessary to be careful. He was quite droll, particularly when he related his encounter with two men-of-war off Sicily; he believed they were Turks."

Shortly afterward Abel was pleasantly surprised by another letter from Holmboe; the faint suggestion of reservation between them had been dissolved. On June 15, 1826, Abel replied from Bozen with a long description of his new adventures:

"This moment I received your letter dated May 22, and a thousand thanks for it, you cannot believe how I appreciate hearing something from home and especially from you. I am glad that on the whole you like my travel route and I feel myself it is not badly planned. You add, it must be a happy life. True, I would not have missed this trip for anything, but you will perhaps be surprised when I tell you that I am quite satisfied to have come this far, and particularly to have got out of Italy. What I have seen has interested me greatly, but it is a terrible country for travel. I shall tell you briefly about my journey.

"I left Vienna for Graz with Möller and Tank on the 25th of last month at ten o'clock in the evening, by the express mail coach, so named because it goes quite fast, but not as we ordinarily drive in Norway. In North Germany such mail is called Schnellpost, or in derision, Sneelpost [Snailpost], since it goes rather slowly.

"It is a strange feeling to leave forever a great and multitudinous city, particularly a place where one has enjoyed oneself greatly. I was in bad humor and spent a miserable night, almost sleepless as you can understand. At the glimmer of dawn I began to observe my traveling companions, and after a while I discovered that aside from the three of us, there were two Germans and three Italians in the coach, all terrible blokes, especially one 'Merchant of Venice' who made an awful racket.

"Halfway between Vienna and Graz the road leads through a pass in the Alps called Semmering, and here lies the border between Austria and Steiermark. The countryside again becomes very beautiful; I could believe I was in Norway, so much does Steiermark remind me of it. The road went through a very narrow valley next to the river Mur. This enlivened the scene, every moment new views. But if the country was pretty, the population was not. Everywhere one sees people with goiter; it looks awfully disgusting. It is said to be caused by the drinking water. South of Graz the disease is more rare. About eight o'clock in the evening we arrived, very tired, at Graz and after a meal went to bed. Möller and I spent the next day seeing the beautiful surroundings. There is an especially charming view from a mountain hard by the city. Just as we were eating dinner Boeck and Keilhau came in the door. They had walked afoot from Vienna by another route a few days before us. This amused us greatly, for we did not know where they were, and it was entirely by chance that they came to our place. They had had a very enjoyable trip, but been greatly hampered by snow.

"Graz is a beautiful city. It has 40,000 inhabitants, and a new theater which we attended every evening, since we shall soon take our leave from the German theater which has given us so much pleasure. On May 29, I left Graz with Boeck, Keilhau, and Möller. We rented a coach which should bring us to Trieste in four and one-half days for about 21 daler. We had a pleasant journey: the landscape was extremely beautiful, fertile fields, large rivers — Mur, Sau, Drau, and high mountains created a good effect. The nights, on the other hand, were not so pleasant, for the inns were bad, everything swinish, but very cheap.

"The strangest sight on the way was the famous subterranean grotto at Adelsberg, some distance from Trieste. This cave extends many miles into the mountains, and it requires 24 hours to walk as far as it has been explored. It goes still farther, but at this point a broad and deep hole creates an insurmountable obstacle. We proceeded only a short distance. Through the same mountain runs a river which is hidden from view for a distance of 20 miles; we saw both the entrance and the exit.

"On the fifth day we crossed into Italy, and had dinner in the first

Italian town, Sesana. The people were German, but the food was Italian macaroni. Since it was Friday we had to be content with Lenten food. Here the red wine is called black wine, and it is a name it deserves; it looked doughty, but was not particularly good.

"We were now approaching the ocean and suddenly came to a place where it was in full view. We descended from the coach to enjoy the scene better. The Adriatic was before us, far below Trieste. Numerous ships lay in the bay; on one side was the coast of Istria, on the other the coast line stretched toward Venice. The view was undeniably beautiful, but far from comparable to Ekeberg [near Oslo]. But for us who so long had missed the ocean, it made a very pleasant impression — especially since it was the Adriatic which we saw for the first time.

"We rolled down the hill, and soon reached Trieste, where we lodged in the Albergo all'Aquila Nera [the Black Eagle]. Before we could get our things arranged we mixed four languages: Norwegian, German, French, and Italian; and these four we used daily as long as we were in Italy. We decided first to go swimming, but we had great trouble in finding a rowboat, for no one understood German or French, and our Italian was extremely poor. Finally a fifth language — English — helped us out of our embarrassment. By a fortunate chance we met an English sailor, and Möller speaks English.

"Trieste is a beautiful city, has 36,000 inhabitants, and a lively trade. There are innumerable nationalities represented, certainly all European ones including Turks and Greeks, and, in addition, Arabs and Egyptians. In the harbor we found four Norwegian vessels with cargoes of fish, two from Bergen and two from Trondheim. We visited three of them. One skipper from Bergen and another Norwegian, Larsen from Arendal, previously consul in Genova, we invited for a dinner where we lived high on classical wines. I wrote a little note to Lector Bohr in Bergen, which I sent with the skipper, together with some books which I asked him to forward to you. Will you kindly receive them and keep them until my return? In Trieste I saw my first Italian comedy, *Il dottore e la morte*. Outside the theater some of the most remarkable scenes were depicted, and the title was painted in yard-high letters.

"Midnight, June 7, all five of us left Trieste with the steamship for Venice. At 8 o'clock we caught a glimpse of its towers, and not long afterward we were lying at anchor in this strange city. I could not believe I was in Venice. We disembarked near the famous St. Mark's Square, and were immediately surrounded by a mass of gondoliers, all intent on making money. These gondolas are long and narrow and propelled by one oar. In the center there is a little shelter under which one sits. We took one of these, but not until we had agreed on the fare; otherwise one would be cheated. Everything in Venice is designed to dupe the public. There is such a horde of good-for-nothing beggars and scoundrels that one must constantly be on guard.

"We had disembarked at the Hotel Europa, which had been recommended as being one of the best. Actually, it was rather poor, and very expensive. We immediately engaged a guide to show us the city and the sights. We rented two gondolas and set out, for just as one drives or walks through the streets in other towns, one here moves through the canals which take the place of streets. However, it is possible to reach any point in Venice on foot, but since the streets are very narrow and winding, the passage over water is preferred.

"It is a melancholy sight to pass through Venice; everywhere one sees signs of decayed splendor and present misery. Wonderful palaces stand quite deserted and almost decrepit; ugly, ramshackle houses with one or two rooms inhabited, ruins of crumbled or wrecked buildings which once have been beautiful, all testify to decadence. Venice now has not more than 80,000 inhabitants; I would estimate that more than half the city lies waste.

"The most wonderful locality in town is St. Mark's Square. It is extremely beautiful, surrounded by exquisite buildings and infinite colonnades. It is particularly crowded in the evening and late at night, when people visit the innumerable coffeehouses in the archways. I counted 25 on one side, some of them very large; on the other side there are magnificent shops.

"On St. Mark's Square stands an isolated, very tall tower. We ascended to the very top, and had a delightful view of the city. It is, I believe, unique, for everywhere one looks out over water, no land except far in the distance. Across from the tower lies the celebrated St. Mark's Cathedral, built entirely in marble, and splendidly ornamented. All the walls and floors have mosaic inlays. Next to it is the ducal palace. Under its roofs were formerly the lead chambers, well known from Casanova's life story, since destroyed by the French. I could tell you much more about Venice, but I must be brief; I shall write also to my fiancée today.

ABOVE *The market place in Predazzo, with the inn Nave d'oro at the left.*
BELOW *Carl Friedrich Gauss, the leading German mathematician, and the
Marquis Pierre Simon Laplace, the "Newton of France"*

"We left Venice on the 10th, and rowed in two gondolas to Fusina, where we ordered a veturino to take us to Padua. Shortly afterward we were there and found a large and comfortable carriage. We drove along the river Brenta through the most fertile and thoroughly cultivated land imaginable. The whole landscape was as flat as a lake, and quite like a garden, with grain, vines, and fruit trees on every spot.

"After six hours' ride we came to Padua, an awfully ugly city, the worst I have ever seen. We visited some churches, viewed a house in which Titus Livius had lived, and spent an expensive day and night in a poor hostelry. The next day we drove on to Vicenza, located in charming surroundings. Here we dined, and came to Verona in the evening after a pleasant journey.

"We saw several remarkable sights; for instance, a Roman gateway, a bridge built by Vitruvius over the River Etsch which runs through the city, and above all a tremendous amphitheater from antiquity, able to hold 23,000 spectators. On the 12th we left Verona, and traveled along the Etsch through a narrow valley surrounded by extremely high mountains. We entered Tyrol, and arrived yesterday, the 14th, here at Bozen. We shall now make an excursion, lasting a few days, into the Fassa valley and the surrounding mountain districts. Then we shall drive with all possible speed to Schaffhausen, from where Möller and I go on directly to Paris, where we hope to arrive in a month or less."

Abel could not deny himself the pleasure of a last fling in the company of his friends. He joined them in a two-week geological excursion to the Fassa and Fiemme valleys, and to the mines at Agardo. These localities Keilhau considered the most essential to him of all those visited on the whole trip, and here he expected to put his own theories to a crucial test. "We proceeded further, about twelve miles, to Predazzo which has become one of the most renowned places in the geological sciences," Keilhau wrote. They stayed almost three days, using the inn Goldenes Schiff as their headquarters. When in Dresden they had belonged to nobility for a day; here they registered themselves as the venerable members of the scientific community which they once hoped to become:

Keilhau, professore della mineralogia.
Boeck, professore dell'arte veterinaria.
Abel, professore della geometria.

The host was somewhat more prosaic in his appraisal, and noted that they were five "studenti da Norvegia," who were making geological studies. They returned to Bozen, and Keilhau reported to Hansteen on June 28: "Here Tank, Abel, and Möller have left us; they drove yesterday to Innsbruck to hurry to Paris." Keilhau and Boeck spent the summer together on mountain tours in Switzerland before separating, Boeck to study in Munich and Keilhau in Paris.

It had been an unforgettable journey. Boeck wrote to his father from Bozen: "We have again turned toward the north, after having seen a little of Italy and a part of Tyrol since I wrote you from Trieste. Aside from a few discomforts it has been a trip so interesting that I shall never forget it. The districts we passed through, the cities of Venice, Padua, Verona, and Vicenza, had so much new to offer that I shall always remember the tour as in a dream. Tomorrow I continue to Schaffhausen. Thus we have, in a short time, covered quite some ground. We have seen more than the majority, for we have trotted around energetically, and not saved our legs. But the journey has had a disastrous effect on the purse, for it was frightfully expensive, particularly in Venice and Padua."

A few months later, Tank wrote from Norway in his florid style, inspired by Steffens: "Thanks, my dear honest friend Boeck, for your kind letter from Munich. It proved to me that my memory is still sympathetically retained in the mind of a precious friend, and that the warmth of the south and the vast distance between us cannot diminish Nordic friendship. Yes, have thanks for this latest pleasure, as well as for the many agreeable hours we passed together in the great Nordic trek, which to the last will remain to us a rich and enjoyable memory. What you so charitably say about the discussion of 'warmth over differences of opinion' I should rather consider to be as the tendons in the muscles, which contribute to their strength. What is born in heat always promises to be of use in this world. For me, the string of recollection still vibrates, perhaps because I was the weakest among us. It will be a continued delight to listen to its song about a pleasant time in rich provinces, among beloved countrymen in the flower of their youth."

Even Hansteen was aware that it was of little use to sulk or preach. He wrote a letter to Vienna, embracing all three, Abel, Boeck, and Keilhau; but it was delayed and reached them only long afterward. In his next letter to Schaffhausen he concluded with the best wishes for the company and the tour. "Now be you commended to God, all three of you. Enjoy yourselves in the Alps and under the Italian sky, and write letters when you have leisure. But be warned that I can repay but for few of them; I wanted to do more, but I am unable to. Your devoted friend C. H."

Hansteen's letter contained splendid news for Keilhau. It seemed likely that his appointment to the university would be approved, and he reported also that the finance minister was willing to grant Keilhau an advance on his salary: "I called on Collett today in regard to the 100 daler. He said, 'Why does not Keilhau personally address himself to me? I have shown him every possible attention, and with the greatest readiness. I have procured all that he so far has received from public funds.' I replied that it was probably caused by modesty. The final outcome was that Keilhau will receive the 100 daler, payable in francs, when he arrives in Paris."

Hansteen added a special greeting and apology to Abel, but said nothing about his future: "Finally, my good Abel, I must thank you for your friendly letters. I am infirm, loaded down with duties and rarely in good working condition. This is the reason why I have had to let you wait so long for an answer. Be assured that I and my family clearly recognize all the things which are good and agreeable in you, but we also perceive certain weaknesses. Others have had to wait equally long for reply, yes, even longer.

"Dean Hertzberg has a lawyer on my neck, who has laid down severe conditions; he has been ordered to call on me three times a week until I reply. I have amicably advised the lawyer to disassociate himself from this commission, for I have a steep stairway, a quick temper, and a pair of loose fists. Under these conditions the correspondence naturally becomes irregular."

12

MATHEMATICIANS IN PARIS

⚜ EN ROUTE TO PARIS Abel traveled with Tank over Innsbruck as far as Basel. His intentions were the best, but he could not bring himself to pass Switzerland without seeing a little more of the Alps and a few of the most famous localities. When the two finally started in earnest toward Paris, Tank was informed that a calamity had ravaged his home town of Halden, a little border town surrounding one of the strongest fortifications in Norway. It was a historic place which had figured heroically in the wars between Sweden and Denmark-Norway. A century earlier, it had voluntarily been put to the torch by its patriotic citizens, intent upon driving out of its shelter the beleaguering Swedish army under Charles XII.

Tank later wrote to Boeck: "In Basel I was informed that the town of Halden, with its suburbs and the fortress, the faithful rock, had burned. I could no longer expect any letters without again going toward the south where, on the way to my cousin in Naples, I might have found you and Keilhau. But it seemed to me that under such circumstances, this was not the time to travel idly around, so in 15 days I exchanged Basel for this ash heap where — God be praised — I have had plenty to do and have done it eagerly. On the stage of my life this last half year there has been exclusively lumber and brick; but truly, I have many times had the same pleasure as I formerly had at Sonntag's and Krone's. One hundred fifty houses have been rebuilt and also the greater part of the fortress which some infamous persons wanted to abolish for economic reasons. It seems that in a few years the town will be more beautiful than ever.

"The occasion of the conflagration was strange. It was caused by the cannonade from the fortress to celebrate the birth of the first Bernadotte in Scandinavia. Thus it happened that this sacrificial fire burned upon the same altar which shone at the fall of the last great Vasa king. May it stand ready to be lighted again if required! There are now plans afoot to increase and strengthen the fortress considerably.

"You were so kind as to inquire about our losses. I can reassure you that they were relatively small, for our large pier loft and office building were among the few undamaged houses. Since we ourselves live outside of town, we had an opportunity to assist many during the long period when they needed it. At my sister's place there are still 250 persons, and at my brother-in-law's and here we had over 1000 persons during the first days. If this be counted as a loss, it is a most cherished one.

"You know, people were not in their worst spirit when the walls which separated them burned down; there was a small period almost of inspiration. Now they are building them up again, and more and more I turn back to my former life, to my books, to the free life in the wonderful nature of Norway, to the thoughts of my journey which ended in Basel."

He added, "A short time ago I talked with Hansteen who brought me regards from Abel, who continues to move along his trajectory, although at times it is quite curved."

Otto Tank's hope to return to his books and scientific studies was not fulfilled, nor was his journey ended in Basel. Later he became deeply influenced by the simple and sincere faith of the Moravian Brethren, joined the group, and moved to the Herrnhutian center in Christiansfeld, South Jutland. He married the daughter of one of their elders and was placed in charge of some of the industrial undertakings of the community. In time, he felt it his duty to take an active part in the missionary work. After a training period he was dispatched to Surinam, in Dutch Guiana, as the leader of the mission station of the Brethren. For seven years he worked devotedly among the natives, trying to improve their lot. He could evoke not only the treasures of heaven for his congregation, but also earthly riches which neither moth nor rust corrupt. By virtue of his geological training, he discovered gold deposits which produced a great income both for himself and for the Dutch government.

After his wife died in Surinam, Tank gave up his mission work and went to Holland to attempt to reform the government's backward policy of colonial administration. He married again, this time a wealthy lady of a distinguished Dutch family. He could not return to Surinam; as an opponent of slavery he was *persona non grata* to the plantation owners. During a visit to Norway, he heard of a small group of Norwegian Herrnhutian brethren struggling under great handicaps near Milwaukee in the United States. Here again was an outlet for his humanitarian impulses. Shortly afterward, inspired by the example of Count Zinzendorf, the great leader of the Brethren, Tank conceived a magnificent utopian project.

Tank left for the United States in 1849. Few immigrants have settled in the West in greater style, nor did anyone have greater resources; even the Oleana planned in Pennsylvania about the same time by his countryman Ole Bull fades by comparison with the Ephraim which Tank envisaged. He and his aristocratic wife arrived with a large shipment of valuable Dutch furniture, a library of several thousand volumes, and, according to a contemporary newspaper report, one and a half million dollars in gold. Tank bought 10,000 acres of land in the Green Bay section of Wisconsin, offered free soil to all the Brethren, and assisted them economically in building homes and buying equipment. Faithful to his own higher education, he also founded an academy, the first Norwegian institution of higher learning in America.

In spite of Tank's philanthropic idealism and his personal friendliness, a group directed essentially by one man was not adapted for survival in the land of liberty. Dissatisfaction and suspicion arose, and the group made another exodus, the deserted Tank remaining on his land until his death in 1864.

From Basel Abel drove without halt to Paris, attempting to regain a little of the precious time he had lost. He had traveled as a tourist since his departure from Freiburg, four months earlier. He arrived in July, during the hottest part of the summer. It was vacation time in Paris, the university lectures were over, the libraries closed, most professors had left town. However, this suited Abel's plans quite well. He needed to learn more French before he initiated his round of official calls; furthermore, he wished to commence his ambitious program of mathematical production.

Abel had written incessantly in Berlin, completing one remarkable article after the other. Now, after many months of enforced abstention from his mathematics, his fingers itched to begin afresh: to analyze, to compute, and to fix on paper the numerous ideas which had come to him during his apparent idleness. In addition, there were a few important topics which he had long worked on; the results had been essentially established and could be made ready for publication in short order.

In his letter to Degen during the spring of 1824, more than two years previously, Abel indicated some of the results on integrals which he had achieved. He had purposely omitted them from his first round of publications in the *Journal*. As he mentioned to Degen, the results connected with his general theorem on integrals — later called the great Abelian theorem — he expected to present to the French Institute as his introduction to the French mathematicians; to this plan he faithfully adhered.

The second topic which held Abel's interest in the fall of 1826 was the theory of elliptic functions, a field in which he was greatly advanced as early as the summer of 1823, as evidenced by his letter on the subject to Holmboe from Copenhagen. He had developed his ideas into a coherent mathematical theory, and stimulated by Crelle's optimism in regard to a publisher, he now delved into the subject with renewed fervor.

As soon as he arrived in Paris Abel wrote to Crelle, explaining and illustrating his new discoveries. Crelle had become his most faithful correspondent — even his dear Crelly did not write as often. He knew Abel's poverty, his uncertainty in regard to his future prospects at home, and if Crelle could not grasp entirely the implications of all Abel's mathematical creations, he certainly came nearer to it than any other mathematician Abel had met. The mathematical missives passed back and forth; Abel continued to describe his work to Holmboe also, but in general terms without details; to Hansteen he rarely mentioned any mathematical problem.

Paris abounded with famous mathematicians and physicists at this time. Abel mentioned a considerable number of them, occasionally with an impertinent observation to characterize them. He was obviously disappointed that many were so old that only their fame remained.

Abel first called on Bouvard, the amiable director of the observatory who, among other achievements, had been the first to suggest that some irregularities in the movement of the planet Uranus might be due to some unknown planet — Neptune. Hachette, who introduced Abel to many of his colleagues, was a professor at the Sorbonne. Poisson was one of the most active of the mathematicians, and highly esteemed for his studies on probability, heat, and electricity. Such great men as Fourier, Ampère, and LaCroix Abel mentioned only in passing. He bought and shipped a trunkful of their works to Holmboe for safekeeping: "I have bought what I believe we do not have at home, and have still more here, which I shall send in the spring."

The most famous of them all was Pièrre Simon de Laplace, the Newton of France, who had been made a marquis for his services to science. In spite of his old age he had just completed the fifth and final volume of his monumental work, *Mécanique Céléste,* which Abel thought a suitable gift for Hansteen: "Among the books is the fifth volume of the *Mécanique Céléste.* Perhaps you will be good enough to deliver it to Hansteen with my regards. So the *Mécanique* is completed; anyone who has composed such a work can look back upon his scientific career with satisfaction." Abel confirms his great admiration for Laplace in a marginal observation in his mathematical notebook: "It is readily seen that any theory written by Laplace will be superior to all produced by mathematicians of lower standing. It appears to me that if one wants to make progress in mathematics, one should study the masters and not the pupils."

There were at the time two mathematicians in Paris destined to play a particular role in Abel's own scientific life. One was Adrien Marie Legendre, who in spite of his seventy-four years still was very active in research. Throughout a long life he had made discoveries in many fields: number theory, geometry, geodesy, and astronomy. His works were among the most read in the mathematical literature. Almost simultaneously with Gauss, Legendre had introduced the so-called method of least squares, which since has formed the basis for the analysis of all observational material in astronomy and geodesy. But Gauss, a little ahead of him, had received the lion's share of the credit. Here, as well as in other fields, Legendre was a bit jealous of the master in Göttingen.

More important for Abel was the fact that Legendre was the foremost authority in regard to the elliptic integrals. For forty years he had worked sporadically on the subject, and had just presented a large work in two volumes, *Traité des fonctions elliptiques,* to the French Academy of Science. Unfortunately it did not appear in the bookshops until shortly after Abel's departure. Abel paid his respects to Legendre after his arrival, and saw him at various meetings, but no scientific contact was established between the two. Certainly had Legendre realized the importance of Abel's ideas for his own work, as he subsequently did, he would have shown the same delight which he later was unable to restrain.

The other mathematician whose evaluation of Abel's work became of extreme importance to him was Baron Augustin Louis Cauchy, the leading active mathematician in Paris. His scientific production was enormous. For long periods he appeared before the Academy once a week to present a new paper, so that the Academy, largely on his account, was obliged to introduce a rule restricting the number of articles a member could request published in a year. As a mathematician he was a many-sided genius, but at present he is principally known as the creator of the theory of functions of a complex variable and one of the initiators of the modern exact direction in function theory. Among his colleagues he was not always popular, often considered hypocritical and egotistical. In his preoccupation with his own work he showed little interest in that of others. Abel does not seem to have liked Cauchy personally, but he never made a secret of the fact that he considered him to be the only one who knew how mathematics should be presented and demonstrated.

In France, as everywhere else, Abel was greatly interested in the opportunities for getting some of his articles published. The work containing the great integral theorem he had reserved for one of the series of the Institute, the most distinguished scientific publications in France. A purely mathematical journal, well established and privately published, was the *Annales de Mathématiques pures et appliquées,* usually referred to as Gergonne's *Annals,* after its founder and editor, Joseph Diez Gergonne, professor of geometry at the university in Montpellier. Crelle had used this publication as the model for his *Journal,* in name, form, and content.

A few years before Abel came to Paris, a quite unusual publication had appeared, *Bulletin universel des sciences et de l'industrie,* one of the first scientific review journals in the world. As customary, the name was shortened to Ferrusac's *Bulletin* in honor of its editor, who had the formidable name Étienne Just Paschal Joseph François d'Audebart, Baron de Ferrusac. The baron had been an army officer, but he had resigned to devote himself entirely to science, and had conceived the ambitious plan of creating a magazine which in brief reviews would give the content of all new publications, books, and articles concerning the natural sciences. He had succeeded in engaging some eminent scientists as his collaborators, and a whole series of volumes had already appeared. The project had caused a stir in the scholarly world, and it was natural that Abel should have tried to establish contact with de Ferrusac; however, the baron was not in town when Abel called. But he made the acquaintance of the young editor of the mathematical and physical section of the *Bulletin*, Jacques Frederic Saigey, who promptly engaged him as a new member of the staff.

Saigey was also a mathematician, although he was more interested in astronomy than pure mathematics. He knew Abel as a prominent contributor to Crelle's *Journal*, and the two became fast friends. Abel was not particularly enthused over the idea of writing reviews rather regularly, but the work gave him various advantages, perhaps he was even paid a little. He became acquainted with a circle of young scientists similarly occupied and he obtained free access to de Ferrusac's fine private library, a meeting place for the scientists.

One of his first assignments was to review the first issues of Crelle's *Journal*, a task which pleased him since it suited Crelle's desire to make the *Journal* internationally known. The first article Abel tackled was his own proof of the impossibility of a solution of the quintic equation in radicals. It was an unusually extensive and detailed review, giving all his main arguments, so it was practically a new paper which he presented to the international public of the *Bulletin*. Saigey added a postscript, pointing out that Ruffini some years earlier had given another proof which Cauchy regarded favorably. "Other mathematicians confess that they had been unable to understand this proof and some have made the correct observation that Ruffini, perhaps by proving too much, had proved nothing in a satisfactory manner. Monsieur Abel has shown by a more penetrating analysis that there can be no algebraic [radical] roots, but he does not deny the possibility of transcendental roots. We recommend this problem to the attention of mathematicians specializing in this field."

Abel wrote short accounts of other articles, both his own and those of others, but since the reviews are unsigned, it is impossible to decide which came from his pen. But from Hansteen's *Magazin* only one article is discussed, the unfortunate computation of the effect of the moon upon the pendulum. The content with its slip is quite kindly reviewed, and there can be no doubt that it was Abel who had the desire to explain the error from his early youth.

The only authentic portrait of Niels Henrik Abel, executed by the painter Görbitz in Paris in 1826

After a month in Paris the first report was sent to Hansteen on August 12, 1826:

"Finally I am here in Paris, the focus of all my mathematical ambitions. I have been here since July 10. You may feel that this is very late and that my Venetian detour was not justified. Dear Herr Professor, it grieves me deeply if I have done something which does not meet with your approval, but now that it has been done I must appeal to your kindness. I hope you have enough confidence in me to believe that I want to utilize my journey for the best purpose; indeed, this I shall.

"I have nothing to say to excuse myself except that my desire to look around was great. Does one travel exclusively to study strictly scientific things? After this I shall work with so much greater eagerness. In Bozen I left Möller, Boeck, and Keilhau and traveled as quickly as possible to Paris. From Innsbruck we drove to the Bodensee — I hope you will not blame me for seeing a little of Switzerland; it cost me a few pennies more than the direct route. I passed through Zurich, Zug, Vierwaldstädtersee, and Luzern to Basel. I was also on Mount Rigi, between the Zugersee and Vierwaldstädtersee, from where one has the widest view in Switzerland. From Basel I drove in one stretch to Paris, three days and four nights.

"To improve my French I have taken lodgings with a French family, price 120 francs a month, all included. The husband and wife seem very obliging and I am content, except that the room is very bad and we eat only twice a day. I had great troubles in finding such a place, and I would not have succeeded had I not been fortunate enough to recall the painter Görbitz whom you had mentioned. He has been as kind and helpful as anyone could wish. I visit him often; he wants to be remembered to you and expects to visit Norway next summer.

"I have called on the director of the observatory, Monsieur Bouvard, and delivered the letter of recommendation from Littrow. He was quite friendly, showed me the observatory which naturally was excellent, and has offered to introduce me to the most prominent mathematicians whenever I appear at the Institute. I have not yet made use of this offer, since I want first to be able to speak a little French.

"Furthermore, I should like to have completed a memoir I am working on and wish to present to the Institute. I expect it to be finished shortly, and shall then go to the Institute. In this article I have succeeded extremely well, it contains much that is new and, I believe, worthy of attention. It is the first development of a theory for an infinite class of transcendental functions.

"I have the hope that the Academy will print it in its *Memoires des Savants Étrangers*; if not, I shall either print it privately or send it to Gergonne in Montpellier to be included in the *Journal de Mathématiques*. I shall shortly also send him something else. I have a number of articles ready, some will appear in the aforementioned *Journal*, some in Crelle's *Journal der Mathematik*, some in Littrow's *Annalen der Wiener Sternwarte*, and finally some will be presented to the Institute. So you see I do my best.

"Three issues of Crelle's *Journal* have appeared, and it seems to be doing well; this pleases me since I have a share in its initiation. If I am not mistaken, there are six papers of mine in these three issues. I have not received more than the first, but expect to receive the others from Crelle shortly. The first number I sent from Trieste to Bohr by a fisherman from Bergen, but I suppose he will not return home for a while.

"I have been to see Legendre with my landlord, who is a rascally dilettante in mathematics. Legendre was on the point of driving out, so that I exchanged only a few words with him. He appears to be an excellent old man. As a mathematician he is well known; once a week there is a soiree at his home where I hope to be admitted. I have also called upon Baron Ferrusac, the publisher of the *Bulletin*, but he was not at home. Once a week I can go to a soiree at his house; then I also have an opportunity to obtain all possible periodicals and new books, an excellent thing, particularly in these days when all libraries are closed. Poisson I have only seen once on the public promenade. He appeared to be very pleased with himself, although this is said not to be the case. *Voilà toutes mes connaissances*, but it will not be long before I have acquired some more, for I have been able to quicken my French tongue.

"I wrote to Bernt Holmboe from Bozen; I hope he has received my letter, I am eager for a reply. Please remember me to him.

"Otherwise I live quietly, write all day long and only take walks to the Jardin du Luxembourg or Palais Royal. Think of it, I have not yet been to comedy. The actor François Talma has been near death, but is now out of danger.

"I suppose you have had letters from Keilhau or Boeck. I have heard nothing since we separated in Bozen, but I expect Keilhau soon; it is likely that we will stay together in Paris this winter. Möller returns home shortly, he is tired of traveling. I must confess that I also yearn for home. Paris probably will not be the most agreeable place to stay, for it is so difficult to become acquainted with people. It is not like Germany."

Möller did not stay long in Paris, but shortly after his departure Abel had the pleasure of welcoming Keilhau. He also moved in with Abel's hosts, Monsieur and Madame de Cotte, in rue Ste. Marguerite 41, Faubourg St. Germain. Keilhau had had the best intentions of accomplishing an inordinate amount of work, but his normal energy had given way to a spell of laziness, and he had not been able to get started. However, he and Abel never forgot their duty to Hansteen, and made a long series of careful observations of the magnetism in the Luxembourg garden, surrounded by a curious group of very youthful Frenchmen.

During the first days of October they sent a common letter, written by Keilhau, to inform Boeck in Munich of the great news: The first of the triumvirate, Keilhau, had achieved the long desired goal, a permanent position as lecturer in mineralogy at the university. "His Majesty's appointment is dated August 11, and in the accompanying letter from the Church and Education Department, it is added: With the obligation to undertake travels in the less explored parts of the country as long as this may appear necessary and useful." Secondly Keilhau had been awarded a prize of 200 daler from the Danish Academy of Science for a geological memoir, submitted the previous year in response to a proposed prize question. He did not receive the coveted gold medal of the Academy, but the money was a considerable consolation prize.

Keilhau admitted that he had done little work in Paris. "I have never been a poorer correspondent than at present — not because I have had too much to do, on the contrary, I idle the day along. Why don't I do anything? Aside from my natural laziness, it is because the Natural Science Library, to which I have been admitted — the Bibliothèque Royale and the library of the Institute have been closed until now — is located so far away from my residence. You know I am very pedantic in my study habits; I must have the books at home and everything very comfortable in a certain disorderly order or orderly disorder — otherwise it doesn't work — and this arrangement I cannot make during my brief sojourn here. At Ferrusac's I can read journals, but even this opportunity I have not utilized much, for the above-mentioned reasons.

"As you have probably guessed we very frequently go to the theaters here. Some of them present wonderful things, and what I have seen at the Théâtre Français surpasses all in Germany. Talma does not dare to play any more, but Mademoiselle Mars compensates us largely for this loss; she is more than human. . . . So we drag along together as previously; billiards daily and Madame de Cotte growls over the large quantities of her wine which we consume."

So to Abel's great disappointment, the Paris sojourn of his friend Keilhau came to an end. Keilhau had made his plans; early the next summer he intended to conduct an expedition to the north to study the geology of Finnmark.

In spite of his many good prospects Keilhau had no money. The 100 daler from the Finance Department had not arrived; his bills and voyage had to be paid for. He had found a shipping opportunity from Le Havre and it would take too long to receive reinforcements from Oslo. In short: "I was in a hell of a financial fix," as he expressed it himself. So Abel had to come to his aid with all he could spare, and perhaps a little more than that; it was agreed that upon Keilhau's arrival in Oslo the money should be paid to Holmboe and forwarded.

Abel had to take advantage of this excellent opportunity to send letters to Norway. He wrote some loving words to his sister Elisabeth at Rector Treschow's:

"I shall not neglect to send you a few lines on this occasion when Keilhau returns home. I think of you so very often, dear sister, and always wish you happiness. You live well, don't you, among the good people you stay with, but how is my mother, my brothers? I have heard nothing about them. It is already a long time since I wrote to my mother; the letter has arrived, that much I know, but I have heard nothing from her. Where is Peder? does he still live? and where? I am very concerned for him; when I left it did not augur well for him. God knows how many times I have felt sorrowful on his account. I don't believe he is very fond of me and this grieves me greatly for I have never willingly done him any harm. Listen, Elisabeth, you must absolutely write me and tell me all about him and about my mother and other brothers.

"Here in Paris I live quite pleasantly and study a good deal. From

144

time to time I visit the curiosities of the city and take part in the entertainments I like; but I long for home and I would leave today were it possible, but I must still remain for quite some time. In the spring I shall return. Actually I should stay abroad until next August, but I feel that I will not benefit particularly by further foreign study. I expect to return by ship or perhaps by the way of Berlin, where I should like to visit before coming home. But I don't know whether the money will last.

"My fiancée is in Aalborg with her sister and I have not heard from her for a considerable time. I am quite concerned, but I hope she lives well. She has probably written, but the letter must have been lost.

"How is Fru Hansteen? I hope she is well, do not forget to remember me most obligedly to her and equally to Professor Hansteen; I wrote to him some time ago. To the rector and his wife you must present my humble respects.

"Keilhau has been kind enough to take with him a small gift for you. I should have wished it could have been more considerable, but for the time I cannot afford it. It consists of a couple of bracelets, a buckle for a belt, and a small ring. Please accept them and think occasionally of your devoted brother N. H. Abel.

"When you write you must put on the outside of the letter:

> Monsieur N. H. Abel à Paris
> Rue Ste. Marguerite No. 41
> Faubourg St. Germain

"The letter should not cost you anything, at least not more than two pence.

"Live well, my beloved sister, and do write as soon as you receive this letter."

13

WISTFUL WAITING

⟶§ ABEL'S LONELINESS became intense after Keilhau's departure from Paris. He had few acquaintances, and the mathematicians he felt unable to approach, either personally or scientifically. Most of all he desired to go home, but a winter in Paris was an unavoidable condition of his fellowship; also, he was compelled to submit his large memoir to the Institute, as he had long planned and promised. Fortunately, the manuscript was nearing its completion, and Abel was convinced it would prove to be the key which would magically open the entrance to the exclusive circle of the French scientists.

A week after the departure of Keilhau, Abel wrote to Holmboe: "I must grant you that you are strong in your intent not to let me hear from you. You have no idea how sorely I have awaited a few words from you. The only reason I can see for your silence is that you have not received my last letter dated Bozen, and that is now four months ago or more.

"Show me now, my friend, that you do not want to disappoint me. Send me a couple of words for consolation and encouragement in my loneliness. Although I am in the noisiest city on the continent, I feel as if I were in the wilderness; I know practically no one, for the reason that everyone is in the country during the summer; thus no one is visible. To this moment I have only met Legendre, Cauchy, Hachette, and a few lesser, but quite clever mathematicians: Monsieur Saigey, editor of the *Bulletin*, and Herr Lejeune-Dirichlet, a Prussian who called on me one day, taking me for a fellow countryman. That is a very ingenious mathematician [he later became the successor of Gauss in Göttingen]; with Legendre he has shown that the equation $x^5 + y^5 = z^5$ is impossible in integers, and other beautiful things.

"Legendre is an extremely amiable man, but unfortunately hoary

ABOVE *Baron Augustin Louis Cauchy and Adrien Marie Legendre.* BELOW *Carl Gustav Jacob Jacobi and Heinrich Christian Schumacher*

with age. Cauchy is 'fou,' and there is no way to get along with him, although he is at present the mathematician who knows best how mathematics ought to be treated.

"His things are excellent, but he writes very obscurely — earlier I understood practically nothing of his works, but now it is easier. He has published a series of papers entitled *Exercises des Mathématiques*. I buy and read them diligently; nine parts have appeared since the first of the year. Cauchy is immoderately Catholic and bigoted, a very strange thing for a mathematician. Otherwise he is the only one who at present works in pure mathematics; Poisson, Fourier, Ampère, etc., are exclusively occupied by magnetism and other physical theories. Laplace presumably does not write any more. His last contribution was an addition to the Théorie des probabilités. He maintains it is by his son, but it must in reality be his. I have seen him often in the Institute. He is a small, lively man, who suffers from the same fault as the devil charges Zambullo with [in Le Sage's novel: *Le diable boiteux*], namely, to interfere with the speech of others. Poisson is a short man with a pretty *embonpoint*; he carries himself with dignity, as does Fourier. LaCroix is quite bald and aged. On Monday I shall be introduced to some of these gentlemen by Hachette.

"On the whole, I do not like the French as well as the Germans; the French are extremely reserved toward strangers. It is very difficult to become more closely associated with them, and I dare not hope for it. Everybody works for himself without concern for others. All want to instruct, and nobody wants to learn. The most absolute egotism reigns everywhere. The only thing the French look for in foreigners is the practical; no one can think except himself, he is the only one who can produce anything theoretical. This is the way he thinks and so you can understand it is really difficult to be noticed, particularly for a beginner.

"I have completed a large memoir on a class of transcendental functions to be presented to the Institute; it will be done on Monday. I showed it to Cauchy, but he would hardly cast a glance at it, and still I dare say without boasting that it is good. I am curious to hear the judgment of the Institute; I shall let you know in due time."

Abel continued to describe his other papers and his work for Ferrusac's *Bulletin*: "For the same Bulletin, I have written some articles and shall do others. It is damned tedious work, but I do it for Crelle, the most honorable man one can imagine."

Abel also mentioned his progress on one of his principal problems: "I now work on the theory of equations, my favorite topic, and have finally come so far that I see a way to solve the following general problem: To determine the form of all algebraic equations which can be solved by radicals. I have found an infinite number of fifth, sixth, seventh, etc., degree which no one else has even scented so far. At the same time, I have the most direct solution of equations of the first four degrees with clear indication why just these and no others can be solved.

"I really cannot expect to get anything out of all this until I have completed my foreign travels, and have settled quietly at home, if this will happen. I regret having applied for a two-year fellowship. One and a half years would have been ample. I am very homesick, and from now on cannot benefit too much from my sojourn here or elsewhere. I am now familiar with everything important and unimportant existing in mathematics, and I long to devote my time to work with what I have accumulated. There are so many things I wish to undertake, but while abroad it does not progress as it should.

"I wish I were in Keilhau's shoes in regard to the lectureship! I cannot be confident, nor am I too concerned, for if the ice should break in one place it will support in others. How large is your salary? Will you get married? Are you engaged? And to whom? You must answer these questions to me, for my thoughts so often revolve around you and all connected with you. I don't have such a superfluity of friends that I am in any danger of forgetting those I have.

"I live an extremely virtuous life: study, eat, drink, sleep, and on occasions I see a comedy. This is the only so-called amusement I indulge in, and it is a great pleasure. I know of no greater enjoyment than to see a play by Molière in which Mademoiselle Mars plays. I am really quite enthused; she is 40 years of age and still plays very young roles.

"Talma, the famous tragedian, died a couple of days ago. On this occasion Théâtre Français, as well as all the other theaters, was closed for two days. A tremendous crowd followed his bier. It was brought directly to the cemetery without being placed in a church as is customary, for as an actor he is excluded from the society of the faithful. Ridiculous, but unimportant. His children are all illegitimate and they have been brought up in the Protestant faith. In life he suffered from three capital faults: he was devoted to gambling, to women, and to extravagant building, all three in the highest degree. The actors at Théâtre Français have contributed 12,000 francs for a monument to him.

"Occasionally I visit Palais Royal, which the French call *un lieu de perdition*. There one sees *des femmes de bonne volonté* in considerable numbers, and they are not at all intrusive. The only thing one hears is: 'Voulez vous montez avec moi? Mon petit ami, petit méchant.' Being an engaged man I never listen to them and leave Palais Royal without the least temptation, although many of them are very beautiful.

"The other day I attended a diplomatic meal, a dinner at the residence of His Excellency, Count Löwenhielm, the Swedish envoy, where Keilhau and I became a little under the influence, but very little. He is married to a young French lady. He told us that every Christmas Eve he held a party at which he drank all his countrymen under the table.

"I lodge with a family where I have room, meals, and washing for 120 francs a month. The husband is a bit of a mathematician, but very dumb, and the wife is a somewhat wild one of 35 years of age or more. At the table one always talks in equivocal terms about *les secrets de ménage*, etc. The other day it went so far that a lady suggested that the goose on the table had been changed into an *étron*. To talk about chamber pots is quite decent, so I always drink coffee out of *mon petit pot de nuit*. Otherwise I eat quite well, but only twice a day; in the forenoon a *déjeuner à la fourchette*, and in the afternoon at half past five a long dinner, with one to one-and-a-half bottles of wine each day. Now I am completely alone, for Keilhau left for home by sea a couple of days ago."

The strange ménage at de Cotte's amused Abel, and later at home he liked to tell stories about them. Hansteen often retold the following: "Abel used to fool around with Madame de Cotte, who seemed to enjoy his *courtoisies*. The husband was henpecked, and once when he dared express himself in a determined way about something, his wife exclaimed, 'Ah, Monsieur de Cotte, si vous prenez le haut ton, moi je prendrai la bas ton [bâton].' "

As customary, the controversies between Church and State were in full swing in France. Abel wrote about the Jesuits with a tolerance similar to that of the Norwegian constitution, which until 1956 forbad the Jesuits access to the realm: "The Jesuits want to govern and the newspapers are full of disputations in regard to them. A Satanic rabble.

A few days ago a young Jesuit denounced a whole group of his confreres, and intends to do so with 300 more. According to his description they must be the most abominable persons in the world. He narrowly avoided being murdered."

In his letters, Abel often touched only in the last few lines upon the problem which weighed most heavily on his mind. So also to Holmboe:

"Keilhau borrowed 180 marks from me, which I have asked him to deposit with you, if you would be kind enough to receive them. May I trouble you to buy a draft on Hamburg for me? And one thing more, but this is only a modest query: Do you think it might be feasible for you to lend me 220 marks so that the total will be 400? You would show me an excellent favor thereby, for I am so damned anxious to go to Berlin before I return home, and I also wish to buy a few things here, which I cannot obtain at home, or at least, it costs three times as much. Please do not feel ill at ease at my request and reply as soon as possible. Finally, do not forget, at your earliest convenience, a long letter with much news. Remember me to all our good friends and do not forget your friend, N. H. Abel."

The following Monday, October 30, 1826, Abel attended the session of the Institute when his memoir was submitted for publication. Fourier, the secretary of the Academy, read the introduction to the work: *Mémoire sur une propriété générale d'une classe très étendue des fonctions transcendantes* presented by Monsieur Abel, Norwegian. The memoir was referred to Legendre and Cauchy for evaluation; the latter acting as *rapporteur*, that is, the committee member in charge of drawing up a report.

Abel was firmly convinced that the paper was good, even excellent, and was optimistic enough to hope that the commendatory decision of the Institute would not be long delayed.

This article, like almost everything else Abel wrote, was composed in a very clear style. It has often been said by mathematicians that, as far as presentation is concerned, his papers belong with the most lucid in the mathematical literature. But this paper was exceedingly long, longer than anything Abel so far had written. In his collected works it covers sixty-seven large-format printed pages. Furthermore, the ideas were entirely new and extremely general, so certainly, at first, they would be difficult for anyone to absorb.

A detailed examination of the content of such a memoir could not be quickly accomplished and Abel undoubtedly underestimated the obstacles which it presented to the readers. Even under normal conditions it would not have been unreasonable for the referees to require a considerable period before the report could be completed. Unfortunately, Cauchy was in no way suited to this task. He was preoccupied by his own projects, ideas, and papers, and had but little time to contemplate the creations of others; it appears that he laid Abel's memoir aside, perhaps in the vain expectation that he would have more leisure at a later time. This was by no means the only incident of its kind in the Academy, and Cauchy has repeatedly been reproached for this negligence in his duties. Psychologically it is understandable, but it is tragic that his indifference should cause severe harm to two of the most remarkable young geniuses the world has ever seen.

While Abel waited in Paris he had too much leisure to meditate upon his own worries. From Oslo he rarely heard anything; from the family at Gjerstad he received no word, but from other sources he heard that his brother Peder was still in trouble. His relations with his beloved Crelly grieved him more. They were evidently not as they had been. During the journey she had written only sparingly, and now seemed to have given up the correspondence altogether. She had tired of staying in Norway after Niels Henrik's departure and had returned to Denmark to live with her sister, who was married to a physician in Aalborg. Crelly was undoubtedly disappointed; Niels Henrik's honest pessimism must have made it clear that the prospects for a marriage as they had planned had to be projected far into an uncertain future.

At times, Abel clung to the hope that the lectureship in Oslo might still be created; at other times he was depressed. Nothing was being said, but something had to be under consideration. There actually had been a small opening which he could have filled. A military academy had been created in Oslo, for which two teachers in mathematics were required, one in pure, the other in applied mathematics. This was at least instruction at a higher level than in the schools, and although the positions were not full time, they paid reasonably well. Unfortunately, the vacancies had been filled the same summer by Holmboe and Hansteen.

Meanwhile, Crelle labored assiduously to create a position for Abel in Berlin as editor of the *Journal*. The income would be modest, but Abel would be able to devote himself to his science. It would be possible to supplement his salary in various ways, and in any case, the position was only meant as a beginning. Crelle had more ambitious plans for his young protégé. On November 24, 1826, he wrote from Berlin:

"Dearest friend: Both your letters, of October 23 and November 1, I have received and I thank you. I am very glad you are well, but it saddens me that you cannot come to Berlin: If only my project in regard to the *Journal* could be brought in order, I could even offer you some money. There is some hope, but as yet nothing has been settled. Originally I did not intend to tell you anything before a decision had been made, but since it takes so long I shall tell you about my plan. Perhaps my expectations will give you some pleasure. I have addressed myself to our government, and requested that it grant a subvention, so that the undertaking can be brought properly in swing. I have proposed that a considerable number of copies be subscribed to by the higher schools.

"All the gentlemen I have spoken to have been very kindly disposed to my idea and proposal. However, the minister of Church and Education does not feel that he alone should present the application to the king; thus I must seek to influence certain other gentlemen to offer their support. Just now some of them are away, and the decision is being delayed. One cannot say anything definite in advance, but I shall spare no effort. If my request is granted then I can give an honorarium to you. This must remain between us, because I cannot pay all others. This is the money I mentioned to you previously.

"Even if my plan should fail I shall do everything within my power to continue the *Journal*, be it through personal sacrifice. But then I would not be able to pay for articles, and would have to rely upon the interest among the friends of science. I believe a decision will have been made before the end of the year.

"Please continue to enlist contributors in Paris. If I should succeed in my intentions that would make it still more splendid. Only inform them that I have addressed myself to my government with a request for support, and have the best hope of obtaining it — such as is really the case — because the Prussian government is eager to promote the sciences. This, particularly, should encourage the contributors there, for if the government of a great country should assist it, the *Journal* would acquire a much more highly esteemed position.

"As soon as the matter has been decided upon here, I shall ask you to send many of your works, which will all be included in the *Journal*. The fourth number has left the press and contains your article on the binomial series. Kindly make use of your acquaintance with the gentlemen Hachette, Dirichlet, and others to the advantage of the *Journal*. I count quite especially upon cooperation from France. The fourth issue contains some of the work which Herr Hachette sent me.

"So I ask you kindly to reply by return mail, and I state definitely: Unpaid. Steiner and all your friends send their regards, as does also my wife. I am, and remain, your sincerely devoted friend, Crelle."

Even Abel's appearance as the ambassador of Crelle and the *Journal* did not bring him in closer contact with the influential French mathematicians. Only Saigey and the little circle of young scientists reviewing for Ferrusac's *Bulletin* became his associates. They probably gave hearty support when Abel vented his disappointment over the indifference of the Academy. At least one young man among them clamorously denounced the Academy, both because his own works had suffered a similar fate and because he saw in the actions of the members another instance of the vicious social injustice which plagued France.

François Vincent Raspail had originally been a cleric and a teacher of theology, but this career he had been obliged to give up on account of heretical ideas. He was well on his way to becoming a scientist of acknowledged standing. He wrote reviews for Ferrusac on botany, was a pioneer in plant physiology, and later made fundamental studies in organic chemistry. His name became a household word in France because of his immensely popular books on the home treatment of diseases. However, this is still not the reason why the Parisians have honored him so distinctively in the Boulevard Raspail. Throughout his life he was a revolutionary combating the injustices of French society by all the means at his disposal. He was among the first on the barricades in the revolutions of 1830 and 1848. Repeatedly, even in his old age, he was compelled to serve long jail sentences for his merciless exposures of the corruption and incompetence of those holding the powers of government. Many years after their association he recalled the sad fate of Abel, and brought it forth accusingly in the Chamber of Deputies as a tragic example of the egotism of the academicians.

Some years later Saigey gave a few details of his acquaintance with Abel in Paris. "Abel spoke equally well French, German, and the Scandinavian languages. He was a little above medium height, his face was lean and sallow and looked anxious and tired. His mild character manifested itself in modesty and great embarrassment. His pecuniary resources were small as one could see from his simple attire, the single meal he could afford each day, and the modest lodging in rue Sainte-Marguerite. Once he encountered a person who showed him the hurts he had suffered from some assailants. 'I have nothing to fear from robbers,' Abel responded with a smile when asked by the man to watch his belongings.

"In reality, Abel was in the same condition as the philosopher who could carry within him all his wealth wherever he might go. Viewed in this way his riches were immense, for he had read and meditated upon the works of all mathematicians. Not a single word of Monsieur Cauchy's many articles had escaped his attention, and even if there should be the danger of reducing the excellent opinion which the Academy now has arrived at concerning Abel's achievements, I must confess that he had the very greatest esteem for the publications of this academician, and even went so far as to assign Cauchy the first place among mathematicians."

With very few acquaintances and low ebb in his purse Abel could do little else than write mathematics, and the last months in Paris turned out to be extremely fruitful. A few days after his great memoir had been submitted to the Institute, he completed a lesser paper on equations, which he presented to Gergonne's *Annals*. He then again concentrated upon two principal topics — the solution of equations and the elliptic functions — and created a combination of the two, a field in which he had particular qualifications.

Let us say just a few words about his ideas, which, unfortunately, can be made intelligible only to those with a background in mathematics. Abel had long pondered this problem: How had the great Gauss arrived at the idea basic to his ingenious studies on the division of the circle in equal parts, that is, the construction of regular polygons by compass and ruler? In examining the so-called division equation for elliptic functions and how it could be solved, he realized that this was a much more general problem than that for the circle, and the principles became completely lucid. "On the same occasion I have lifted the mystery which has rested over Gauss' theory of the division of the circle; I see now clear as daylight how he has been led to it," he wrote to Holmboe.

154

In his chef-d'oeuvre, the *Disquisitiones Arithmaticae*, Gauss made a cryptic and apparently unmotivated observation in connection with the construction of the polygons, to the effect that something similar is possible for the lemniscate curve. The lemniscate is a curve of fourth degree, about the shape of a figure eight, much used as an example in analysis and geometry, an heirloom in mathematics from the time of the Greeks.

From the pinnacle of his general theories, Abel could view the special problems of the division of the circle and the lemniscate into equal parts. He wrote to Crelle and Holmboe with obvious excitement over his results, and informed Holmboe that he was preparing a memoir on elliptic functions "in which there are many queer things which I flatter myself will startle someone; among other things it is about the division of arcs of lemniscates. You will see how pretty it is! All I have described about the lemniscate is the fruit of my efforts in the theory of equations. You will not believe how many delightful theorems I have discovered."

The contrast between Abel's rich fund of scientific treasures and his earthly penury became more evident each day. He was aware that what he had left would not sustain him for many weeks in Paris, even at the low level on which he now subsisted. But still more serious was the realization that even when the loan to Keilhau had been repaid him, as well as a small amount which Boeck owed him, he would not have nearly enough to provide for the remaining period of his fellowship. A further half year was the least he would have to remain abroad, even to approximate the terms of his appointment. If he did not receive aid he had no choice but to return home as quickly as he could. In his letter to Holmboe of October 24 he had cautiously inquired about a possible loan, and to his great relief Holmboe replied both expeditiously and favorably. Shortly before Christmas, Abel sent him a last letter from the city on the Seine:

"Dear Friend: Many thousand thanks for your two highly welcome letters, especially because you were so prompt. If I had known that you had written, I would not have dared to ask for such a sacrifice. Please do not frown upon my request for money; I have only two real friends, and so I am compelled to bother them against my will.

"Possibly I can spare you the loan, but it is probable that I shall have to rely on your generosity, not yet, but when I return to Berlin. I shall leave Paris shortly, since here is nothing more to gain, and go to Göttingen, primarily to beleaguer Gauss, if he is not too strongly fortified

155

by his arrogance. I would rather stay in Germany to learn some more German, because this will be of the greatest importance to me in the future. French, I manage well enough to write a memoir, and I would like to be able to do the same in German."

Between Christmas and New Year's Abel left Paris without sorrow. In Berlin life was more comfortable and friendly: Maschmann was still studying there and could assist if necessary. Crelle, his fatherly friend, could also be approached in case of acute distress. Besides, his consuming loneliness would be over. Many of his friends among the students and young mathematicians were still in Berlin, and he could meet them in the customary haunts when the desire for company overcame him.

A stay in Göttingen was out of the question; his purse was so empty that he could barely scrape enough together to reach Berlin. Thus he never made the acquaintance of the great Gauss, who so often had figured in his thoughts.

The mail coaches were unhealthy conveyances in the middle of the winter, drafty and cold; but only seldom did they fail to produce some adventure. Shortly after his arrival Abel wrote to Boeck in Munich:

"My trip from Paris was extremely lean. I traveled with the diligence over Valenciennes to Brussels. On this tour I was alone with a danseuse, not of the great opera, but one of the very smallest theaters, a very dangerous neighbor during the night. She slept in my arms, obviously, but that was all. I held edifying conversations with her about the transitory things of this world.

"Brussels is a very beautiful city. I stayed there a day and a night, running around town all the time. I continued with the diligence over Liége to Aachen. For company I had a decent chap from Frankfurt am Main. As far as Liége everybody speaks French, but in Aachen it was more homelike. After a stay I left for Cologne, a terrible old and ugly city with many whores, remained one day and two nights, and took the mail coach to Kassel by the way of Elberfeld and Arnsberg. The countryside is said to be extremely beautiful, but the night and the winter prevented me from seeing it. Between Elberfeld and Arnsberg we had an accident, the coach ran over a boy 7–8 years of age. He lay dead in the road; the coach passed over his stomach. We continued without halting.

"I stayed overnight in Kassel, a beautiful city. There I went to a comedy; the theater is very nice and the acting was good. In Cologne I also went to the theater, but it was poor. From Kassel I traveled by extra coach to Magdeburg with a merchant going to Berlin and Königsberg. We came over the Harz which must be very beautiful in summer. The road between Quedlinburg and Magdeburg is the most outrageous I have ever traveled; although there were only two of us in the coach and we had four horses in harness, we only passed with the greatest difficulty.

"I stayed overnight again in Magdeburg and then traveled by hired coach to Berlin; the road was excellent, but the company was disgraceful, a shoemaker, a glovemaker, and a discharged soldier, who all drank brandy continually. I was bored and no one was happier than I when we passed through the Brandenburger Tor in Berlin. I descended at the Kronprinz. I now live in Französische Strasse 39, on the second floor, near Gens d'Armen Markt. A quarter of an hour later I was at Königstädter and enjoyed seeing familiar faces and hearing voices I knew."

It was a relief to be back in Berlin, and a weight fell from Abel's heart when he found a letter from Crelly waiting, stating that all was well. But the money situation was still extremely distressing and he had to write to Boeck for an immediate remittance: "I presume you will be surprised to see me so soon in Berlin, but for the lack of money I could not remain any longer in Paris; I had to leave in a hurry, the sooner the better, while I still had money enough to pay for the journey. When I arrived here five days ago, January 10, my whole fortune consisted of 14 taler. I have borrowed 50 from merchant Backer. What you owe me I must ask you to send me as early as possible, preferably in Prussian currency."

Abel continued, describing his trip from Paris and giving news of their friends: "Maschmann lives well and wants to be remembered, he is peeved because you have not written. Lately he has been bored, he says, to an unholy degree. He is traveling southward in May; about the same time I expect to be going north. Maschmann now speaks German very well, probably you do the same. I have not forgotten anything, but it does not come fluently. I have been once to Schauspielhaus. An apothecary Monrad from Bergen is here with wife and mother. I have made their acquaintance — they are agreeable people. Otherwise I expect to be very busy here. I heard nothing before my departure about the memoir I presented to the Academy in Paris. . . . I would have written you a longer letter if I did not have so many others to write: To my fiancée, who lives well, to Hansteen, Keilhau, Bernt Holmboe, Möller, etc., something which I should have done a long time ago. I expect a letter and draft from you as soon as possible. Yours very devotedly, N. Abel."

Some days later he was obliged to turn to Holmboe to remind him of the promised loan:

"Many thanks for your two letters. I really ought to have written to you a long time ago, but I first awaited the outcome of the article I submitted to the Institute. Legendre and Cauchy were referees, Cauchy reporter. Legendre said 'ça prendra.' Then the journey to Berlin came over me in a holy hurry. Even this time you don't hear much from me, I have so damned much to do, both for Ferrusac's *Bulletin* and Crelle's *Journal.*

"But now to what I really wanted — money. You have been good enough to promise to help me. Since I am in a hell of a pinch I should of course like as much as you can spare, and as soon as possible. Please do not be vexed because I trouble you so much, but what shall *ein armer Teufel* do?"

During his wait for money Abel probably managed by loans and aid from friends. He mentioned repeatedly that he regularly associated with the apothecary Monrad and his wife. Monrad was a relatively young man who had been interested in the promotion of the sciences in Norway, so he undoubtedly knew Abel by reputation. Abel continually won money from them at cards, almost a regular income. He fooled them, as he related, but it is entirely possible that he was the one to be deceived, and that it was a quiet satisfaction for the apothecary to assist the needy young man in a discreet manner.

Meanwhile Abel became ill and was compelled to stay in bed some time during the first part of February. Holmboe's loan he received after six weeks, but the letter to Boeck still had produced no results. Abel was obliged to remind him again of the amount due:

"Many thanks, dear Boeck, for the letters you forwarded to me; both arrived from Paris. So you finally received the letter from Hansteen addressed to Vienna. I was pleased to receive it and many thanks for letting me see it. A couple of days ago I had a very long letter from Fru Hansteen and the professor, six large quarto pages, most of it from Fru Hansteen to me. The letter had gone to Paris, and was dated January 25; presumably you have more up-to-date information."

He reproduced university gossip from Oslo and the news that Hansteen had become a member of two scientific societies, the Academy in Copenhagen and Werner's Geological Society in Edinburgh. "How he has been elected to the latter he does not understand, for he knows nothing about rocks. His wife has a baby son. That is all.

"Immediately upon my arrival in Berlin, more than a month ago, I wrote to you in regard to the small amount which you owe me. Please do not forget to send it to me before you leave Munich; I am badly off Yesterday I received 293 marks from Bernt Holmboe, that is all I have. He had been to Stockholm and Uppsala and enjoyed himself greatly on the trip. In May I shall leave on account of my distress, without regrets. Hansteen believes that I shall receive an appointment at the university when I come home. He also mentioned the possibility of tormenting me at some school for a year, but to that I shall rear on my hind legs.

"Maschmann lives well and sends regards, he is bored and travels southward after Easter. Apothecary Monrad, his wife, and mother, who has trouble with her eyes, are here. Maschmann and I visit them every evening to play cards; I really clean them out, but I need it and it seems fair. I hope to hear from you before you leave Munich. If I can assist you with the magnetic formula I shall do so with pleasure.

"I have a formidable number of letters to write, also I have been sick some time and stayed in bed, now I am well again. It has been terribly cold and snowy; the temperature has been down to 9° F. Adieu, my dear Boeck, yours Abel."

Financial tribulations rarely reduced Abel's mathematical productivity; on the contrary, it seems that his pecuniary difficulties made him concentrate more on his scientific work. Nor can illness have hampered him noticeably at this time for, during the first days of March 1827 he reported with evident satisfaction that he had completed another large memoir begun in Paris. He had produced a masterpiece and was greatly pleased over the new mathematical horizons which it revealed.

Crelle's encouragements had contributed largely to the creation of the *Recherches sur les fonctions elliptiques*. Again it proved difficult to find a publisher for the large manuscript; the only possibility was to print it in the *Journal*. In its final form, the *Recherches* is of book length covering 120 pages in Abel's collected works. However, in Berlin Abel completed only the first part, about two thirds of the opus. For Abel himself, the *Recherches* contained relatively few new discoveries; it involved mostly results which he had obtained as a student in Oslo.

The inversion of the elliptic integrals — his first main idea — he had mentioned in a letter to Holmboe from Copenhagen in 1823, other discoveries he reported to Degen in the spring of 1824. In the first part of the *Recherches* Abel developed a great variety of results for his elliptic functions, double periodicity, series and product expansions, multiplication theorems, and division equations. Among the topics which he postponed to the second part was the so-called transformation of elliptic functions, also indicated to Degen; he must later have regretted bitterly that he did not include this.

The *Recherches* was scheduled for publication in the second volume of the *Journal*, but this time the printing did not proceed as expeditiously as before. Crelle had serious difficulties in financing the *Journal*, and his negotiations with the Prussion government had failed in the main. Instead of the 800-taler annual subvention he had requested, the ministry only approved a subscription of 20–30 copies for schools and libraries.

In almost every letter from Berlin Abel returned to his perennial concern: the position in Oslo. Hansteen had nothing definite to report, except that it had become evident that for the current year at least there would be no expedition to Siberia. "The government refused to include my journey to Siberia in the budget," Hansteen wrote to Boeck. "I had to write to the king and various influential men to procure a royal resolution that it should be listed. An amount of 4500 daler has been proposed, but the present Storting is so unusually niggardly that only God knows the fate of the project."

The longing for Norway dominated Abel's sentiments more than ever. He had to go home regardless of what was in store for him, but at the same time he was flattered by Crelle's insistent efforts to keep him in Berlin. In his first letter to Boeck from Berlin, Abel was strikingly depressed by the thought of conditions at home. The debility of his finances and the pressure of ever-mounting debts; the uncertain aspects of his marriage; the sad condition of his family; the psychic effect of his illness — all plagued him:

"The day before I left Paris, December 29, I received a very long letter from Keilhau. He asked me to report to you that he has not forgotten you in the least, and you can soon expect a long letter from him; perhaps it has already arrived. He wishes that he were again back abroad while, strangely enough, we who are here want to return home. I believe in the end it is better abroad. When we return home we shall probably feel as Keilhau does. He predicts there will be many unpleasant things for you to deal with when you return. My own position will be the best, he says; perhaps publicly; but *unter uns gesagt,* I forsee many ghastly things, I am really worried about my future.

"I should almost like to remain forever in Germany, which I could do without difficulty. Crelle bombards me terribly to make me stay here. He is a little peeved because I refuse, and cannot understand what I want to do in Norway, which seems another Siberia to him."

In his letter of thanks to Holmboe Abel is a little more philosophical in regard to his concerns:

"Some days ago I had the proof of your honorable character, my good Holmboe, in receiving 293 marks through Cordes in Hamburg. This was a great blessing to me, for I was poorer than a church mouse. I shall live on this as long as I can and then I shall sweep northward. I expect to stay awhile in Copenhagen where my fiancée will meet me, then move homeward, where I shall arrive so empty-handed that I shall have to panhandle at the church door. However, I shall not be disconcerted, because I am really well accustomed to misery and wretchedness; it will work out somehow."

He then proceeded to discuss the *Journal,* and the results on equations and elliptic functions, but the topic overwhelmed him, so that he was compelled to break off and reserve the rest for conversations after his homecoming:

"On the whole I have made an outrageous number of discoveries. I wish I had them all arranged and written down, for most of it is still in my head. But this I cannot think of before I am home and in order. Then I shall slave like a workhorse, but with pleasure of course.

"My life is quite tedious, no great variations. I study, eat, sleep, and not much else. A couple of times a week I play cards at apothecary Monrad's from Bergen, who is here with wife and mother. I really take advantage of them. Crelle is still the same honorable man, and I visit him often. I have been ill and in bed some days, now I am well and speak better German than last year. Maschmann is an expert, sends regards. The winter has been doggishly cold, but it seems to be over.

"I long to come home, for there is no particular benefit in staying. At home one has such damned different ideas about the foreign countries from what one ought to have. They are not too good. On the whole, the world is rather sad, but quite direct and honest. Nowhere is it easier to get ahead than in Germany and France; in Norway it is ten times more difficult.

"I hear you were in Uppsala and Stockholm. Why didn't you come to Paris? That is a place I must visit again before I die.

"The enclosed letter I must ask you to deliver personally to Professor Hansteen. I received a letter from him the other day over Paris. I shall not ask you to write to me, but if you want to spend the time and postage on me — one can no longer mail unpaid — then you know how dear it would be to me. In such case it would have to be soon. Tell me something about the steamer! Remember me to friends and live well. Yours, Abel."

Toward the end of April, Abel left Berlin, first heading for Copenhagen to visit the Tuxen family and to meet Crelly. Then he intended to travel by "steamer" to Oslo. All Norway was agog over the modern era in communications being inaugurated by the two steamships, the *Constitution* and *Prince Carl*, purchased by the government. In spite of the one's name, the constitutionality of the transaction had been disputed. The contract for the construction of the vessels had been forced through and signed rather highhandedly by the minister of finance, Jonas Collett, Boeck's uncle and future father-in-law. On April 1, 1827, the first of the smoking wonders arrived in the harbor at Oslo, cheered wildly by the excited crowds, while the peeved Storting tried to impeach Collett. But the minister was acquitted and his name was praised unanimously along the coasts. The greatest disadvantage of the paddlewheelers was that they could not be used in ice. During the winter they were laid up and communications reverted to their old conditions.

Before Abel left Berlin he wrote a last letter to Fru Hansteen, and told her how warmly he anticipated being able to visit her again. Next he fired a salvo directed against the peculiar Frenchmen, with whom it had proved so impossible to come into contact:

"I am now in Berlin, and I am happy over it, because the French did not please me. They are cold, prosaic people. They deal with everything in the same impersonal manner, discussing with equal emphasis the most serious as well as the most frivolous topics. Never do they show any confidence; a Frenchman is on the same level of intimacy with nearly all people; extreme egotists. When they hear that foreign countries have something they have, or perhaps they don't have, then they are surprised and say 'diable!' and so they are constantly surprised.

"And then the dear female sex! They are so neat, so ingratiating, and dress so prettily, but *voilà tout*. They lack much of the modesty and bashfulness which men like so well to see in women. The French say so themselves: 'Les étrangères sont plus modestes que les françaises.' The German girls are certainly to be preferred.

"I am really envious when I think of all the enjoyment you and Hansteen must have had while Fru Fridrichsen and Charité stayed with you. You know how fond I am of both of them. I am looking forward to seeing both when I come to Copenhagen; it will not be terribly long. My fiancée, who is in Aalborg, will also come. In Copenhagen I have always had the most pleasant life.

"I had a letter from Boeck yesterday; he has had a cold and other sufferings, but now he is well. His mother died. He leaves for Paris in the middle of April, and returns by the way of Berlin. A good fellow. He is not in the best of spirits.

"It was extremely good to hear that my beloved sister is doing so well. Her happiness, and the delight I derive from it, is all due to you, dear Fru Hansteen. You must absolutely remember me to her most lovingly when you see her. I am always thinking of her.

"Otherwise, as you may think, my life is very quiet and monotonous. All my outer pleasures consist in infrequent visits to the theaters, and every Monday attending Crelle's assembly.

"So adieu, my most beloved motherly adviser. Reserve some tiny spot in your heart for your Abel."

In Copenhagen, Abel was in familiar places and among good friends. The Tuxen family had again been increased, but this did not prevent Captain Tuxen and his wife from planning a visit to Norway during the summer. The wonderful "steamer" made the trip so delightfully simple. They intended to go to Oslo first, and then visit relatives and old friends in the vicinity of Risör and Arendal; particularly the apothecary Ole Tuxen in Arendal and his brother-in-law Sivert Smith, who was now the sole owner of the ironworks at Froland.

Christine Kemp also awaited him in Copenhagen. All misunderstandings and disappointments seemed to vanish, and love blossomed forth more warmly and understandingly than ever. Marriage was distant, but they could at least make plans to be together from time to time.

The Return

14

AT HOME

꘎ On May 20, 1827, Abel arrived in Oslo on the government steamship. Perhaps the home town appeared provincial to the traveled young man, but in any case it was wonderful to be back. Friends and acquaintances welcomed him, eager to hear his tales of adventure. He paid more formal visits to the university professors, first of all to Rector Treschow, where his sister Elisabeth lived. It was a mature scholar who returned, carefully dressed, experienced, and with better manners. His friends noticed the change and Möller wrote to Boeck: "I have seen Hansteen. He was extremely pleasant that day, and spoke most amiably about you all. He was pleased that Abel's manners had improved, and gave you credit for it."

It did not take Abel long to realize that in regard to a position no preparations had been made, either at the university or anywhere else. But the good will among the faculty was evident, and he was advised to notify the Collegium officially of his return, so that a natural occasion would be created for the consideration of his case. In a letter of June 2, Abel followed this suggestion, stating that he had attempted to the best of his judgment to achieve the proposed aims of the journey: "In presenting my respectful thanks for the assistance of the Collegium in reaching this goal, I recommend myself to its continued favorable grace."

The Collegium was ready to help, and shortly afterward the case had been acted upon. A warm, but somewhat indefinite, recommendation was made to the rector that he use his influence to procure support of some sort for Abel: "The Collegium has considered it to be its duty to report this to your Honor. We regret that the financial condition of the university is such that it is impossible for it to offer Herr Abel the support of which he now, being without position, is in need. We therefore highly recommend him to be considered for some temporary assistance from public funds, as a man whose acknowledged extraordinary talent for his science should make it important to preserve for his country, in particular for the university. The Collegium takes the liberty in the interest of the service to request the influential support of your Honor in this respect."

At the same meeting, another matter was up for consideration. One of the professors had asked to be granted a leave in order to accept another government position, suggesting that the university recommend this transfer on the ground that the number of students in his classes had been very small. The discussion developed into an argument about university principles, in particular, whether instruction or scholarly productivity should be the prime concern of a professor. Hansteen, opposed to using the lack of students as a justification for the transfer, commented: "It seems to me that we can so much the less make this recommendation as we in our letter to the rector have indicated the importance of an appointment for Abel to the university, and still it seems to be taken for granted that he never will be able to give lectures, at least in such a way that anybody will understand them."

Another member of the Collegium, probably Professor of Law Steenbuch, who always maintained a formalistic point of view, wrote the following opinion: "Since the university teachers by oral lectures should expound the sciences, and since there is at least no formal duty compelling them to write, it would be highly incorrect to recommend Abel for an appointment if he could not give intelligible lectures, a fact of which I am not at all convinced. Also Holmboe denied him this ability, but without giving reasons. If the university were a scientific society he would still be acceptable, but language usage and the laws connect other concepts with the salaried teachers at the university."

These statements seem to mirror the opinions of a previous debate, and make it likely that a principal objection to the appointment of Abel as successor to Professor Rasmussen had been a strong conviction of his inability to lecture intelligibly.

Rector Treschow supported the proposal of the Collegium in regard to Abel and added in transmitting it to the Church Department: "So I do not doubt that a similar support as previously will gracefully be granted him through the resourceful assistance of the government, to continue until such time when he receives appointment to a suitable office, this in order that the fruits of his extraordinary talents for higher mathematics as well as the grants expended upon them should not be lost to the nation."

The Church Department, as was customary in cases involving financial expenditures, forwarded the proposal to the Finance Department, which lived up to its reputation of being an effective machine moving on the rails of principle. A proposal for a new position not scheduled in the budget was highly irregular and the department put an unsentimental end to it:

"In remitting the request of the Collegium Academicum, which was received with the letter of June 13 from the honored department, about temporary assistance for Student Abel, it is advised that no grant from government funds can be made for this purpose. Jonas Collett."

Abel had returned to his mother and brothers at Gjerstad during the summer. He had not visited them for several years, and there was little reason to stay in Oslo during the university vacation, living on his credit while the department arrived at a decision. None of his friends from the journey were in town; Maschmann and Boeck had not returned, Keilhau was studying the geology of Finnmark, Tank was busy in Halden, and Möller had joined a mining company.

The conditions at Lunde had not improved and Niels Henrik did not return as a well-to-do son who could contribute from his opulence. One of the obligations which weighed on the family was the annual grain contribution which Pastor Abel had enthusiastically made to the university in 1811. It had in the meanwhile been converted into a cash impost, but after the first year nothing had been paid by Pastor Abel, or by his widow. Fru Abel had vainly applied to be relieved of the charge, but she had only obtained a deferment after Pastor Aas had informed the Collegium that she was attempting to raise the amount by selling her husband's books. It was a recorded lien on the farm and if the authorities should proceed with severity there was a possibility that it might be foreclosed and the family would lose its refuge. The total was not large, but Fru Abel had previously been summoned to court by her neighbors for much smaller amounts than this.

On July 10, Captain Tuxen and his wife arrived in Oslo on the *Constitution*, and after a brief stay in the capital they continued to the south coast to visit their family. Gjerstad was included in the itinerary, although the relations between the two sisters were no longer as cordial as they had been. The visit was probably brief because the Tuxens were going on to the Smith family at Froland Works. They invited Niels Henrik to accompany them on the trip before he returned to Oslo, an invitation which he was pleased to accept since life at Lunde was not too interesting. The Smiths led a manorial life at Froland; their large home had been constructed by Sivert Smith's wealthy father and the surrounding garden was one of the sights of the district. The family was large, eleven children altogether. Smith happened to mention that they needed a governess to take charge of the education of the youngsters, and Abel immediately saw an opportunity for bringing Crelly to Norway again. Here, in the house of an old friend of the Tuxens and of Pastor Abel, she would find a good home and be treated as a member of the family. Upon the warm recommendations of the Tuxens, she was accepted. Niels Henrik wrote her immediately, and shortly afterward Christine Kemp was on the way to her new position.

Meanwhile, Abel had been informed of the sharp refusal to the request of the Collegium for some kind of position or support for him. His friends at the university declined to consider this a final defeat; to strike another blow for the young mathematician and his science they encouraged Abel to apply once more for aid. This he did during the summer; in his second letter of July 23, he described himself and his work in greater detail:

"Long ago I conceived the ambition to devote myself entirely to the study of mathematics, with the object of qualifying for a position as an academic teacher. I flatter myself that now, after completed foreign study, I have acquired sufficient knowledge so that when conditions warrant I may count on such a position at the university.

"However, until the time such an appointment is granted me, I am entirely without means to procure the necessities of life, and have been so since my return. To be able to live I would be compelled to put aside my studies almost entirely, particularly painful to me at the present moment, since I had hoped to complete several articles which I have begun. It would be quite detrimental to me, as it would interrupt the literary career which I initiated abroad as writer for the *Journal für die reine und angewandte Mathematik*, published by Crelle in Berlin. I take the liberty to enclose the issues which have hitherto appeared.

"I dare to apply, therefore, to the high Collegium for a subvention on whatever terms the Collegium may find suitable."

At this time the plans for the expedition to Siberia had begun to take shape, the government had approved the appropriation, and details were being arranged. Hansteen went abroad during the summer to confer with scientists willing to participate and did not return until the beginning of the fall term. But beforehand he had discussed with the members of the Collegium the best strategy to be adopted to promote Abel's petition. This time the Collegium could utilize the impending Siberian journey as an argument in favor of the young mathematician. After giving a résumé of the principal points in the case the Collegium continued:

"After the Royal department has informed the Collegium that after consultation with the Department of Finance it feels unable to grant any support for Herr Abel, the Collegium nevertheless considers it to be its duty to reiterate its recommendation in this matter to the influential concern of the Royal department.

"It appears superfluous to the Collegium to expand further than has already been done upon Herr Abel's unusual talent for his science. His literary achievements are already known, not only in this country, but abroad. The Collegium wishes only to add the observation that Herr Abel has already received so strong an encouragement from the government that it seems that he should have some claim upon its future concern, as he considers himself obliged to devote his efforts and talents primarily for the benefit of his country.

"It would undoubtedly be less justified now to leave him as the only alternative the necessity of setting aside his science to earn a modest subsistence, at a time when he has reached a high level in his science, and has not disappointed the expectations which his excellent talent provoked. It is probable that the temporary support in question will be of short duration, since there is now the prospect that Herr Abel's services will be required during Professor Hansteen's projected journey to Siberia."

The Collegium concluded with a definite proposal that "Candidatus philosophiae Niels Henrik Abel be awarded an annual support of 200 daler from government funds, to run from the date of his return from abroad until he receives an appointment."

This was an excellent presentation of Abel's case, and the idea that Abel should again receive his old fellowship seemed a reasonable and modest proposal. But the Department of Finance had already laid down its veto, and the Church Department dared not disregard it. However, it was willing to make one small concession. If it were possible to spare the 200 daler from the university budget, the department would not oppose advancing it to Abel, but stipulated that the amount was to be repaid in case Abel should be appointed as a substitute for Hansteen.

Abel already had a superfluity of debts and loans, and the proposed arrangement meant that he would contract a still larger loan. The Collegium was also dissatisfied and courageously set out on a course of action of its own. On September 4, 1827, it granted Abel a fellowship of 200 daler from its own funds, with no reservation as to repayment. The fellowship became payable from July 1. To provide a little immediate relief in his straitened circumstances the treasurer was instructed to pay 100 daler at once, and the rest in twelve installments.

While all this official correspondence was in progress, Christine Kemp came to Norway, stopping on the way to visit old friends in Son. Abel went to meet her, and on August 5 they arrived together in Oslo on the *Constitution*. Crelly stayed for a week, and then continued her voyage to Arendal, where she was met by a carriage from Froland.

In summertime travel to the southern coastal towns had been transformed by the steamers into a most pleasant excursion. The steamers had also changed the habits of Oslo. The great events were their arrivals; crowds would gather and the more distinguished families would dispatch their maids to pick up their mail directly. Abel, more in love than ever, was anxious to be informed of Crelly's safe arrival at Froland, but he had been invited for dinner at the home of Holmboe's brother and was prevented from being at the pier. He knew, however, that Fru Hansteen expected letters from her husband who was abroad, so he wrote her a little note, in French, begging her to instruct the maid to ask for his letter from "celle que j'aime le plus." The maid was to bring it to him "chez Monsieur le professeur Holmboe, demeurant au second en face du théâtre, dont les habitués ont été réjouis tant de fois par vos charmes. Agréez, Madame, l'assurance de ma plus parfaite considération avec la quelle j'ai l'honneur d'être votre serviteur très humble et très obéissant." Even the fashionable Charité would have been impressed by such a letter from a man of the world.

It was good to be back in Oslo again, but life was no longer as carefree as it had been in student days. Abel was melancholy and concerned, and felt lonesome even at home. Crelly was too far away, his student friends were scattered in positions around the country, and his best friends — Boeck, Keilhau, and Maschmann — were still traveling. Keilhau's expedition to Finnmark had been extended to Spitzbergen and the Arctic islands. Boeck had been in Paris after Abel's departure and was now turning slowly toward Norway. When he returned to Hamburg he lodged in the same inn where the company had stayed while traveling south two years earlier, and he related his feelings to Elisabeth Collett: "It was so strange for me to enter the same lodgings as two years ago; I felt as if I were home and could almost have kissed the droll innkeeper." He had just heard that Abel had arrived home: "This I did not know. Then you have had occasion to hear much about our journey."

Money remained the most urgent problem for Abel during the fall. The advance on the university fellowship had been used to pay his most pressing debts, and it was impossible to live on his small monthly stipend. He was aware that he was himself largely to blame for his financial misery; he had been using money generously while he was in Berlin, and the extravagant trip to the south had completely wrecked his economy. But there were many other circumstances which had contributed to the quagmire of debts and obligations in which he found himself.

One of Abel's first items of business upon his return to Oslo was to obtain some arrangement in regard to his mother's debt to the university. He discussed the matter with the university treasurer, Mandall, who brought the situation to the attention of the Collegium, and informed them of the suggestion he had made: "The farm is owned by the widow who still lives there, and is said to be in very straitened circumstances. There remains 26 daler on the above mentioned contribution and her son, Herr Student Abel, in expectation of an appointment at the university, has promised me orally that he will assume the charge, provided he will be permitted to pay it off in installments."

It seems likely that there were other and larger debts which Niels Henrik had to assume for the honor of the family. His brother Peder had continued to hover around the university without doing anything useful, and probably had taken advantage of his brother's credit wherever it was good. The next year when his finances improved, Niels Henrik began to pay small amounts on the various charges, giving account of them to the supervising Fru Hansteen. But the debts were much larger than anything he could possibly run up in the half year of modest

173

living while waiting for his substitute position: to the merchants, 103 daler; to the madam in his former eating place, 82 daler; to the cloth dealer, 45 daler; and smaller amounts to the tailor, the shoemaker, and his new eating place.

The heaviest debt was to Holmboe, but he also owed money to Fru Hansteen, who had given more to Peder than Niels Henrik had advanced to her. Hansteen's own financial position was not good, and the obligation to Holmboe he wanted to discharge as soon as possible. Thus, in October 1827, Abel applied for a loan of 200 daler from the Bank of Norway to consolidate these debts. The loan was granted over the signature of his old friend Rasmussen, and since the applicant had no security to offer, repayment was guaranteed by Professor Hansteen and the two brothers Holmboe.

It was necessary to look for work and Abel reverted to tutoring, a field in which he had so much experience during his student years. He advertised for pupils in mathematics, both for laggard students and for schoolboys preparing for the entrance examination to the university. He may even have stooped to instruct in German, French, and the ordinary elementary school subjects. He obtained a number of pupils; some of them later related that Abel was an excellent teacher whose presentation was clear and easy to follow. Turning over the leaves of his notebooks, one finds the most profound studies of elliptic functions, equations, and series mixed with card game scores, washing lists, and elementary school mathematics, traces of the many times he used the books to convey to his schoolboys the rudiments of his science.

Aside from Saigey of Ferrusac's *Bulletin*, his untiring friend Crelle was his only mathematical correspondent during that fall. Crelle was deeply concerned about Abel's circumstances and had begun thinking in terms of a permanent position for his friend in Berlin. But to create a new scientific position required a good deal of preparation, however favorably inclined toward the sciences the Prussian government might be. Crelle's hopes lay in a new polytechnic institute in Berlin, with a mathematical seminary, whose creation had long been contemplated by the authorities.

Not a word arrived from the Institute in Paris in regard to the great memoir which he had presented a year earlier. He often wondered, but refrained from writing to expedite the referees. He was encouraged a bit by receiving an academic honor — the only one in his life — election

to the Royal Norwegian Society for the Sciences, a venerable but somewhat isolated institution in Trondheim. At the same time the society
published one of his lesser papers, an early article probably submitted
by Hansteen, who had more manuscripts from Abel than he dared use
in the *Magazin*.

Aside from the tutoring, Abel had a good deal of leisure in his poverty,
and his science benefited from it. He worked on a great variety of mathematical problems, but concentrated on completing the second part of
his memoir *Recherches*. It was to contain that part of the elliptic functions which was later called the transformation theory, as well as the
division properties of such functions, in particular, the lemniscate. These
lemniscate problems brought Abel to consider a large class of equations
with special properties, which interested him greatly. With his characteristic ability to crystalize the essential of every problem, he created
the theory of Abelian equations as they have since been known in the
mathematical literature.

The *Journal* resumed publication after a short delay, the first issue
containing a small paper by Abel, and the second, dated September 20,
1827, including the first eighty pages of his *Recherches*. Abel, isolated
in Oslo during the winter, far from the centers of scientific activity,
had no inkling of the stir which *Recherches* had caused among the most
eminent mathematicians in Europe, nor did he realize the tense expectation with which some of them looked forward to the promised continuation. Without knowing it himself, Abel had entered the elite of the
world's mathematicians, and nothing he produced could from now on
be neglected.

Hansteen and several of his colleagues felt ill at ease over Abel's
miserable situation after his return, but could do little except strengthen
his credit whenever it was needed. In his last column on "Our traveling
young scholars," Hansteen wrote a few lines evidently for the benefit
of Abel:

"These young men are the hope of our future. Our humane government has willingly contributed to the cultivation of their talents. We
are convinced that there should be no delay in bringing them into
spheres of activity suitable for their ability and knowledge, until such
time as we retire incapacitated, with our bodily and spiritual powers
expended."

Abel's prospects became brighter as the realization of Hansteen's plans drew nearer. The Storting had appropriated 4500 daler for the expedition, an enormous amount by Norwegian standards of that period. In the middle of September 1827, the Church Department informed the Collegium that the grant had been made and that it was necessary to make provision for Hansteen's duties during his absence. The department also instructed the Collegium rather ominously to "give an opinion whether it believed that the arrangements would entail increased expenditures for the university treasury."

On October 6, Hansteen reported to the Collegium in regard to his expedition, and proposed Abel as a substitute in his post:

"Since my Siberian journey will begin in March of next year, it will be necessary to make a temporary appointment of a docent from the first of the year 1828, who can take over my lectures during my absence, which presumably will last one-and-a-half to two years. The lectures which are required for the present are only an introduction to theoretical astronomy for the students wishing to take the philosopical examination, and in case any geologists should register, lectures on the principal theorems of mechanics. Herr Studiosus N. Abel has declared himself willing to take over these duties."

Hansteen had prepared the manuscript for the almanac for several years ahead; it was undoubtedly important for him to be able to collect fees before his departure. The last sentence in the letter from the Church Department had evidently shocked Hansteen. He guessed that the department might consider requiring him to pay for the substitute during his absence. This may explain the rather facile evaluation which he gave of the burdens of his office. Hansteen urgently requested a statement from the Collegium and the faculty in the matter. Obviously the Collegium had the same misgivings as Hansteen, for, when it finally replied to the department shortly before Christmas, it did so in terms which could not be misunderstood:

"The Collegium has found it desirable to request the opinion of the Philosophical Faculty in this matter and this has declared that it knows of no one to take charge of Professor Hansteen's duties except Herr Candidatus Philosophiae N. H. Abel. It believes that this task has been facilitated by the fact that Professor Hansteen has computed the almanac for the coming three years. The Faculty also believes that this appointment should be made contingent upon Lecturer Holmboe taking over the responsibility for the astronomical instruments in case their use should be required, a charge which he has declared himself willing to accept.

"In regard to the expenditures in connection with the appointment of a temporary docent, the Faculty expressed the opinion that for Professor Hansteen's journey to Siberia, no expense should be charged to the university budget, since this is a government matter. Since the government has approved the purpose, it must also approve the means."

At the same time Professor Hansteen informed the military academy that he would be unable to give his lectures, and that, after conference with General Aubert, the director of the school, he had approached Studiosus Abel, who was willing to give the instruction in mechanics and theoretical astronomy. The remaining third of the job, the practical use of instruments, would be entrusted to a captain in the engineering corps.

The prospects for 1828 looked more favorable for Abel. Shortly after the New Year he began his classes at the military academy; his salary was to be two thirds of Hansteen's annual remuneration of 200 daler. Not long after he commenced his university course, Introduction to Theoretical Astronomy. The appointment had to pass several official stages and this took some time, but in March he was informed that he had been named a temporary docent at an annual salary of 400 daler.

If Abel had not been weighted by his many obligations he would have had no reason for concern. In those days, 533 daler a year was an ample income for a bachelor. In any case, both he and Crelly undoubtedly appreciated the added prestige which the position entailed. From now on Abel always, certainly with a touch of pride, used the official title docent.

Even if his brother Peder and other members of his family may have continued to exploit Niels Henrik a little, his modest way of life made it possible for him to begin paying off some of his debts. The figures were considerable according to his report to Fru Hansteen. The total, including the bank loan, was nearly a full year's salary, so that with a substitute job lasting perhaps a year and a half, there was reason to be careful. The prospects after Hansteen's return were more than dubious. The attitude of the department in refusing the proposal for a position gave little cause for optimism. Alone he could of course manage in one way or another, but the feelings of Crelly most certainly had to be considered. They had already been engaged for several years, and she naturally hoped for an early marriage. So far he had had nothing to offer her except the hard lot of making her own living. It did not improve his spirits that his best friends had already been appointed to the positions they had wished for so wholeheartedly during the journey. Keilhau had been a lecturer for more than a year; immediately upon his return Boeck had been named a lecturer in the veterinary sciences and could marry his Elisabeth Collett.

It was cheering to have the ever-active Boeck in town again. Brimming with scientific plans, one of his first undertakings was to organize a scientific society in Oslo: The Physiographic Association. On the journey, Boeck and Keilhau had often discussed the plans for such an organization and had drawn up its program and bylaws. Keilhau, Boeck, Professors Hansteen and Maschmann were among the founders; in the first session on February 4, 1828, Abel was elected a member. In many ways, the association, albeit more formal, was a direct continuation of the scientific club of their student years. They met the first Monday of every month at 5 o'clock, the meeting place alternating among the homes of the older members. The program embraced a scientific lecture with subsequent discussion, probably followed by supper and a few glasses of punch, precisely the sort of session which Abel enjoyed. According to the minutes he was a most faithful member, ever present except when he was absent from town during the vacations. The Physiographic Association remained active until, in the 1850s, it was superseded by the Scientific Society in Oslo, which in turn became the Norwegian Academy of Science in Oslo. Boeck was a prominent member in all three organizations.

Immediately upon its creation, the association was entrusted with an important scientific mission, namely, the responsibility for the publication of the *Magazin*. It relieved Hansteen that Boeck was designated to succeed him as editor; he had often been concerned for the future of the publication. Hansteen's colleague, Professor Keyser, more than willing to serve as editor, had proposed that the *Magazin* be transformed into a popular scientific monthly, undoubtedly to improve its financial outlook. Hansteen maintained strongly that its strictly scientific character should be preserved and expressed himself quite cynically about the lay public who should support it:

"None of this pleases me. It is quite contrary to the principles which

I have hitherto followed, and which so far have made it possible to keep it going and even create a kind of reputation for it in this country as well as abroad. Whether the good people here understand it or not is quite indifferent to me. It is not written for their sake, and still less for their entertainment. They shall only be awarded the honor of maintaining it by their subscriptions. This they will do in good humor, as long as they believe that something good is published which at least will benefit the foreign scholar, for Ola Norwegian is fond of being praised abroad. But if he discovers that it is only a hodgepodge of valueless articles and still more expensive than before, then he will say: Upon my soul, I will rather drink another schnapps a day than throw my money down the gullet of printer Gröndahl. Then the *Magazin* caretaker can lock the door and become a homeless tramp, that is my prediction."

15

A QUESTION OF PRIORITY

❧ DURING THE FIRST DAYS of February 1828, Abel completed the second part of his *Recherches* containing, as planned, the lemniscate results and the transformation theory, a field in which he had gone far beyond Legendre. In reality, he had revolutionized the whole subject. He had taken a good deal of time in editing and publishing these results from his student days, but there did not seem to be any particular urgency; there were many other articles which he had preferred to prepare before this, and apparently he was the only one working in earnest in the field. To his great consternation, he discovered that in this conviction he was gravely mistaken. Without his knowledge, important things had happened in the mathematical world during the last half year, and the attention of mathematicians was for the moment especially focused upon the elliptical transcendentals.

During the fall of 1825, when Abel left Oslo on his journey and met Crelle, another young mathematician, the Privatdocent Carl Gustav Jacob Jacobi, began his first series of lectures at the university in Berlin. He was born in Potsdam, the son of a well-to-do Jewish banker. He had begun his university studies when he was only seventeen years old, and now, at twenty-one, he had completed the habilitation degree qualifying him for university positions. Jacobi lectured on differential geometry, a topic which never interested Abel, who was busy with his Norwegian friends and the many articles for Crelle that winter. Nevertheless, it seems reasonable to assume that the two young mathematicians must have seen each other at the time.

Jacobi demonstrated unusual talents as a lecturer; his presentation of advanced topics was clear and well coordinated. When Abel traveled southward, Jacobi had already obtained a better paid position at the University of Königsberg. Jacobi was interested in almost all fields of mathematics, and at the time was working in number theory, the particular delight of Gauss. Jacobi informed the master in Göttingen of his results, and Gauss became so interested that he wrote to his old friend, the astronomer Bessel in Königsberg, to obtain further information about the talented youth.

Bessel was both a friend and an admirer of Jacobi, but even so felt that he could not conceal the fact that the young mathematician was known both for his unusual ability and for his arrogance: "He is undoubtedly very talented, but here he has made almost everyone his enemy since he arrived, because he has said something unpleasant to each, and said it in a manner which they cannot forgive. However, I hope that these small stupidities soon will not be mentioned any more; toward me he has always been a well-behaved young man." Jacobi gradually did improve his insolent manners, as so many young men have done in the course of time. Even at this stage, in the competition which arose between Abel and Jacobi, the two rivals always expressed themselves with courtesy, respect, and admiration for the works and discoveries of the other.

Jacobi, as well as Abel, had early studied the works of Legendre on elliptic integrals, but, as he himself confessed, without inspiration. But during the summer of 1827, while Abel's *Recherches* was awaiting publication, Jacobi also was led to new ideas and mailed two notes, dated June 13 and August 2, to Schumacher in Altona, to be printed in the *Astronomische Nachrichten*. The first presented some special transformations of the elliptic integrals, the second a general formula, but neither contained any proof. Schumacher felt embarrassed; he was no specialist in the field and was reluctant to print formulas stripped of proofs and justifications. Gauss, from time to time, had alluded to profound studies of the elliptic integrals made in his youth; it was also known that he had a large unpublished work on the subject. Thus it was natural for Schumacher to turn to Gauss. He mailed Jacobi's notes to him, explained why he was in doubt, and asked for advice.

The response from Gauss was somewhat peculiar. He first confirmed that the results obtained by Jacobi were in order, and that they followed directly from his own. He added quite curtly that, if in the future Schumacher should receive communications of this kind which he hesitated to print, then Gauss insisted that they not be sent to him. Schumacher was surprised, and did not understand why his friend and correspondent of many years replied so brusquely, but he informed him that in the future his wishes would be respected.

The next letter from Gauss was more explicit, explaining his motives. His intention had only been to protect himself until his own investigations on the subject were published as planned:

"It grieves me that you have interpreted my remarks on Jacobi's communications in a manner which is so unjust to me. I shall always be prepared to examine mathematical papers, even those which do not interest me, if I can be of any service to you. But I do not wish to receive such communications as those of Herr Jacobi, which you do not intend to print, because my own interests are involved. His results are only fragments of my own extensive investigations, which I should like to edit in a comprehensive work some time in the future, if Heaven continues to grant me life, strength, and peace. Then it cannot be indifferent to me that someone might be able to charge that parts of it have become known to me through private communications."

Schumacher was at least reassured that the formulas were correct and he printed them in September 1827, the same month that Abel's *Recherches* appeared. Many mathematicians realized that they were witnessing a revolution in the theory of functions, and that Abel and Jacobi were in the process of transforming completely Legendre's lifework on the elliptic integrals. Several friends turned to Gauss, urging him to publish his own material so that he might not be deprived of the honors of prior discovery. On November 30, 1827, Bessel wrote to Gauss from Königsberg on this matter. To some extent, Bessel was the protector of Jacobi and was well informed of his rapid progress:

"As much as the beautiful results of Jacobi on the elliptic transcendentals have pleased me, I regret that he and Abel, who presumably is stronger than Jacobi, have deprived you of many results which have previously been in your possession. Jacobi does not possess the ability to present this theory in as elegant a form as undoubtedly can be done. Here, as well as in every other direction, your work will again be the classical model. Would you not be so good, since your work has long been ripe, to prepare at least some application of it, and thus secure the priority for yourself?"

It took several months before Gauss replied. Then it was evident that he had changed his mind about protecting his own interest after having read Jacobi's notes. The perusal of Abel's *Recherches* had influenced him, although for the moment only the first part had appeared:

"I shall most likely not soon prepare my investigations on the transcendental functions which I have had for many years — since 1798 — because I have many other matters which must be cleared up. Herr Abel has now, as I see, anticipated me and relieved me of the burden in regard to one third of these matters, particularly since he has executed all developments with great stringency and elegance. He has followed exactly the same road which I traveled in 1798; it is no wonder that our results are so similar. To my surprise this extended also to the form and even, in part, to the choice of notations, so several of his formulas appeared as if they were copied from mine. But to avoid every misunderstanding, I must observe that I cannot recall ever having communicated any of these investigations to others."

Gauss replied in a similar vein to a letter from Crelle. "Since Abel, also in regard to presentation, has exhibited so much elegance and discernment, I feel myself absolutely relieved from the presentation of these topics." In a later letter, dated May 1828, Crelle related this and various other excerpts indicating that the mathematicians had begun to appreciate Abel's writings, and added: "This judgment by Herr Gauss has pleased me greatly."

When the September issue of the *Astronomische Nachrichten* arrived in Paris, old Legendre became aware of Jacobi's formulas, and shortly afterward received a letter from the author explaining the results. Only some time later did Legendre become acquainted with Abel's *Recherches*. Legendre explained in his reply to Jacobi that one of his results was already known; he had just published it himself. But the general formula overwhelmed him to the extent that he could hardly believe that Jacobi had a proof. He himself had vainly worked in the same direction, and eagerly awaited further information from Jacobi in regard to the principles of this new method, so that he might add a supplement to his own great work on elliptic integrals. In a meeting of the Academy of Science in Paris, early in November, Legendre gave an enthusiastic account of Jacobi's discoveries; shortly afterward his statements were reproduced in the periodical *Globe*, and from there it passed to German newspapers, laying the foundations for the fame of the youthful Jacobi.

Legendre had expressed some doubt about whether Jacobi actually was in possession of a proof for his general formula. Schumacher too was dissatisfied with the state of affairs, and wrote directly to Jacobi:

"I am frankly of the same opinion as Legendre. When one publishes such brilliant discoveries as yours, one should not only make an announcement but also prove them immediately. Anyone who really loves his science must feel unpleasantly tense in the interval between the announcement and the presentation of the proof, and one cannot suppress a secret fear that it may not be demonstrated. Permit me, therefore, to ask you to relieve us all from this tension by giving us the deduction."

Jacobi must himself have been unpleasantly tense all that fall, for according to his statements to Bessel and his later explanations to Legendre there is no doubt that in reality he had arrived at his formula through an audacious but correct guess. His reputation as well as his hope for a professorship in Königsberg was at stake, for, in view of the favorable expressions of opinion of several eminent mathematicians in regard to his work, he had applied to have his docent position changed into an extraordinary professorship. He was well aware that any criticisms would be grasped with alacrity by his numerous enemies on the faculty.

Two circumstances brought Jacobi safely over the abyss which had been opened before him: his undeniable genius, and an idea which in all probability was revealed to him through reading Abel's *Recherches*. It was the fundamental principle of using the inverse functions instead of the integrals, an idea Abel had mentioned as early as 1823 in letters to Holmboe. Abel had refrained from publishing it until he could treat it comprehensively in connection with the theories in *Recherches*.

Through days and nights of intense work, according to Jacobi's own confession, he was able to establish a valid proof for the results which had been announced in the *Astronomische Nachrichten*. Greatly satisfied, he mailed the paper to Schumacher for publication. To arrive at his result, Jacobi had been compelled to rely heavily on Abel's idea of the inversion, but references to Abel's *Recherches* were conspicuously absent.

Early in 1828, Jacobi's proof was printed and on its way to Legendre. Jacobi, at twenty-three, also received his appointment to the professorship, just at the age when Abel in vain had hoped for the lectureship in Oslo. But in Jacobi's case, the situation was reversed: It was the Education Department which had to take the initiative in creating the new position, and urge it upon the faculty. The faculty itself had no desire to see Jacobi in its midst; his disrespectful and facetious observations about the professors had alienated too many of them. The department pressed the appointment, emphasizing the necessity of placing scientific progress above personal feelings. The faculty could not deny Jacobi's unusual talents and finally relented. An argument in his favor seems to have been that, as an extraordinary professor, he was not entitled to participate in the faculty meetings.

The elliptic functions became one of the most important research topics in mathematics during the nineteenth century; thus it is not surprising that the question of the equitable distribution of the honors of priority has been a subject which has preoccupied historians of mathematics. The German mathematician Leo Königsberger wrote a book on the subject, and many other mathematicians have since added their contributions. Without going into any details, let us only summarize how matters seem to stand.

Jacobi was an eminent mathematician who continued to write papers and lecture on elliptic functions long after Abel's death. A dominating personality, he exerted great influence on contemporary mathematics through his many excellent pupils; it is natural that Jacobi, in his lifetime, was assigned a somewhat greater share of the honors than may have been just. Abel's letters and many of his manuscripts were only published after Jacobi's death.

On the basis of the material now available, there is no doubt that Abel was in possession of most of the theory of elliptic functions long before Jacobi; nor can it be denied that Abel's *Recherches* was the first systematic account published. Jacobi's notes and proof can in no way be placed in this category. Only in his main work, the *Fundamenta nova* of 1829, does Jacobi expound his views on the general theory; this work and Abel's *Recherches* and later *Précis* must be accepted as the three pillars of the new theory. But justice also requires, according to what we now know, that Gauss' share in these discoveries should be acknowledged. His collected papers were published long after he and the two rivals were dead. His notes, written before either Abel or Jacobi was born, show clearly that he had then mastered a principal part of the theory of elliptic functions.

In reading the correspondence between Jacobi and Legendre, one feels that, in the beginning, Jacobi tended to emphasize his own results at the expense of Abel's. Later he gives Abel abundant recognition in his letters, but rather little in his published papers; it is not, of course, unnatural to find such small weaknesses in an ambitious young man struggling for his career. The only point on which serious criticism has been leveled at Jacobi is the one mentioned, namely, whether he willfully omitted any reference to Abel's ideas in his first proof in the *Astronomische Nachrichten*.

The proof is dated November 18; through a strange coincidence we know that the issue of Crelle's *Journal* containing Abel's article had arrived in Königsberg before October 4, and had been delivered to Jacobi's friend Bessel. On this date the university librarian wrote a letter protesting that this number had been sent by letter mail costing the institution an extra taler. The issue contained a paper by Jacobi; otherwise, most of it was filled by Abel's long memoir, dealing with the topic on which Jacobi was working. It is hardly believable that he had not glanced at it and noticed the main idea stated in its first section. It is impossible to deny that Jacobi may have found the idea of the inversion independently; Gauss' remarks about Abel's discoveries show how readily such a coincidence may occur. But under the circumstances, one is inclined to believe that the idea had been obtained from Abel. The young Jacobi was at a critical point in his scientific career; for several months his only thought had been to search for a proof of the announcements he had made. Suddenly he stood before the goal; the brief paper was probably written in a few hours with only the rapture of victory in his mind, making him forget in the moment that he had, in part, supported himself upon an idea which justly belonged to another.

Toward the middle of January 1828, after his completion of the proof, Jacobi wrote an exuberant letter to Legendre assuring him of his gratitude: "It would be wasted effort to attempt to describe for you my feelings when I received your letter of November 30, along with the issue of *Globe*, which contained an account of the statement which you were so good to make about my articles in the Academy. I felt confused, overwhelmed, both by the superabundance of goodness which you had shown and the feeling that never in my life could I have been worthy of anything of the kind. How could I show my gratitude? What satisfaction it was for me that the man whose works I had admired so greatly while I devoured them had been so kind as to receive my own writings with such an unusual and precious good will. Since I have no words which fully can describe my sentiments, I know of no better way to respond than to multiply my efforts to expand to a still higher extent the beautiful theories which you have created."

After this introduction, Jacobi continued: "Since my last letter some investigations of the very greatest importance have been published by a young mathematician whom you perhaps know personally. It is the first part of a memoir by Herr Abel in Oslo, who according to what I have heard was in Paris two or three years ago." The remaining parts of the long letter consist mainly of an extensive account of the results of Abel's paper, presented in the form preferred by Jacobi; here he shows that he is fully acquainted with the ideas of his rival.

By this time Abel's article had been brought to Legendre's attention by his colleague Poisson; it contained much that Legendre could not understand, but he was fully aware that a new and valuable contribution had been made by the young Norwegian. Perhaps Legendre already had given a concrete sign of his appreciation; there happened to be a vacancy among the corresponding members of the mathematical section of the Academy, and on the list of six proposed candidates presented on New Year's Eve 1827 may be found the names of Abel and Jacobi. Neither was elected; Jacobi received three votes, Abel none.

Legendre was grateful for Jacobi's explanation of Abel's paper. Abel's point of view was too radical for the old mathematician; Jacobi's way of presenting things was much closer to his own. He replied to Jacobi on February 9, 1828:

"I had already become acquainted with Abel's beautiful paper, printed in Crelle's *Journal*. But you have done me a very great favor by giving an analysis of it in your own manner of expression, which more resembles my own. It is a great satisfaction to me to see two young mathematicians so successfully cultivate a branch of analysis which long has been my favorite field, but not at all been received as it deserves in my own country. Through these works, you two will be placed in the class of the foremost analysts of our times. Here there are few talents, and those we have devote themselves to indefinite studies, leaving only indistinct traces in history. It is not sufficient to have talent; one must also be able to understand to what subjects it should be applied."

187

In reality, Legendre never became entirely familiar with Abel's methods, which influenced his valuation of their importance a good deal. From a modern point of view, this appears very surprising. In his biography of Jacobi Königsberger writes: "It is a peculiar fact that Abel's clearly conceived, well-written, and lucidly arranged works to the mathematical world appeared less accessible than those of Jacobi."

In a letter written in the spring of 1828, Jacobi explained that in order to prove certain new results, he was compelled to rely on a formula for the multiplication of elliptic functions established by Abel. In his reply Legendre sounded quite irritated:

"You say that in order to establish the principle of your proof it is necessary to make use of certain analytic formulas for the multiplication, *given for the first time by Herr Abel.* This confession demonstrates your candidness, a characteristic which accompanies true talent; however, it concerns me somewhat, for having justly evaluated Abel's beautiful work, I place it far below your own discoveries, and I should wish, therefore, that the honor of the proofs should also belong fully to you. But, of course, I am easily consoled by the fact that science has lost nothing; the proof belongs to you regardless of where you have found its basis, be it in my own work or in the highly esteemed recent article by Herr Abel."

Gauss at the same time pronounced a judgment exactly opposite to that of Legendre.

Throughout the fall and winter, Abel had lived in complete ignorance of the commotion caused by the elliptic functions among the leading mathematicians in Europe. During the winter the steamship no longer maintained its route to Copenhagen; mail from abroad was slow and uncertain; packages and printed matter arrived irregularly, and not at all when the Oslo fjord was covered by ice. Early in 1828, perhaps toward the end of January, Hansteen showed Abel the issue of *Astronomische Nachrichten* in which Jacobi's notices were printed. It does not appear to have made any deep impression upon him. The second part of the *Recherches* was near completion, and he hurriedly wrote a brief addition to it, pointing out how Jacobi's transformation formulas readily followed from his own results. On February 12 he mailed his manuscript to Crelle for the *Journal.*

But a little later, near the end of March, Hansteen again brought a number of *Astronomische Nachrichten,* and Abel received a shock when he read Jacobi's proof: Here another mathematician, evidently unusually gifted, had moved into a domain which Abel had considered his own; still worse, he had in part made use of methods which Abel had created, but without mention of his name. From a letter to Gauss from Schumacher we may gain an impression of Abel's consternation:

"From Abel I have received an article about the transcendental functions, and I shall reproduce for you a part of the letter from Hansteen who transmitted it to me. I seem to recall that you understand Danish so I shall reproduce it in the original since a translation would deprive it of some of its naiveté:

" 'Abel sends herewith an article about elliptic transcendentals, which he asked to have printed as soon as possible, since Jacobi is on his heels. The other day, when I handed him the last number of the *Astronomische Nachrichten,* he became quite pale and was compelled to run to the confectioner's shop and take a schnapps of bitter to counteract his alteration. For several years he has been in possession of a general method which he communicates in this paper, and which includes more than Jacobi's theorems.' "

Schumacher ingratiatingly added, on his own account, to Gauss: "When in due time you publish your own investigations, it will probably cost him more schnapps."

It was impossible for Abel to estimate how far Jacobi had gone, or how far he was able to go, but it was perfectly clear to him that if he did not want to lose the honor of priority, it was necessary to formulate and write down his discoveries as quickly as could be managed. Immediately after the completion of the second part of the *Recherches,* Abel had begun preparing the manuscript for the Abelian equations, with which he had struggled during the autumn months. It had been planned as a long paper with numerous applications, but with these new circumstances, time became urgent. He cut the paper short after having derived the basic principles of the theory. One thing he had learned from his perusal of Jacobi's papers; from now on he carefully dated his manuscripts. The equation paper was completed on March 29, 1828, but remained unpublished in the *Journal* files for more than a year, while Crelle awaited the promised continuation.

The next immediate aim for Abel was to surpass Jacobi in his own specialty, the transformation of the elliptic functions. He had long been in possession of the solution to a much more general transformation problem than that posed by Jacobi, and in two months' time he had completed a larger article, "Solution d'un problème general," which was dispatched to Schumacher on May 27, 1828. This time he preferred to let it appear in the *Astronomische Nachrichten*, both because this was the center of Jacobi's activities, and because Schumacher was known for his expeditious printing.

"My knockout of Jacobi" said Abel a little facetiously about the paper in a letter to Holmboe, and Jacobi received it with great admiration. But a mathematician as original and talented as Jacobi could not be knocked out, rather it served as the signal for another round in the strange rivalry.

16

HOPES AND DISAPPOINTMENTS

⋘ IT HAD BEEN Hansteen's expectation that both Boeck and Keilhau would accompany him on the expedition to Siberia. However, Boeck was getting married and declined the invitation; Keilhau was willing, but the faculty felt that he could not be spared so long from his newly created post, and denied his application for leave.

About the middle of May 1828 Hansteen embarked upon his journey. The expedition made good newspaper copy and the public was kept informed of its progress through Hansteen's travel letters until he returned two years later as a popular hero. The leading Oslo newspaper wrote about the plans: "From here he is accompanied by First Lieutenant Due of the Navy and in St. Petersburg he will meet Dr. Erman from Berlin, who takes part in the expedition as natural scientist and astronomer." The route was described and the dangers were not minimized: "The last stretch from Yakutsk to Okhotsk is 1014 versts [650 miles], and passes through completely uninhabited territory with 1000 rivers to ford. It is necessary to sleep in tents at night and carry provisions for the whole trip."

After Hansteen's departure, Boeck later related, Abel became more depressed. He was visited by his brother Thomas, but this may not have raised his spirits much; Thomas had abandoned his attempts to make a living in Copenhagen, and now was trying in Kragerö, nearer home, with equally disappointing results. He arrived by the *Constitution* on May 25, lived off his brother, and left him the bills when he departed in July.

Much more encouraging was the fact that Crelly came to town in the company of Sivert Smith, who was taking a business trip abroad. Abel and his sister met them at Dröbak, the last stopping place for the steamer before the capital. They arrived on June 8, and Crelly remained for three wonderful weeks, staying with Fru Hansteen who now was alone. Abel felt he was entitled to a few days off from his intense mathematical activity; the second part of the *Recherches* was in print, and his reply to Jacobi, the "Solution," was scheduled for the July issue of the *Astronomische Nachrichten*.

About the same time exciting news arrived from his friend Crelle. Undaunted by the first refusal, Crelle had continued with unabated energy to seek support for the *Journal* from the Prussian government. In a letter of May 14, 1828, he explained the importance of the *Journal* to the mathematical world, taking the opportunity to enlarge upon the exceptional merits of one of its contributors:

"The *Journal* has, in reality, found uncommonly strong support, and the most eminent mathematicians have of their own accord honored it by their works. During the short period of its existence it has made great progress and has contributed essentially to the propagation and enrichment of science.

"So for instance, Article 8, vol. 1, 'On the impossibility of a general solution of equations of higher degree than the fourth,' is unusually important for the still so obscure theory of higher equations. The author, Herr Abel, a young Norwegian, perhaps one of the greatest talents for higher mathematics at the present time, is almost completely overlooked in his own country and struggles against unfavorable circumstances.

"Article 12, vol. 2, by the same author 'On elliptic functions,' to be continued in the next issue, also initiated the investigations on this important part of analysis which are now being pursued so actively and, according to a statement by Legendre, have been further advanced by Herr Jacobi in Königsberg. This paper encouraged and spurred these studies onward. The continuation of the article by Herr Abel has again produced considerable progress, and impending investigations by the same mathematician may almost exhaust the subject."

To these strong words the minister benevolently replied on June 7:

"The extremely favorable judgment which you have expressed in your letter, both in regard to the excellent talent which Herr Abel possesses for higher mathematics, and his achievements until now, causes me to make an attempt to attract the young scholar to government service here. However, since there at present is no possibility at hand to offer him a definite position, you would oblige me by kindly investigating whether he for a suitable annual salary would be inclined to serve as privatdocent at the university here."

Crelle immediately wrote to Abel, explaining the situation and asking for an early reply. To the minister he expressed his gratitude:

"The acquisition of this young man for government service, as is your Excellency's graceful intention, will undoubtedly be a gain both for the service and for science. I am gratified that the State and the sciences will be indebted to your Excellency for this accomplishment. I have attempted to find out immediately through a letter whether Herr Abel is willing to remove here as privatdocent at the university, but I found it appropriate not to mention the source of my authorization for the inquiry. I shall be honored to humbly inform your Excellency of the reply which I expect shortly."

These were delightful prospects for Crelly and Niels Henrik; the long engagement would be ended, Crelly could take her rightful position at his side, and no longer would they be separated. They already imagined themselves as "Herr Professor und Frau Gemahlin." Abel was reluctant to leave Norway. But if there ever should be any hope of a scientific future for him at home this would be the time to find out. He discussed the problem with Crelly, and wrote an urgent letter to the Collegium. In his eagerness he forgot to date the missive:

"I take the liberty, since there at the moment has been opened a possibility for me to be appointed abroad, namely at the university in Berlin, to inquire from the high Collegium whether there is any prospect that I may be appointed to a permanent position here. It is certainly my most sincere wish to live my life in my own country if this can be done in an acceptable way. But without this, I do not believe I can refuse an opportunity to secure my future, which here appears very precarious to me.

"If no permanent appointment can be granted me, then I presume that my temporary appointment here at the university will not stand in the way of my attempting to secure a position in Berlin. If at some later time there should be the possibility of a position, if I dare nurture that hope, there will be, on my side, nothing to prevent my return. Since I have been insistently instructed to deliver my answer as soon as possible, I dare to ask the high Collegium to consider this case at its earliest convenience.

"This is for me a matter of the greatest urgency for my welfare."

193

The Collegium was again willing to lend its support, but the memory of the department's sharp refusal the preceding year was still fresh; it was not prudent by such repeated requests to irritate the powers which held the purse strings for the university in their hands. The application from Abel was acted upon June 21, 1828, and the recommendation to the rector was subdued:

"The Collegium regrets that it cannot make any proposal for a permanent position for this talented young man, so that he might be preserved for the university and his country. Nevertheless, the Collegium feels it to be its duty to submit the case to the higher authorities, inquiring respectfully whether from the government there may be an opportunity to offer Herr Abel a position consonant with his recognized achievements in the scholarly world, and the prospects he has for promotion at a foreign university where he probably, after a short appointment as a so-called privatdocent, will obtain a professorship."

The Collegium found also that Abel's temporary appointment should be no obstacle to accepting an offer from Berlin, and Holmboe declared himself willing to take over his friend's duties if necessary.

Abel's old friend Treschow had retired as rector. The new incumbent made an endorsement which precluded any hope of success:

"I must declare that I share the wish of the Collegium that such a position could be offered Herr Abel so that this talented young man could be kept in the country, but since I for the moment see no possibility for this, I dare not make any recommendation. Therefore I must console myself in the hope that some time in the future there may be an opportunity to bring Herr Abel back.

"Nevertheless, I shall request to be informed as soon as possible of the decision of the Royal department, in case it, contrary to expectation, should find means for making Herr Abel a suitable offer."

Obviously the application was without a chance of success after such an annotation by the rector, and Abel was advised by his friends to have it withdrawn. He wrote to Crelle and said he would come.

In a later memorandum to the Prussian minister of education, Crelle informed him that he had investigated with the strictest privacy, and "to my great pleasure found that Herr Abel is perfectly willing and prepared to accept the position as privatdocent at the university in Berlin."

"He told me confidentially that his demands were not great, but since he was without means and had acquired some debts through his studies, and partly supported his brothers — he is the son of an evangelical pastor — he should wish to obtain to begin with at least 500 taler, preferably 600 taler, in annual salary, and in addition some travel money, perhaps as much as one quarter's salary.

"If this should be granted him, he will gladly interrupt his stay there. His subsistence is only assured for the time being and not at all for the future, through an appointment as a privatdocent and substitute for Professor Hansteen during his travel in Siberia. He prefers to come here because, during a previous long stay and a journey which he undertook in 1825, 1826, and 1827 to Germany, France, and Italy, he could not fail to observe that at present the sciences are supported and promoted more forcefully by the high Prussian government than anywhere else.'

Crelle had evidently mastered the art of writing to the authorities.

The Smiths had invited Abel to spend his summer vacation at Froland, perhaps his last in Norway for a long time to come. He waited till July 1, pay day, and then boarded the *Constitution* with Crelly. The first stop was at Risör to see his mother. Niels Henrik could at least reassure her that the debt on her property had been paid. He had talked to Mandall, the university treasurer, and had been informed that there still remained 50 daler on his fellowship grant. Abel, under the impression that the fellowship had ceased after his substitute appointment, had drawn nothing on it after the New Year, 1828. This was a pleasant surprise; after paying the obligation on his mother's farm, he still had nearly half the amount left.

The day before his departure, he wrote to the Church Department, requesting that his application be tabled. The department gracefully composed this epitaph:

"Abel, temporary docent, asks that the application for a permanent appointment contained in his letter — N.B. without date — to the Academic Collegium for the time be tabled.

"Resolved: Approved and tabled."

But this did not quite end the matter. The letter must have caused an association of ideas in the mind of some meticulous secretary who, leafing through the copybook, came across the letter from the department to the university written in August. A few days later the university received an order which caused considerable indignation and a heated discussion. The department pointed out that in connection with Abel's last fellowship it had suggested to the Collegium "that an assistance of 200 daler be granted Herr Abel from the university treasury, this amount to be refunded when his services were required at the university. The department is informed that this advance has been paid to Herr Abel, but upon his appointment as temporary docent has not been repaid, either fully or in part. We request, therefore, in the interest of the service, that the honored Collegium will kindly take steps to have the above-mentioned amount refunded to the university through suitable deductions from Herr Abel's salary."

The Collegium was indignant, found the demand highly unjust, and took the responsibility entirely upon itself. It was fully aware how impossible it would be for the debt-ridden Abel to repay the 200 daler. This time the reply was forthright:

"We shall not fail to state that the support granted Herr Abel was given, not as an advance, but as a fellowship. The Collegium did not find it appropriate to stipulate any refund, considering the distant expectations for Herr Abel to obtain a permanent position, since only in such a case would it be fair to think of any restitution to the university, while under his present as well as any other temporary employment it will doubtless be extremely difficult for him to procure the money."

The Collegium could also have retorted, but did not do so, that the department had already received its pound of flesh. Abel's salary had been placed at 400 daler, while in similar previous cases the amount had been 600 daler annually; a possible reason for this may have been Hansteen's rather slight estimate of the burdens of the office. But the Collegium did concede that it was not reasonable that Abel for a certain period had received both fellowship and salary, and it delegated one of the professors to find out privately whether Abel would be able to make restitution for this period.

After the Collegium's courageous stand there was little the department could do except make the Collegium admit that in principle it had been in the wrong, the decision properly belonged to the department: "The department does not believe that the Collegium is entitled to make such dispositions of the means of the university without higher authorization." It suggested that the university ex post facto should request the approval of the government for its action.

But by this time the Collegium was convinced that the liberty of the university in regard to internal decisions was at stake, and it was unwilling to yield an inch on the principle that the amounts granted it through the budget could be distributed for approved purposes without the department's minute control. In particular, the budget provided 1200 daler for fellowships, and the fact that the Collegium had awarded to Abel more than the usual amount could in no way make it subject to renewed approbation. However, the Collegium gave the department an opportunity to retreat gracefully by suggesting it approve the action and leave the matter at this point. The Collegium had been immovable in its stand and the Church Department, losing its desire to discuss the principles of academic self-government with the government, and perhaps the Storting, quietly gave its sanction.

The whole feud had lasted about two months. Abel was probably more bitter than ever before toward these departments which forever placed obstacles in his way, but he soon found other troubles to disturb his peace of mind still more. After his case had been discussed in the Collegium, it was impossible in the little town of Oslo to keep secret the fact that a young Norwegian had gained the rare distinction of being called to a foreign university. It was somewhat of a sensation and on July 7, 1828, one of the papers printed this news item:

"Our young scholar Abel, teacher in mathematics at the university, who a little more than half a year ago returned from his scientific journey abroad, has acquired such a reputation in Berlin that he has received an offer from this seat of science which gives him and his country great honor. One must regret that at present there is no more worthy position vacant for him than the one he nows holds, and we must be glad that he thereby is induced to accept this honorable offer. We cherish the hope that some time in the future he will hasten home to his beloved native country with a famous name."

Crelle had insisted upon discretion, so that the article was most unwelcome. But a few days later a calamity occurred which made all of Abel's dream castles tumble down like card houses: On July 11, Crelle wrote from Berlin that grave obstacles were blocking the appointment.

Fru Hansteen was the first to be informed of the catastrophe:

"'Leider' [unfortunately] — with this ominous word begins a letter which I received from Crelle yesterday, dated July 11, and 'leider' I must confess that the letter has depressed me greatly. Nothing will come out of it.

"Someone else has appeared as if fallen from heaven. He has made his demands and must absolutely be provided for before I can be considered. Crelle does not say who this other person is and I know of no one of this caliber. He says that he will not at present push my case because it will harm more than it will benefit me, God knows for what reason. Furthermore, the minister of education is absent, and will not return for eight weeks; thus he says, no final answer can be given me before October. But his letter is so pessimistic that I have abandoned all hope.

"So now I stand at the same point as previously, but a little worse, for I have been disgraced here and may be so abroad — see the edifying piece in the newspaper. I shall issue no denial in order not to rip open the dirty matter; now it may pass as a newspaper lie; *et enfin le temps tue tout.*

"Whatever may happen, I shall hardly apply for anything more in Oslo, I will rather struggle along with what I have as long as it lasts.

"But I have learned to keep my mouth shut — a good thing. Crelle is probably thumbing his nose at me for tattling, for even if I have not told him what I have said, I feel that he is *au fait*. However, he asks me to say absolutely nothing, thus you must say only that you know nothing, except that I have never received an offer.

"If my brother Peder comes to see you, don't let him hear this, so that he will not refrain from seeking a job as tutor. I hope you don't blame me.

"It grieves me most for my betrothed; she is much too good for this. Except for a little sickness from which I suffered during the first days, I have been very well here with Crelly — or Christine — and I work quite busily.

"Since I was really born to bother you, perhaps I may ask you to send someone down to cash the enclosed draft at the treasurer's office and soon mail me 10 daler in one bill and keep the rest for me. If you write on heavy opaque paper or put the bill in such paper it is not necessary to mark it as containing money. The very best thing to do is to prepare an envelope with sealing wax and put the bill in another piece of paper within. It is best not to mention money on the outside so that the boy who brings the mail from Arendal will not steal. Please do not be angry with me for troubling you, I am provoked enough as is. It is impossible, I suppose, to get the money to me before the first mail day in August. But that will be time enough.

"Crelly sends her best regards, she wrote last mail day.

"I take it like a man.

"The most beautiful Fru Hansteen's most miserable little creep, N. H. Abel.

"How is the husband? I see from the newspapers that you received a letter from him from St. Petersburg dated June 25."

Holmboe was in Copenhagen, but he was informed of the sad story a week later, this time in more lively terms:

"Herr Lecturer: Assuming that you have returned from Copenhagen I write to you, but you need not tell anyone what I write. Namely, the trip to Berlin has gone to the devil, and so I am just as far as before.

"Crelle wrote to me a week ago Sunday that there was someone, *vom Himmel her gefallen,* who had made his claim and had to be taken care of. God knows who he is, but he has pushed me out, the swine. Otherwise, he says that although it looks bad I must not give up all hope, since it may be possible later; I shall know in October. But you must say nothing about all this, only that there never was an offer for me to come to Berlin, in accordance with the truth. Crelle would be greatly displeased if I talked about it.

"I have received a letter from Schumacher; my knockout of Jacobi is printed. I am working on a similar one which will be sent shortly. I have made a couple of beautiful discoveries in the elliptic transcendentals. Perhaps I did not mention that books have arrived for us at Messel's bookstore.

"According to what Hansteen said, it is possible that a teacher in astronomy will be needed at the military academy. In that case, please say that I may be willing to accept it, so that they will not be under the misapprehension that I shall go to Berlin. This I mention only privately to you; if you feel like it, please write me a few words about it. I shall leave here on Friday in two weeks. Remember me to our friends, and live well.

"I hope that you will not be peeved at me if I stay briefly with you upon my arrival, until I find lodgings; nor that I do not pay for this letter; nor that I ask you to forward the enclosed."

The "enclosed" was a short note to Fru Hansteen about money and the affairs of his brother:

"Still another plea to you, good Fru Hansteen. It is possible that Thomas has left without a word to his host Ibsen. God bless you, let the maid go down and ask Ibsen whether Thomas still is there, and if not let her give notice and say that I shall pay upon my return.

"I wrote to you a week ago and enclosed a draft upon the treasury for the salary for the month of July. Perhaps I can expect the ten daler I mentioned. I shall probably not return to Oslo before the middle of August.

"Please do not be angry with me for troubling you; when I come to think of it I could really have asked Holmboe to do it. Crelly sends regards. I have received a present of six pairs of socks from Marie and Crelly, and something unmentionable from Hanne Preus and Lina. May God let you live well, dearest Fru."

But only a couple of days later Abel bothered Fru Hansteen again with his money matters:

"I suppose you received the note with the three daler. I am as poor as a church rat. I have only 1 daler and 60 skilling left, which I need for tips. But I have otherwise not wasted a penny; the merchant has been paid 103 daler, 26 skilling, which was all I owed him.

"I have received a letter from Schumacher; my *Aufsatz* is printed, and on its way to Königsberg. When you see Elisabeth, greet her and the Treschows. Your miserable."

Abel had no inkling of what had transpired in Berlin, and for Crelle it was difficult to explain the events freely. However, the background of the episode seems to have been about as follows:

Crelle served as consultant to the ministry in questions concerning scientific and technical education. After assiduous efforts he had finally convinced the Education Department of the desirability of creating a mathematical institute in connection with the university; to this he intended Abel should be assigned.

But an institute must have a director, and when it became known that the plan was nearing fruition, there occurred behind the stage one of those bitter rope-pulling contests to which the republic of the learned is much too prone.

One faction forcefully maintained that the inimitable Gauss would be a natural choice for the position; to this the department might have been inclined to agree, since the appointment of so famous a scientist as Gauss would be hard to criticize. Gauss was aware of the action and strangely enough seemed inclined to move to Berlin.

But from the other camp, and here Crelle could be found, it was objected that the real need of such an institute was for several young and active mathematicians who could attract great numbers of pupils. This was exactly Gauss' weakness. He showed little interest in youth; furthermore, he had in no small measure avoided lectures and administrative tasks at the university in Göttingen, an attitude not at all suitable for the director of the new institute.

Late in the summer of 1828 it appeared that the faction for Gauss had lost its enthusiasm. The astronomer Schumacher was in Berlin at this time, and made every effort to determine the actual prospects for his friend. On September 7 he reported to Gauss:

"It appears to me that in general your Berlin appointment is not desired. From this statement I except Alexander von Humboldt and the few who are really distinguished there; it is meant for the great gross of scholars. Each of these has his own social circle in which he passes for an oracle, and none of them is inclined to let his reputation suffer the blow of bringing in a tremendous, universally recognized genius.

"If you were not the man you are, but some mediocre intellect with a little reputation, then these gentlemen would receive you with open arms, because they could hope to show their own pre-eminence over a famous man, and so consolidate their authority in their own circle. It also seems to me that they fear that you might show your superiority with too little regard to the weaker ones. You see how little they know your character."

But when even the famous and influential von Humboldt repeatedly evaded the subject when Schumacher approached him, he realized that the call of Gauss to Berlin no longer was under consideration. The controversy had delayed the consideration of appointments to the faculty of the institute, but now after the air was cleared Crelle could redouble his efforts on Abel's behalf.

17

THE DAWN OF FAME

◌§ IN THE MIDDLE OF AUGUST, Abel returned to the capital for his classes. He had been ill at times during the summer, had coughed and was feverish. Not long after he arrived in Oslo he was overcome by the most serious and prolonged attack he had hitherto suffered, and was unable even to leave his sickbed to say good-bye to his beloved Fru Hansteen when she departed for Copenhagen. It had been arranged, probably as a matter of economy, that Fru Hansteen should live with her sister Fru Fridrichsen during Hansteen's absence, and on September 16 she left Oslo on the *Constitution* with her whole household — six children and a maid. Abel wrote to her the following week:

"You were doubtless somewhat surprised, my good Fru Hansteen, at not seeing me before you left, but your surprise cannot have been greater than my sorrow at not coming. I was ill and stayed in bed from the evening you were at Treschow's until a couple of days ago. At present I am, God be praised, very well.

"It is so strange; I cannot get it into my head that you have left. I have often been on the point of going to you. I literally do not associate with a single person. However, at present I do not feel the need, since I have so terribly much to do for the *Journal*. From now on I shall receive one ducat for each printed sheet; Crelle has offered it to me. Of course it does not amount to much, but my straitened circumstances made me accept. Recently, only yesterday, I received a letter from Crelle in which he says there is still hope that I may come to Berlin, and that a decision will be reached soon.

"From little Crelly I can bring you regards. She sends you a small hood, the creation of her own hands, which she asks you to accept in the condition in which it is. The reason it is not quite completed is that she was compelled to send it a week ago, so that you might receive it before your departure. Unfortunately, I only received it on Tuesday, and thus too late.

"I have various things I could write to you about, but the lectures compel me to conclude. Cordial regards to the most sweet Fru Fridrichsen. As ever, my wish for your well being. N. H. Abel.

"Crelly loves you almost as much as I do."

Abel wrote mathematics while he was at Froland, and after his return to Oslo; in fact, he wrote almost continually. One of the papers completed at Froland, a continuation of his "knockout" of Jacobi, was sent to Schumacher. But otherwise he dispatched his whole production to Crelle, always praying for rapid printing. Crelle placed no restrictions on his youthful protégé in regard to the number of papers he was willing to accept for the *Journal*. The volumes for 1828 and 1829 are filled with Abel's works.

No active mathematician could fail to observe this stream of papers on a variety of mathematical topics. Some of the articles were so evidently masterpieces that Abel, in a short time, became one of the most talked of mathematicians on the Continent. Interest was intensified through his prolonged competition with Jacobi — the race for discoveries in the theory of elliptic functions.

The two rivals had different principles in regard to the publication of their results. Abel preferred to write long memoirs, giving the results as well as the methods behind them, while Jacobi was content to publish a series of brief notes, some directly connected with Abel's works, others containing sketches of his own finds. At the same time, Jacobi worked incessantly on his large *Fundamenta nova*, the new foundation for the elliptic functions which he intended to publish as a book at his own expense.

Legendre was dissatisfied with Jacobi's procedure; it gave no key to his thoughts and his contributions did not appear in their best light:

"Herr Abel, on the other hand, publishes in suitable order memoirs which are true masterpieces; because he is not in possession of the means to publish his investigations collectively, he develops much further what he prints in Crelle's and Schumacher's journals. So he gains a certain advantage over you, since you so far have published only notes not showing your methods. Thus there is good reason for hurrying to take possession of that which belongs to you by letting your book appear at the earliest possible date."

A dark cloud hovered over the correspondence between Jacobi and Legendre after the former had been obliged to confess that his first notes on the transformations had been based, not on a rigid deduction, but on an astute guess. Legendre gave him a good schooling in a letter of June 16, 1828:

"In my last letter I could only touch briefly upon what I had to say to you in connection with the candid statement which you made to me concerning the chain of ideas which had led you to the beautiful results about the elliptic functions. I see we have both run a risk: you by announcing discoveries which did not carry the seal of approval which a valid proof affords; I by giving my full approval to them, publicly and without reservations."

Legendre, continuing to have difficulties in understanding Abel's method of presentation, wrote in the same letter:

"In your last and in your previous letters you have shown me the kindness of explaining to me some of Abel's beautiful results, which I find a little confusing although they have been presented in a very methodical fashion by the young and ingenious author."

The explicit expression of his feelings by the old Legendre cleared the air, and through the fall of 1828 the correspondence continued without any discordant note. Meanwhile, Abel's "knockout" had been printed, and Jacobi did not hide his admiration:

"You have undoubtedly received the two memoirs by Abel, one in Crelle's *Journal* [*Recherches* II], the second in Schumacher's *Astronomische Nachrichten*. From the first you will see that Herr Abel has also arrived at the general theorem for the transformation, which I anticipated him by six months in publishing. The second paper, printed by Schumacher, contains a rigorous deduction of the transformation theorems, an appreciable deficiency in my notes on the subject. It stands as high above my praise as it surpasses my own works."

In the same letter, Jacobi related that the *Fundamenta nova* would soon be ready for the press, and that he might possibly come to Paris to place a copy in Legendre's hands in person. But he admitted he had begun to tire. "I shall confess to you, Monsieur, that I am a little weary of this subject which has occupied me almost day and night for 18 months. Nevertheless, the conclusion of my book will not represent the conclusion of my investigations; there will still remain many important questions, but these are associated with great difficulties."

Abel had a certain advantage in regard to the elliptic functions; he had lived with the subject matter for several years, and had already delved deep into many questions. But now his sickness began to undermine his health in earnest; the pace had been too great, and he could no longer cope with all his many tasks and projects.

Crelle was tireless in his efforts; from prominent mathematicians he had quietly gathered opinions of Abel's work as a preparation for the decisive campaign to bring Abel to Berlin. To encourage his young friend he sent a few excerpts to Abel on September 10, 1828:

"Jacobi writes: 'Herr Abel, in a distinctive way, has arrived at my transformation theory in which I had anticipated him, just as well as he has anticipated me in so many others. In your *Journal* appeared an article by Abel, in which he shows that our transformation theory is exhaustive and conclusive. I consider this proof one of the most beautiful masterpieces in analysis.'

Legendre writes: 'What you tell me about the young Herr Abel is in complete agreement with the idea I had formed about his great talents while reading the issue of your *Journal* in which his remarkable memoir on elliptic functions is included. Last year Poisson showed me the number you had sent him, shortly after Jacobi's beautiful discoveries had come to my attention through Schumacher's journal and a letter from the author. These contributions by the two young scholars, until then unknown to me, have aroused my admiration as well as my satisfaction. I perceived that they, each for his part and in different respects, had brought to a high degree of perfection the theory which I through a long series of years had cultivated almost alone, and which by the mathematicians in my own country had been considered with indifference. I am now engaged in printing a supplement to my work which will contain the proof of Jacobi's two general theorems as well as new developments. I have decided to publish later a second supplement, in which Abel's discoveries will be exhibited, together with those which I expect will be made by Abel as well as Jacobi.' "

On September 25 Abel replied with his cordial thanks for the statements and continued: "It pleases me greatly, of course, that the hope of an appointment in Berlin is good and I thank you in advance for your efforts. But I implore you, let me know as soon as possible when anything has been decided, be it favorable or not, for if it does not work out as I hope I must be prepared to improve on my conditions here.

I can take no steps until I know what happens. This request you will certainly grant me." Abel was also eager to hear something about Jacobi's methods. "Please spur him on to reveal something, for it is clear that he is in possession of excellent things."

He was informed that Jacobi's *Fundamenta nova* was under preparation and at first wanted to respond with a continuation of his *Recherches*, which he actually began to write. But gradually he had been led to another conception of the whole theory, and now he decided to place it on an entirely new foundation in another work: *Précis d'une theorie des fonctions elliptiques*. Again it was unthinkable that a publisher would accept it at his own expense, but the helpful Crelle promptly offered his services, promising to print it in installments in the *Journal*, regardless of its length. Crelle still had the paper on the Abelian equations, and was waiting for its continuation. For the first time, Abel had to admit that a task surpassed his strength; his health was giving out:

"It pleases me greatly that you will print my *Précis*. I shall exert myself to make it as clear and good as possible, and hope I shall succeed. But do you not think that it would be better to commence with this paper instead of the one on the equations? I ask you urgently.

"Firstly, I believe that the elliptic functions will be of greater interest; secondly, my health will hardly permit me to occupy myself with the equations for a while. I have been ill for a considerable period of time, and compelled to stay in bed. Even if I am now recovered, the physician has warned me that any strong exertion can be very harmful.

"Now the situation is this: the equations will require a disproportionately greater effort on my part than the elliptic functions. Therefore, I should prefer, if you do not absolutely insist on the article on equations — in that case you shall have it — to begin with the elliptic functions. The equations will follow soon afterward. If you have nothing against it, I would prefer to divide it into short sections, so that something about elliptic functions and something about equations could appear in each issue; for the first issue I should like to send only elliptic functions."

The good Crelle had no objections, and during the fall Abel was busily engaged in writing the *Précis*.

Personal interest in the genius from a distant country awakened as Abel's reputation spread to the scientific centers of Europe. Crelle knew

Abel most intimately, and never concealed his anxiety about the youthful Norwegian's uncertain position and difficult economic circumstances. He wrote about it to the Ministry of Education and doubtless privately to many others, and discreetly supported him a little through small payments for his articles. Abel also corresponded with Saigey, who had known him as a destitute student, and there might have been other channels of information to the Continent. The details might not always have been accurate, some might have been exaggerated, but it was well known that, for the moment, Abel had only a precarious substitute position, and recently had resorted to tutoring to make a living.

Abel's situation was so patently inferior to that which his scientific reputation justified that four prominent members of the French Institute were moved to take a most unusual action. In September 1828, through Count Löwenhielm, the Swedish envoy in Paris, they addressed a petition directly to the Swedish king, Karl Johan, requesting that he use his personal influence to create a position for Abel:

"Sire. Informed and generous princes delight in discovering the merits of the unobtrusive and compensating them for the errors of fortune. They are also pleased to secure for a man of genius the means for throwing such light on the sciences as they will receive through his work, reflecting glory upon the government.

"For this reason the undersigned members of the Institut de France permit themselves to bring to the attention of Your Majesty's royal benevolence a young mathematician, Monsieur Abel, whose works have shown him to be a mind of the first order, and who nevertheless languishes in Oslo in a position little worthy of his rare and precocious talent.

"We have dared to believe that the king of Sweden, in perhaps being sensitive to the recommendation and spontaneous wish of some of the friends of the sciences, will deign to interest himself in the fate of a man so distinguished, by summoning him from a faraway part of his kingdom to the midst of his capital, which at all times has been justly famous through the presence of the celebrated scholars assembled in the Academy of Stockholm. It is in their vicinity and within reach of the reciprocal assistance which great talents afford each other that the place for a mathematician like Monsieur Abel seems indicated.

"But in any case they are convinced that enough has been done for him, if they for an instant have succeeded in affixing favorably upon him the august attention of his sovereign. The undersigned declare themselves with profound respect, Sire, to be his Majesty's most humble and obedient servants. Legendre, Poisson, LaCroix, Maurice."

The competition between Jacobi and Abel had been keen and hectic as long as they attempted to surpass each other in the transformation theory. Gradually the two contenders moved in different directions over the wide field which the elliptic functions afforded, separating as do knights after an indecisive joust, each respecting the skill of his opponent.

However, the two young mathematicians were preparing intensely for another tilt, Jacobi armed with the *Fundamenta nova*, still in progress, Abel with his *Précis*, never quite completed. But Abel had another armory which he decided to open. It contained the ideas of his great Paris memoir, which he now began to utilize. The main theorem that he had derived gave him the means to master a wider analytic theory in which even the elliptic functions were but a small part. In the fall of 1828, Abel completed a paper in which he extended the elliptic integrals to what are now called hyperelliptic integrals. He still did not use the great theorem in all its force, but added only in a footnote that in a memoir submitted to the French Academy in 1826 he had given the proof for a much more general result.

After Crelle had transmitted to him the sympathetic opinions of Legendre in regard to his results, Abel took courage and wrote directly to the famous old mathematician. Abel explained some of his most recent discoveries, also mentioning the hyperelliptic integrals. Legendre was delighted to hear from the other of the two eminent rivals, and replied on October 25, 1828:

"Monsieur, it is with great pleasure that I have received and read the very interesting letter which you addressed to me on the third of this month. I congratulate you cordially upon the great progress you have achieved through your works on the elliptic functions. I was already familiar with the beautiful articles which you had published in the journals of the gentlemen Crelle and Schumacher; the new details which you have been kind enough to communicate to me from your later studies have, if possible, augmented to a still higher degree the claim which you have to the esteem of the scientists, in particular my own.

"In thus rendering deserved homage to your discoveries I cannot deny a feeling of pride in being in some measure connected with your triumphs and those of your worthy rival Jacobi; for it is to a large extent through the study of my own works that you have found an opportunity to exhibit the great talents with which nature has endowed you. In one of his last letters Jacobi writes the following words about your memoir in No. 138 of Schumacher's periodical:

" 'This number contains a rigorous deduction of the transformation theorems, an appreciable deficiency in my notes on the subject. It stands as high above my praise as it surpasses my own works.'

"A confession like this, expressed so candidly, is equally honorable for Herr Jacobi as yourself. Without doubt, you two will prove fully worthy of each other through the nobility of your sentiments and the justice which you mutually yield each other.

"I should like to be permitted to send to you, Monsieur, a copy of my *Traité des fonctions elliptiques* in two volumes, which appeared in January 1827 and contains a variety of things which do not appear in my *Exercises de calcul integral.* But it is difficult to dispatch it to you in a secure manner. You will not be able to learn anything from this work, on the contrary, it is I who must rely upon you two gentlemen to greatly augment it by your precious discoveries, which I never should have achieved by my own efforts, for I have reached the age where research is difficult or impossible.

"The conclusion of your letter almost confuses me by the comprehensiveness which you have been able to impart to your study of the elliptic functions, and even for more complicated functions. I am very anxious to become acquainted with the methods which have led you to such remarkable results. I do not know whether I shall be able to comprehend them, but in any case I certainly have no idea of the means which you have been able to devise to penetrate difficulties such as these.

"What a head there must be on the young Norwegian."

Legendre had just completed and printed the first supplement to his *Traité.* The old master was struggling against age and bodily infirmities, but he exerted himself to the utmost to follow the stimulating events which occurred in the field which he so long had cultivated almost alone. With the supplement, Legendre dispatched a letter to Jacobi on October 15:

"The journey which I had contemplated did not take place. I have rested and taken advantage of an interval of some months, during which my health improved a little, to work on my supplement. I have used up the little strength I had left, for now my catarrh again threatens to attack me, and soon I may be unable to occupy myself with the second supplement.

"But at this the learned world forfeits nothing, for I shall rest secure upon the indefatigable efforts of two athletes, you and Herr Abel. The latter has, in Crelle's *Journal*, published the concluding part of his beautiful work where, among many other very interesting things, one finds a proof for your general theorem about transformation, a proof which you modestly have placed above your own. Then, in Schumacher's periodical, he has printed other investigations in which he shows great profundity and ingenuity. But in regard to yourself: you have not lagged behind, and in the same journals you have continued to bring forth a large number of new results which should prove highly interesting to the analysts, particularly if you produce the proofs."

In the preface to the first supplement, Legendre explained the reasons for composing it: "For many years I had been engaged in the study of the elliptic functions, of which the immortal Euler had laid the foundations. I believed that I should gather the results of this long labor in a treatise which was published in 1827. Until then, mathematicians had taken almost no interest in this type of investigation; but when my work barely had appeared and hardly before its title could even have been known to foreign scientists, I was informed, to my great surprise as well as my satisfaction, that two young mathematicians, the gentlemen C. G. Jacobi in Königsberg and Abel in Oslo, through their results, had succeeded in bringing to perfection some of the highest levels of the theory.

"The works of these young mathematicians are characterized by a profound knowledge of the most beautiful methods in analysis, as well as the application of several ingenious ideas of their own. By their work science has attained such heights that one can expect that the results which they have already obtained will be followed by many others of no lesser importance."

Legendre had already begun writing his second supplement which, to an even greater extent, should be devoted to Abel's studies.

To hear one's works praised in such a fashion and from so many different sides was quite wonderful. Legendre's obvious admiration particularly flattered Abel. No longer could he visit Fru Hansteen in person, but she received all the news in letters to Copenhagen. He confided to her about his relationship with Crelly, and the new understanding which had grown up between them; about his finances, which were miserable, but improving a little; finally about the acclaim which he had received from abroad:

"Perhaps I have not always behaved toward Crelly as I should, but now we are of one mind, and understand each other. I have improved considerably and I hope that sometime we shall live happily together, but when this fortunate moment will arrive I do not know. May it only be not too far away. I pity my Crelly that she shall be obliged to slave this way.

"She wants dearly to be remembered to you and would appreciate a few words from you. You cannot believe how much it would encourage her, for she cherishes you so highly. I wrote her a couple of days ago and sent her your regards, so that she may see that you have not forgotten her. But, dear Fru Hansteen, do not be concerned because she has worked for you. She did it not to return your goodness in a feeble way, at least that was not the main thought. You know, love often shows itself in trifles and she wanted to express hers. Nothing would cause her greater pleasure than to know that she had given you joy, a tiny bit of joy.

"It grieves me that you are not in the best of spirits, but I can understand that many things must weigh on your mind. And, of course, you are particularly anxious because of Hansteen's absence. It is quite natural, but recall how happy you will be in a not too distant future. One believes so readily in what one desires to happen, and you, dear Fru Hansteen, really have all chances in your favor.

"My salary is 400 daler as before, and I am immersed in debts up to my ears, but I am working myself a little out of it. However, my former landlady, the Queen, has not received a penny, and I owe her 82 daler. I have worked the bank down to 160 daler, and the cloth dealer from 45 to 20 daler. Furthermore, I owe the shoemaker, the tailor and my eating place, but I borrow no more. But please do not pity me for this. I suppose I shall get out of it somehow.

"I have no gossip to report, but it is the gospel truth that a son of magistrate —— has been arrested for theft, and worse still, for a break at Professor Bugge's house, where he smashed a window and stole the silver. Among the ridiculous items, let me mention a minister who had his portrait painted in full vestments with his fiancée on his lap.

"There is yet something I must tell you. Lately I have become very proud on account of some letters I have received from abroad. I shall quote a couple of instances for you, since you well know I do not do it to be arrogant. Perhaps you recall a mathematician called Jacobi, who anticipated me, and also an article which I sent to Schumacher in the spring. This article has proved a success. Jacobi has stated in a letter to Crelle: 'I consider this to be one of the most beautiful masterpieces in mathematics.' "

Abel continued quoting Crelle's and Legendre's letters and concluded:

"To state the plain truth, I have quoted this to show off a little, dear Fru Hansteen; in part, because I believed it would please you to see the progress I am making, since you have always shown such interest in my welfare. So, you must not consider it boasting. To your amiable and, to me, so precious family I send my most kind regards. It is always a special pleasure to hear that they live well.

"Good-bye, dear Fru Hansteen, and believe me when I say that I am your sincerely devoted and respectful Abel."

Had the petition of the French Academy members to the king been known to him, he would probably have been still more swelled with pride.

On November 25, 1828, Abel replied to Legendre:

"Monsieur, the letter of October 25 which you were kind enough to address to me has given me the greatest joy. I consider it to be one of the happiest moments of my life when I saw that my attempts had been worthy of the attention of one of the greatest mathematicians of this century. It has greatly stimulated my enthusiasm for my studies. I shall continue them assiduously, but if I should be fortunate enough to make any discoveries, then they should rather be ascribed to you than to me, for doubtless I could have achieved nothing without having been guided by your lights."

Abel continued with several pages of description of his own recent discoveries. It was an important letter so he prepared a first draft in his study journal, and here he described his situation as follows: "Unfortunately, it is absolutely impossible for me to print this work, for there are no publishers here who will accept it at their own risk, and

212

I am myself without means; on the contrary, it is difficult for me to find the necessities of life." Perhaps he felt that this last statement was a little too strong; in any case, it was omitted from the letter which was finally mailed to Legendre. He concluded:

"I hope, Monsieur, that I have not displeased you by daring once more to inform you of some of my finds. It is my wish, if you will permit me to correspond with you, to communicate to you a great number of other results on elliptic functions and still more general functions as well as on the theory of algebraic equations. I have been fortunate enough to arrive at a definite rule by which to decide whether an arbitrary given equation can be solved by radicals or not. A consequence of my theory is that it is impossible to solve the general equations of degrees higher than the fourth."

As a postscript he added:

"I am eager to become acquainted with Jacobi's work; there must be remarkable things in it. Herr Jacobi will certainly perfect to an undreamed of degree not only the elliptic functions but the mathematical science as a whole. No one can place him higher than I do."

The correspondence with Legendre had a couple of strange aspects. One was that Legendre never informed Abel of the petition to the king on his behalf, and it probably never came to his attention. Secondly, it was peculiar that Abel did not remind Legendre of the great memoir which he had submitted to the French Academy two years earlier. Abel knew that Legendre was one of the referees, and even some of the results he inquired about could be found in it. It seems that Abel no longer felt the same anxiety about its fate; he had probably come to consider it a hopeless project. In his latest paper he had utilized the idea in a special case, and he must have decided to make the whole Paris manuscript superfluous by printing a similar article in the *Journal*.

Legendre, on the other hand, had unquestionably forgotten the article as well as the fact that he had met Abel in Paris. The manuscript sank deeper and deeper in the piles in Cauchy's study, and Legendre later confessed that he had never had it in his hands. But in the paper on hyperelliptic functions which had just been printed Abel mentioned its existence in a few words. Such was his new importance in the mathematical world that the detail could not avoid being noticed and commented upon. Bessel wrote to Gauss on January 2, 1829:

"I have been very surprised about Abel's theorem, which makes it possible to discover the properties of integrals without executing them. I believe an entirely new phase of the integral calculus has been brought to light. I wish that Abel would pursue it further in many applications. It appears unintelligible to me that such a theorem has been presented to the Academy in Paris, and yet remains unknown. I should like to hear your opinion, possibly I overrate the value of the theorem." The response from Gauss is not known.

18

THE END

‍&S FOR ALL HIS SCIENTIFIC WEALTH, Abel had felt lonesome in Oslo during the fall. One of the few families where he could feel at home was the Treschows'. The rector had retired, his wife's health was failing, and the responsibility for the household had largely been taken over by Elisabeth Abel. Old Treschow was still fond of having his jokes, and more than once he subjected Niels Henrik to the mental tests which mathematicians know by sad experience that they must suffer from their fellow man: "One day he said to Niels Abel: 'Listen, Niels, if one and a half herring costs one and a half penny, what does a dozen herrings cost?' 'Eighteen,' said Niels Abel and Treschow laughed, rubbing his hands in enjoyment.

"Someone might not find this particularly remarkable, but it is true and that is something," added the old lady who included the story in her recollections.

Christmas was approaching and Abel longed for Froland and Crelly. He was feverish and restless; the continual writing until late at night gave little opportunity for relaxation. At Froland he would celebrate Christmas among friends and loved ones, would receive care and attention, and find good company. But during the winter the road was long and required several days of driving in sleds. The doctor strongly advised against the trip, as did his friends. Fru Treschow wrote to Fru Hansteen in regard to Abel's illness. "If only you had been in town he might have been content to remain. But he tried to hide how ill he really was, although I could plainly see the weakness which the pains in his feet caused him."

The thought of the comfortable home at Froland, and a pleasant family Christmas with Crelly was irresistible. He had been invited especially and knew that he was heartily welcome in the Smith family. About December 15, the fall term at the university and the instruction at the military academy completed, Abel departed from Oslo, warmly dressed and carefully wrapped.

Abel had been encouraged to apply for a raise in his salary from 400 daler to the customary 600 daler, a move which seems to have been under consideration for some time. Before he left he submitted his petition, addressed to the king, as was customary. After giving a résumé of his case he stated:

"Although this remuneration was less than that which had been granted other docents appointed to the university, I had to consider myself fortunate, owing to my poor economic condition, to obtain any position compatible with my study which promised a modest living. I also found it unsuitable to apply for an increase in the gracefully determined honorarium until such time when I had demonstrated my *dona docendi*.

"During the time in which I have lectured on astronomy at the university and thus discharged the duties incumbent upon Professor Hansteen's position, I have had an opportunity to judge whether the time involved for me could be considered to be sufficiently paid, and the university authorities on their side have had an opportunity to decide whether I was capable of the assigned task.

"Therefore I dare most humbly to hope that my petition will not be considered out of order or immodest when I request that from January 1 next year I be placed on a level with the other docents at the university, so that I may in grace be awarded an annual salary of 600 daler. Most humbly, Niels Henrik Abel."

The Collegium gave its unreserved support, stating that since Abel performed the duties of Hansteen's office and for two terms had shown his teaching ability, justice and fairness dictated that he should also enjoy the regular salary.

Abel arrived in Froland on December 19. It was bitterly cold and he had put on whatever clothing he had available, pulling socks over his hands and forearms. He did not look at all well, but jokingly attempted to dispel any discussion of his health. Hanna Smith, one of the elder daughters in the family, many years later recorded her recollections of Abel's visit. She wrote that he complained about coughs, cold chills, and not feeling as he should. But he could not abstain from writing mathematics, and preferred to work in the parlors with people around him, even if it meant frequent interruptions and disturbances by the gay youngsters.

Crelly and Niels Henrik must occasionally have daydreamed about their future, and wondered when they themselves would have a home. Unfortunately there was nothing definite on which they could build their dream castles; perhaps Crelly also perceived more clearly than Abel how precarious was the state of his health.

A permanent position was the absolute prerequisite, but in spite of the support of Abel's friends and the flattering comments by famous men abroad, it still remained very much a dream. Abel's substitute position in Oslo had lasted one year, and he expected to retain it for another; but, to judge from the attitude of the departments his chances for continued employment at the university seemed small. There was a possibility of taking over Hansteen's instruction in astronomy at the military academy, but this would not suffice for a married couple. Whatever hope there was had to be staked on the kindly Crelle, who again sounded quite optimistic.

Between Christmas and the New Year, Crelle concentrated his efforts afresh to obtain a decision from the Education Department in regard to Abel's call to Berlin; this time he had a powerful ally in the great naturalist Alexander von Humboldt. Von Humboldt had himself gathered statements and recommendations for Abel from various scholars, among them Gauss and Legendre. As a most welcome guest at the Prussian court, he could make his influence felt.

In his letter of December 28, 1828, Crelle informed the minister that he had, as requested, explored the conditions under which Abel would accept an appointment. While at present there was an excellent opportunity to obtain his services, Crelle advised quick action, because other institutions had also shown their interest.

"I shall only add the wish that your Excellency obligingly will soon bring the appointment of Herr Abel to execution; for now, when his great talent has become known, it is possible that he may be invited to other places. I have by chance been informed that there has been a plan afoot to gain him for the university in Copenhagen, whereby he would be lost for the service here."

Crelle continued his presentation by referring to a very laudatory letter from Legendre to von Humboldt, and finally emphasized the unique opportunity for the development of German mathematics:

"The gentlemen Dirichlet, Abel, Jacobi, and Steiner, who all, except Abel, already are in the service of the Prussian government, represent in reality a group of young mathematicians giving the greatest expectations for the advance of science. Perhaps they, in time, will become mathematicians of the very highest rank, for in spite of their youth, science already owes essential progress to them. At one time the Prussian government attracted the most meritorious mathematicians — Euler, Lagrange, Lambert, etc. — and offered them what they could not find in other countries: an honored position enabling them to rise above their period and above contemporary science. Again the Prussian government is in a position to support talents so great that nature only rarely produces them. For this science will be in a debt of gratitude to your Excellency.

"Thus it will also be possible for me personally, in my great devotion to the sciences, to entertain the joyous hope that here in my native country we stand on the threshold of a new epoch in mathematics which history may call distinguished in comparison with other periods."

Crelle was overly cautious in his evaluation of the four young men; they were all among the most eminent mathematicians of the nineteenth century.

Abel's application for a raise in salary passed through the regular channels, and at Christmas time had reached the Department of Finance. Perhaps the department simply perceived that this was a very reasonable request, perhaps influence had been exerted from the very highest authority after the petition of the members of the French Academy, or perhaps it was only that Boeck had pleaded with his father-in-law on behalf of his needy friend; whatever the cause, the department made no objections, and shortly afterward the appeal was granted.

On January 6, 1829, Abel completed the article he had been working on during Christmas, signed and instantly mailed it to Crelle with a short note. The experiences with Jacobi had taught him how unwise it might be to let his discoveries await publication too long. Among his many mathematical results this was the masterpiece for which he least of all wanted to lose the honor.

He had arrived at the firm conclusion that the Academy in Paris had no intention of printing the large memoir which he considered his

218

monumental work. If he wanted to ensure for himself the credit for its creation, he would now have to unveil it.

The paper was only two brief pages, but of all his many works perhaps the most poignant. He called it only "A Theorem"; it had no introduction, contained no superfluous remarks, no applications. It was a monument resplendent in its simple lines — the main theorem from his Paris memoir, formulated in few words.

Abel fully understood the beauty of his result. He was unaware that it was the last work which fate had granted him leave to produce; in the last few lines he promised to give many applications which would throw new light on analysis.

The departure from Froland had been fixed for January 9, and the sled and driver ordered for the early morning. Abel had wished to stay longer but his duties could not be neglected. During the last few days of his visit he had been miserable, complaining of coughs and chills, and, most unusual for him, had retired to his room a good deal. On the morning of the scheduled departure he was caught in a violent coughing spell; no longer could it be hidden that he was spitting a good deal of blood. Crelly and the whole Smith family were seriously alarmed and a messenger was immediately dispatched to the family physician, Dr. Möller in Arendal. Examination revealed the dangerous condition of the patient; absolute rest in bed and careful attendance was prescribed. The desperate Crelly took charge of the nursing, still hopeful. After several days of bed rest, sedatives, and cough medication, Niels Henrik felt better and the piercing pains in his chest abated. The improvement seemed to continue and the physician was satisfied; two to three weeks later he even encouraged the patient by letting him know that he might be approaching the convalescent stage. Abel was permitted to sit in a chair a few hours each day, but he had to be reasoned with firmly when he again attempted to work on his mathematical papers.

A letter arrived from Legendre, dated January 25. His second supplement on the elliptic functions was nearing its completion; he had studied Abel's paper on the hyperelliptic functions and had resolved to write a third supplement on this topic. His gift, the *Traité*, and the first supplement had been shipped: "It is on its way and will reach you in a short time. I present it as a tribute I owe to your works. They increase the value of my own, particularly if I shall be able to include a greater part of them in supplements which I intend to publish from time to time, if only heaven will grant me still a couple of years of life."

Legendre continued to discuss some of the interesting information he had received in Abel's last letter, but the memoir on hyperelliptic functions had completely fascinated him:

"But your article, *Remarques sur quelques propriétés générales*, seems to me to surpass everything which you have published until now, both in the profundity of the analysis which permeates it, and in the compass and beauty of the results. The article is not extensive, but includes many things; it is edited with great elegance and insight in almost every detail; if it had been possible to extend it, I should have preferred if you had proceeded in the reverse direction and concluded with the most general cases.

"But, however this may be, I can only express my felicitations to you for being able to surmount such obstacles in such an excellent manner, for even if it surpasses the strength of a near octogenarian to verify all your results I have examined them enough to be convinced that they are entirely correct."

He finally made an appeal to Abel not to procrastinate in the publication of his remarkable method to decide when an equation could be solved by radicals.

"I urge you to let this new theory appear in print as quickly as you are able. It will be of great honor to you, and will universally be considered the greatest discovery which remained to be made in mathematics. Good-bye, Monsieur, you must be happy over your success, over the content of your works. It is my hope that you will become still more so by finding a position in society which will permit you to devote yourself entirely to your genial inspiration. Your humble servant, Legendre.

"P.S. Some time ago I received a letter from von Humboldt, wherein he informs me that the Ministry of Education in Berlin has received royal approbation for the foundation of a seminary for mathematics and physics, to which you and Herr Jacobi will be called as professors."

The eulogy on the mathematical discoveries of Jacobi which Legendre had delivered in the Academy in Paris proved to be the foundation of the fame of the young German mathematician. The old man now felt strongly that he owed a similar tribute to Abel, and a suitable opportunity presented itself at the meeting of February 23, 1829. Cauchy had just explained his methods for the numerical solution of equations, when the astronomer Arago asked whether he was familiar with Abel's investigations on the same subject. This was in reality a rather naive question, for the approximate solution of equations in numbers had little or no connection with Abel's much deeper results on the exact formulas for the roots, but at least it provided Legendre with a platform from which he could speak in praise of Abel.

He reminded the Academy of the flattering testimony he had had occasion to present in regard to Jacobi's works, but on this day felt it his duty to speak on behalf of his young rival, Monsieur Abel. These two mathematicians had enriched science with a large number of discoveries of the highest importance, but at this time he would primarily restrict himself to Abel's results concerning equations, his criterion for an equation to be solvable by radicals, a special consequence of which was that equations of higher degree than the fourth could not generally be solved. This was a fact which mathematicians long had suspected, but not until now had full clarity been achieved. Legendre was not familiar with Abel's proofs, but in view of Abel's great talents, he did not hesitate to consider this fundamental point in science finally elucidated.

After this declaration by Legendre, Cauchy made the entirely correct observation that Abel's works, which he did not know, had but little relation to his own paper, but Abel's investigations appeared to him to be very important.

The improvement in the state of Abel's health proved to be temporary, and the family at Froland began to understand that, at best, the illness would be of long duration. A certificate from the physician, dated February 21, 1829, was sent to Holmboe, asking him to report on Abel's condition to the Collegium:

"At the request of Herr Docent Abel, and in the capacity of being his physician — since he is himself unable to write — I shall report to the high Academic Collegium that shortly after his arrival at Froland Ironworks he suffered a severe attack of pneumonia with considerable expectoration of blood, which ceased after a brief period. But a chronic cough and great weakness have compelled him to rest in bed, where he must still remain; furthermore, he cannot be permitted to be exposed to the slightest variation in temperature.

"More serious, the dry chronic cough with stinging pains in the chest make it very probable that he suffers from hidden chest and bronchial tubercles, which easily can result in a subsequent chest phthisis, particularly on account of his constitution.

"Due to this precarious state of health of Herr Docent Abel, it is most unlikely that he will be able to return to Oslo before the spring. Until then, he will be unable to discharge the duties of his office, even if the outcome of his illness should be the most desirable.

"My hopes for his improvement and complete recovery have prevented his report to the high Collegium Academicum; otherwise it would have been previously presented."

Crelle, in Berlin, was informed of the serious situation; he was desperate over the slowness of the authorities which made it impossible for him to bring the help and cheer which he still believed could save his young friend. Crelle had been informed of the intervention of the French mathematicians, and was concerned that a position in Stockholm or Copenhagen might prove more attractive to Abel. He again turned to the minister of education, urging the greatest haste, and emphasizing the smallness of the amount involved and the modesty of Abel's demands:

"To the reasons mentioned, an additional consideration makes it urgent to come to a quick decision in regard to the appointment. Herr Abel has for a long time been seriously ill, and according to the last letter of March 8, he is still incapacitated to the extent that he is unable to write personally. He has long suffered from a weakness of the chest, and while in the country 300 miles from Oslo has been subject to an attack of blood coughs. Thus it would also be desirable, on account of this condition, that he receive an early improvement in his prospects which until now have been so unfavorable, and a hurried transfer to a milder climate to preserve and strengthen his health.

"Therefore, all considerations urgently point to the desirability of bringing Herr Abel here as soon as possible, and so I dare present this proposal to your Excellency. First, it is perhaps only at the present moment that this man may be acquired for the service here; secondly, it is perhaps the only way in which he at all can be saved for science, and it is possible that he may be entirely lost if he is obliged to remain in his present place and position."

On April 8, a delighted and hopeful Crelle could write to Abel that his intense request had brought a favorable response:

"Now, my dear precious friend, can I bring you good news. The Education Department has decided to call you to Berlin for an appointment. I heard it this very moment from the gentleman in charge of the case in the department, so there is no doubt.

"In what capacity you will be appointed and how much you will be paid I cannot tell you, for I do not know myself. I only spoke with the gentleman in passing in a large gathering, so that in the moment I heard nothing more. As soon as I obtain further details I shall let you know.

"I only wanted to hurry to let you hear the main news; you may be certain that you are in good hands. For your future you need no longer have any concern; you belong to us and are secure. I am so glad — it is as if the wish had come true for myself. It has cost a good deal of effort, but, God be praised, it succeeded.

"Later, when I see you here, I shall tell you to whom you owe special thanks. Only prepare quietly for your journey so that you may be ready to depart the moment you receive the official request. But, until such time, I must again ask you to say nothing until it has arrived; the official notice will follow shortly, at most a few weeks.

"Above all, see to it that you get well again, and may heaven grant that this letter finds you improved. I wrote to you last March 27. I pray you, reply immediately to this letter, be it only a couple of words. Be in good cheer and rest entirely at ease. You will come to a good country, to a better climate, closer to science, and to sincere friends who appreciate you and are fond of you.

"So reply to me by return mail and cherish in your memory, Your devoted, Crelle."

At Froland Abel was surrounded by solicitous attention and nursed lovingly by Crelly, assisted by the two oldest daughters in the Smith family, Marie and Hanna. The latter wrote a few recollections of Abel's last hours.

During March it became apparent that the end was near; the weakness and cough increased and he could remain out of bed only the few minutes while it was being made. Occasionally he would attempt to work on his mathematics, but he could no longer write. Sometimes he

223

lived in the past, talking about his poverty and about Fru Hansteen's goodness. Always he was kind and patient.

Crelly's sorrow was so great that she had difficulties containing it in his presence, so Marie or Hanna were always present with her at the sickbed. Niels Henrik suffered from insomnia as the cough became more severe; he was afraid of being left alone, and a nurse was engaged for relief during the night watches.

"He endured his worst agony during the night of April 5. Toward morning he became more quiet and in the forenoon, at 11 o'clock, he expired his last sigh. My sister and his fiancée were with him in the last moment, and saw his quiet passing into the arms of death."

Some months later one of the Oslo newspapers contained a report of the burial, undoubtedly by Abel's good friend Keilhau, who had just visited Froland:

"The general sympathy which the early death of our already famous countryman, the mathematician Abel, has provoked, makes the writer believe that the public will be interested to know that this burial, which took place in a remote part of the country, was not devoid of the solemnity with which the survivors desire to see honored the memory of their dear departed.

"During the illness of the deceased, Herr Smith, the owner of the ironworks, had shown him an excellent hospitality connected with many sacrifices and at the interment he also demonstrated his great esteem.

"At the house of bereavement there appeared, upon the invitation of Herr Smith, a tremendous crowd of officials and citizens from the surrounding districts, as well as from the neighboring towns of Arendal and Grimstad; this in spite of an extraordinary snowfall and almost impassable roads. The youngest among them carried out the well-appointed bier, decorated with a wreath and the name of the deceased; eight workers clad in black then placed it on the waiting sled. The whole group accompanied the bier the three miles to the Froland church. Here an avenue of freshly cut pine trees had been erected, and after the coffin had been removed from the sled the young men carried it through the alley into the church. After a short eulogy by Pastor Natvig, the coffin was carried to the cemetery, which thus received the sorrowful honor of holding these precious remains. During the next summer, Herr Smith intends to honor this resting place by an iron monument with a suitable inscription."

The ministerial book at Froland church contains only this entry:

"Bachelor and mathematician Niels Abell, died Froland Works, 26 years of age, April 6, 1829, buried April 13."

On April 11, Crelly gathered her strength and wrote to Fru Fridrichsen in Copenhagen, asking her in an anguished letter to inform Fru Hansteen of Niels Henrik's death:

"My dearest love, yes, only duty could make me demand this, for I owe your sister, Fru Hansteen so much. I take the pen with trembling hand to ask you to inform her that she has lost a kind, devout son who loved her so infinitely.

"My Abel is dead! he died on April 6 at four o'clock in the afternoon. I have lost all on earth. Nothing, nothing have I left. Pardon me, the unfortunate can write no more. Ask her to accept the enclosed lock of my Abel's hair. That you will prepare your sister for this in the most lenient way asks your miserable C. Kemp."

Epilogue

19

PRAISE AND BLAME

ৰ্জ SIVERT SMITH, who had felt himself almost a father to Niels Henrik, made the announcement of his death in the Oslo newspapers:

"Hereby it is sorrowfully brought to attention that the highly honored, and for his mathematical knowledge so widely famous, Niels Henrik Abel, docent at the Royal Frederik's University, died in my house, after a 12 weeks' illness, on Monday, April 6, in the 27th year of his age.

"Froland Ironworks, April 11, 1829. Sivert Smith."

It was a little strange that no newspaper printed a necrology immediately after Abel's death, for it was generally known that a remarkable and eminent scientist had been lost. His friend Holmboe, most familiar with Abel's life and activities, was, in the absence of Hansteen, clearly the only one qualified to write his life story. Holmboe may have been criticized for his delay, for later he explained rather profusely that he felt it was necessary to await the permission of Crelle in order to make use of quotations from his letters. As was customary, a couple of publications contained elegies by well-meaning poets who stood absolutely helpless before the mysteries of mathematics. One of these impersonal tributes ran to twelve, another to seven, verses.

Crelle expressed his grief and his deep admiration for Abel's human greatness and exceptional importance in mathematics in a eulogy in the *Journal*. He knew little about the details of Abel's early life; for these he received assistance from Holmboe. This memorial to Abel was read by wide circles of mathematicians, was reproduced in Ferrusac's *Bulletin*, and was translated and reprinted in Norwegian newspapers.

Crelle briefly told of Abel's early youth, his school and university years, his journey and his share in the foundation of the *Journal*, and praised him as one of its most faithful and important contributors. His works, said Crelle, demonstrated that he was truly one of the most eminent talents in science, and that his loss to mathematics was so much the more regrettable, since he had stood at the beginning of his career:

"All of Abel's works carry the imprint of an ingenuity and force of thought which is unusual and sometimes amazing, even if the youth of the author is not taken into consideration. One may say that he was able to penetrate all obstacles down to the very foundation of the problems, with a force which appeared irresistible; he attacked the problems with an extraordinary energy, he regarded them from above and was able to soar so high over their present state that all difficulties seemed to vanish under the victorious onslaught of his genius.

"If one will remember the article, published in the first volume of the *Journal*, about the possibility of solving algebraic equations of higher degree than the fourth, his works on elliptic functions, his article on general properties of certain transcendental functions, and so on, one will find that we have not exaggerated.

"Abel's unique talent has recently become generally recognized; verily, had he been a contemporary of Newton, this master would have been able to exclaim as he did about Cotes: Had he lived longer we would have learned something."

Crelle continued by referring to the competition between Abel and Jacobi, Abel's difficulties in finding a living in his own country, and the petition of the French mathematicians to the Swedish king, and reported with understandable pride that the Prussian government had been the first to offer Abel a permanent position.

"But it was not only his great talent which created the respect for Abel, and made his loss infinitely regrettable. He distinguished himself equally by the purity and nobility of his character and by a rare modesty which made his person cherished to the same unusual degree as was his genius. Envy of the achievements of others was entirely alien to him. He was far estranged from this greed for money and distinction or even fame which so often leads to the abuse of science by making it the means for success. He valued too highly the sublime truths he was seeking to be willing to sell them for so base a price.

"He found the reward for his efforts in the results themselves; whether a new discovery was made by himself or others he was almost equally delighted; all means to personal advance were unknown to him, he worked not for himself, only for his beloved science. It is possible that such an insouciance is not appropriate in this world: he sacrificed his life for science without thought of self-preservation.

"But no one can maintain that such a sacrifice is not as great and as noble as those which are made for any other lofty and worthy purpose, which one, without hesitation, rewards with the greatest honors. So let us pay homage to the memory of this man who to an equal degree distinguished himself by a most unusual genius and the purity of his character, one of these rare beings which nature produces hardly once in a century."

Even the reserved Gauss expressed the great loss to science, and his sincere desire to know more about the life of Abel. He had no inkling of the deterrent influence which he himself once had exerted upon the young man. Schumacher wrote to Gauss on May 12, 1829:

"I suppose you have seen the news of Abel's death in the papers. Legendre has just published a second supplement, and in the introduction he talks about Abel in such a manner that one has the impression that he places him after Jacobi. From you I know that exactly the opposite is the case."

To this Gauss replied a week later:

"I had not seen any report of Abel's death in the newspapers; it is a great loss for science. If the life story of this highly remarkable head should be published somewhere, and a copy come into your hands, I must request you to let me know. I should also like to have his portrait if it is available anywhere. I had discussed him with von Humboldt, who had the firm intention of attracting him to Berlin."

The address of the four French mathematicians, seeking the creation of a position for Abel through royal grace, had led to no immediate action in Stockholm. The envoy in Paris repeatedly reminded the court secretary, Count Lewenhaupt, that no reply had been tendered to the members of the Academy. As late as April 10, 1829, Count Lewenhaupt wrote to Paris:

"The response to the four members of the Academy has not yet been dispatched, because the Crown Prince desired to obtain information about Herr Abel, and the viceroy in Norway, who should produce it, has been so occupied by the canal projects that it has been impossible to obtain a result. I have reminded him of the case more than once. Nevertheless, I hope to inform you shortly that the letter has been sent." Possibly the petition might have brought a result, for, on May 26, 1829, the viceroy wrote a note to Crown Prince Oscar:

"The deservedly esteemed Abel has terminated his career just in the moment when I had hoped to fulfill the encouraging wish of Your Royal Highness in his regard."

In Paris the four scientists continued to await an answer, and on June 2, 1829, shortly before the report of Abel's death had reached Paris, Baron Maurice again turned to the envoy:

"Count Löwenhielm: You have shown the goodness to accept with great willingness an address which I had the honor to present to your Excellency almost nine months ago, and agreed to transmit to your court this letter dated September 15, 1828, signed by certain members of the French Institute. They permitted themselves in this letter to indicate an eminent scientist, Herr Abel, then teacher in Oslo in Norway, to the high benevolence of your honored sovereign. It appeared to them, on behalf of the sciences which Herr Abel has cultivated with such extraordinary success, that it would be extremely desirable for him to be appointed to a less distant position. You were even so obliging as to add the promise that you would especially call the attention of His Royal Highness, the Crown Prince, to the wish of the French scholars.

"In spite of this, my Count, we in Paris do not know whether Herr Abel has been approached from Stockholm. Thus, if it should not be too indiscreet to make such an appeal, I dare to ask your Excellency to let me know whether there exists at the Swedish court any intention of doing anything for a scientist whose fate, without his knowledge, interests his scientific colleagues most intensely."

Late in the summer of 1829, Count Lewenhaupt shamefacedly was compelled to confess that the original document had disappeared from the royal archives, and requested the envoy in Paris to let him know the names of the gentlemen who had signed the petition. Whether they ever received an acknowledgment of their petition we do not know, but by this time even the royal grace could no longer have modified the decision of fate.

During the last year of Abel's life, Legendre had indicated constant wonder at the uninterrupted sequence of discoveries brought forth by the two geniuses, in part on the foundation of his own works. On April 8, 1829, he again wrote to Jacobi:

"I have just received the last issue of Crelle's *Journal*, where I find three articles by Abel and yourself, and also the résumé of your own investigations which you have communicated to me. You proceed rapidly, gentlemen; it is almost impossible to keep up with you, especially for an old man like myself, who has already passed the age at which Euler died, an age at which one must struggle against many infirmities, and the spirit no longer can sustain the intense strain which is required to surmount the difficulties and to adjust oneself to new thoughts.

"Nevertheless, I congratulate myself upon having lived long enough to witness this generous competition between two equally gifted athletes who use their strength for the benefit of science and push the frontiers farther and farther back. This sight interests me so much more, since it gives me the means to complete my own works by taking advantage of the precious materials which you produce through your learned studies."

Upon finishing his next letter, on June 4, Legendre received the tragic news:

"At the moment when I was prepared to seal this letter I heard to my profound sorrow that your worthy rival, Herr Abel, is dead in Oslo, as a consequence of a chest illness, from which he had suffered some time, and which was aggravated by the severe winter.

"It is a loss which will be deeply felt by all who are interested in the progress of mathematical analysis at its highest levels. But during his short life, he has erected for himself a monument which will suffice to give us a lasting memory, and to yield an idea of what he could have attained, had fate permitted it."

Jacobi was informed almost simultaneously, and wrote to Legendre:

"A few days after my last letter I received the sad news that Abel was dead. Our government had called him to Berlin, but the invitation found him no longer alive; so I was bitterly disappointed in my hope to meet him in Berlin.

"The wide scope of problems he proposed for himself, to find a necessary and sufficient condition for an algebraic equation to be solvable by radicals, for an arbitrary integral to be expressible in finite form, his wonderful discovery of a general property shared by all functions which are integrals of algebraic functions, etc., etc. — all these are questions of a form which is peculiar to him; no one before him had dared to propose them. He is departed, but he has left a great inspiration."

On June 22, 1829, Legendre officially informed a session of the Academy of the death of Abel. About the same time, it received a copy of Jacobi's book, the *Fundamenta nova*. Because of the great importance of this work for the sciences, Poisson was entrusted with the task of presenting a résumé of its contents to the Academy. Subsequently, the report was printed in its proceedings. It took the form of an homage to both Abel and Jacobi, giving a sober and fair presentation of the place of each in the new theory of the elliptic functions. On June 28, 1830, the Academy awarded its Grand Prix for outstanding mathematical discoveries to Abel and Jacobi, Abel's share of the prize money, 3000 francs, to be paid to his surviving family.

Legendre spent his last active years in mathematics in completing his third and final supplement; only in the year 1832 could the octogenarian let his pen rest. The work was presented to the Academy as the keystone of his life's mathematical activities. A copy was sent to Crelle to be reviewed in the *Journal*. In the accompanying letter Legendre explained:

"You will see that, on the basis of Abel's beautiful theorem, I have succeeded in creating an entirely new theory, which I have called the theory of ultraelliptic functions. They are much more general than the elliptic functions, but are closely related to them. It has been a great satisfaction to me to pay homage to Abel's genius by showing the value of the brilliant theorem he discovered; it might be called his *monumentum aere perennius*."

In spite of this laudatory opinion, Legendre deals only with special instances of Abel's theorem; the general scope he seems never to have grasped fully. But throughout the third supplement, one finds interspersed his admiration for Abel's theories, expressed in various ways.

No one was better qualified to evaluate Legendre's work than Jacobi, so Crelle turned to him for the review. A brief preface by Crelle preceded the article:

"This publication is interesting in many ways. First, it is important because it is a new work by the venerable veteran in mathematics, whose name assures us of its value. Secondly, it is of interest because it concludes his great work which, for years, until the writings by Abel and Jacobi, was the only one of its kind in this important field, which recently has witnessed such pleasing progress, and now again has been examined by its former explorer.

"Finally, this work acquires a peculiar value because it creates a worthy memorial to the genius of Abel, who was called away so regrettably early in the far north. Almost devoid of facilities, at the age of 24, he soared over those barriers to science which even Euler and Lagrange had been unable to pass. Unfortunately, it is very probable that he has taken with him to his grave precious treasures of new discoveries from the land of truth, mathematics.

"One is uncertain what to admire most highly: the ability of an octogenarian to proceed in the most abstract domains of his science with the force and enthusiasm of youth, and to penetrate obstacles which previously have stood in the way; or his willingness to recognize the merits of others, even if they may be due to a youth who could have been the grandchild of the celebrated scientist!

"Were only such an attitude universal, it would be worthy of the sciences. Goodness and justice are joined also here. Abel himself had this ability to recognize the merits of others with the true and natural conviction of his heart; jealousy he did not know."

Jacobi's review of Legendre's third supplement naturally was quite technical, but he also touched upon Abel's singular theorem; he was dissatisfied with Legendre's new name, the ultraelliptic functions:

"Let us rather call them the Abelian transcendentals, since they were first introduced in analysis by Abel, who demonstrated their importance through his far-reaching theorem. This theorem itself should preferably be called Abel's theorem as a most beautiful monument to this exceptional mind. We gladly express our concordance that it carries the imprint of the profundity of his thoughts.

"As it stands, in simple form without calculations, expressing the deepest and the most far-reaching mathematical thoughts, we consider it to be the greatest mathematical discovery of our time, although only profound future investigations, which may take time, can completely clarify its meaning."

Holmboe's necrology of Abel did not appear until the end of November 1829, more than half a year after the death. It had originally been intended exclusively for the *Magazin,* but there appeared to be some public demand for it, so that it also appeared for sale as a separate pamphlet: *Short Account of the Life and Activities of Niels Henrik Abel.* But before the article had been printed a newspaper reprinted excerpts from it; the editor asked Holmboe why the biography appeared so late, when German publications had already carried stories "about this, our rare countryman." Holmboe had a series of good reasons; first, he had been obliged to await permission to quote certain letters; second, he had been absent from town; third, the printing had been delayed.

Holmboe's account of Abel's life was written soberly in a somewhat heavy style, but it contained many items of information which since have reappeared in all biographies. To convey Abel's mathematical greatness was as difficult for Holmboe as for anyone else who has attempted to write a popular life story of Abel. He sought refuge in the testimony from letters of Crelle and Legendre:

"His life and scientific activity were brief; nevertheless, he achieved great things for his science. All his articles bear witness to the most penetrating ingenuity, and demonstrate fully that he was one of the most eminent mathematical minds ever created. Those who cannot form a judgment by reading and understanding his works will be convinced of the truth of this statement by the acclaim the most famous mathematicians have accorded them."

From his student days Abel had been well known in Norway as a most promising young scientist, a genius in the field of mathematics; now the confirmation poured in from all sides. In laudatory necrologies famous foreign mathematicians hailed his discoveries with admiration, he was recognized as an eminent mathematical author; the French mathematicians had addressed the king on his behalf; the university in Berlin called him. Abel's fate was discussed and the question was unavoidable: Why had not the University of Oslo created a position to give him a secure livelihood? During the last years many other young men had been appointed to scientific positions; huge amounts had been placed at the disposal of Hansteen's expedition; why had not the genius Abel been provided for?

His two friends Boeck and Keilhau considered the university's negligence to be a bitter injustice, and they made no secret of their feelings. In his necrology, Holmboe had passed over the question of a position for Abel with great care; for good reason the vacancy left by Professor

Rasmussen was not mentioned. In regard to the situation after Abel's return from abroad he commented: "He wanted to be appointed to the university, but since it already had two teachers in mathematics and the government did not find it opportune to appoint a third, he remained without a position until March 16, 1828."

Boeck, editor of the *Magazin*, after reading Holmboe's manuscript, could not refrain from adding a postscript giving his own view on Abel's fate:

"Abel was not of strong constitution, he had a tendency to lung ailment, although this was not clearly discernable until the last years of his life. Usually he was very well, and at the time we traveled together abroad he was never really sick.

"To those who did not know him intimately, his temperament may have appeared to be gay; those who only saw him occasionally, in the company of friends, and were not on close terms with him, may even have considered him frivolous. This, however, was not the case; on the contrary, his mind was serious and he felt deeply. Often he would be very melancholy, but he tried to hide it from most by a forced gaiety and an indifferent attitude.

"There were few to whom he gave his full confidence and he was very reticent in revealing his true character; so even among his close associates few really knew him or judged him correctly. The journey abroad was a great encouragement to him, and in Berlin he was extremely satisfied with his pleasant and useful association with Crelle; but still he often drifted into very dark moods.

"Concern for his prospects completely depressed him, and he very often talked about his infelicitous future. Only rarely did he seem to have a ray of hope that a position might be provided for him, but mostly no reasoning could encourage him. Then he tried to escape from such thoughts at his desk, and usually he arose from it with satisfaction. By clearing up some theorem he was working on he could, for a few moments, forget everything else; he was perfectly happy.

"Upon my return from abroad in 1828, I found him very discouraged, and still more so after Professor Hansteen's departure. The letters from Crelle gave him hope of an appointment in Berlin, but it did not cheer him as one might have expected, although it did give him satisfaction, particularly on behalf of his fiancée, a girl whom he loved with greater tenderness than he made apparent to most of his acquaintances.

"He felt sad at the thought of leaving Norway. Many times when he talked to me about a possible position abroad, he found it terrible to go into exile in this way, to move to strangers, perhaps never to see his native country again. In discussing these things he was always deeply moved, he could not conceal the pain he suffered by not being able to work for his science in his own country. Thus there were moments when he determined to refuse all offers from abroad, in spite of his precarious position.

"He knew that upon Hansteen's return he would be without support, with no prospect of a permanent position. He did not expect that the university would take any forceful or decisive action; perhaps there was some reason for such a thought — has it not been said that Abel caused it embarrassment, that he would be a burden to the university? For he was not in possession of the formal degrees.

"In his own country he hardly found recognition for his knowledge and no encouragement; abroad the famous scientists praised the works of his genius, his discoveries, and his scientific merits; a foreign university, one of the best known in Europe, considered it an honor to count him among its teachers; a foreign government wished to provide for his welfare and give him an honored position. This must have depressed his hope and courage.

"Under such circumstances only his own studies and efforts could serve to secure a more kindly future; he was compelled through his work to maintain and increase the esteem and fame already achieved, which promised to open brighter prospects for him. But his labor contributed to his early death. He sought little rest or diversion; excessive studies influenced his nerves; the sedentary life had a harmful influence on his chest — then another tiny thrust and he succumbed.

"His wish that his native soil should hide his remains was fulfilled. Now his troubles are ended; he did not seek his bread among strangers, and yet Norway lost its son. His precious memory lives in the recollections of his friends; future generations will mention his name with honor; the Norwegians will be proud of their departed countryman."

These were strong words from a young man; their effect was reinforced by the fact that Boeck was connected with the university and edited the only scientific publication in the country. His comments were eagerly discussed in the capital and in the provinces; it was evident that the university could not avoid making an explanatory statement. Abel

238

had many friends among the faculty, they had supported him through personal sacrifice. It was bitter to stand accused of inactivity in regard to his future, and even be charged as accessories to his death.

The members of the Collegium were enraged, but the records show that they had difficulties in formulating a suitable defense. Originally they gave free rein to their wrath against Boeck:

"The purpose of these lines is unmistakable. They throw a shadow on the university and its board for their relations to Abel, as if we, for some reason, did not wish to see him in a permanent position or even secretly opposed such an appointment. The intention of the author seems to have been to reproach the Academic Collegium and its members for an unforgivable ignorance of his talents and literary achievements.

"Therefore, the undersigned members of the Academic Collegium consider it a duty which they owe to the university, their predecessors, and themselves to bring a public review of the actions which at various times have been taken on behalf of the deceased Docent Abel. The Collegium assumes that the necrology indicated, with its added note, will be reproduced in scholarly journals abroad. Since it cannot be indifferent to the Collegium how foreign opinion judges its treatment of young scientists in general and Abel in particular, it feels itself strongly induced to present the following facts to correct the distortions in the remarks to which it objects."

After some hesitation, the Collegium omitted the entire introductory passage and limited itself to a very impersonal presentation of its own view on Abel's case; even so it proved difficult to formulate the statement; it was rewritten several times and discussed in two meetings of the Collegium.

The declaration from the Collegium was published in several newspapers. It consisted largely of excerpts from the official documents and copies of the minutes. It mentioned the support of Abel by the professors, the university fellowship, and the large travel grant from the government. The Collegium also explained why Holmboe, rather than Abel, had been chosen as successor to Professor Rasmussen, giving the two reasons then advanced: Abel was abroad, and he would not be able to lecture to the younger students in a satisfactory manner. However, the Collegium had expressed the hope that eventually a position for advanced mathematics could be created.

The Collegium then proceeded to explain the conditions upon Abel's return; the refusal of the department of his application for a position, and the petition to have his student fellowship renewed which was also turned down "for the reason that no such sum had been budgeted." But the department had sanctioned the advance of 200 daler from the university treasury, and the Collegium had awarded him this amount without conditions.

The substitute position during Hansteen's absence was also mentioned, as well as the fact that the salary had eventually been raised from 400 daler to the customary 600 daler. No reference was made to the request of the department that Abel make restitution for the 200 daler in fellowship money, although on this occasion the Collegium had rallied courageously in support of Abel.

When it appeared that Abel could obtain a position in Berlin, but preferred to remain in his own country, the Collegium had deplored that it could not propose a permanent position for him, but nevertheless it had forwarded his case to the department. The concluding statement was quite weak: if Abel had decided to accept a position in Berlin, the Collegium would not have let his substitute duties stand in the way.

The presentation was strictly factual, but in spite of the constant good will the Collegium had shown toward Abel, the record for the last few crucial years was unimpressive and not at all likely to quiet the critics.

One paper took the liberty of making an insertion at that point where the Collegium explained that nothing could be done because the expense was not included in the government budget. "Nor was there any sum in the budget for the interest-free loan granted Herr Professor Hansteen immediately after his departure on the Siberian journey, and still the Storting unanimously granted the amount he had requested."

Here the newspaper alluded to an episode in Hansteen's journey which was well known in the capital. In the correspondence between the two brothers Aubert, acquaintances of Abel, one reads: "Hansteen has received a barbed letter from His Majesty, but since you are probably unfamiliar with this incident, I shall give you some details. No sooner had Hansteen arrived in St. Petersburg than he wrote to the government that after a conference with his commissary there, he had found that the travel money granted him could bring him no farther than to Irkutsk or where the devil it might have been. According to the scantiest of estimates he would need 5000 daler more in order to complete the expedition, which departed in the firm hope that this would be granted. The cabinet had been in the greatest perplexity, but finally agreed to make a favorable recommendation. The royal resolution runs about as follows:

" 'His Majesty has learned with the greatest displeasure of the incomprehensible negligence with which Herr Hansteen has prepared the estimates for those travel expenses which the government so gracefully awarded him. We should have preferred to leave him shift for himself, were it not that the national honor would be prostituted by it. But, since the matter is of national importance, an interest-free loan of 5000 daler is awarded to him; there will, in due time, be made a decision in regard to restitution, but the government has been required to order from him the strictest accounting for the use of the money. Also, the department has been requested to send him a literal copy of the decision. — This is not undeserved.' "

Upon Hansteen's return from Siberia the Storting unanimously remitted the loan.

The Collegium was in an extremely difficult position when it issued its public statement in regard to Abel. It was handicapped on every side; it could not explain that Abel's economic difficulties were in part due to his own heedless extravagance during his journey and to the importunities of his own family; out of consideration for Holmboe it could not admit, even had it been willing to do so, that the choice of a successor to Rasmussen was based on an error of judgment. But from the declaration it appears most distinctly that the Collegium carefully avoided making any statements which could be interpreted as a criticism of the departments. This was not an unnatural attitude, for the welfare of the whole university, its grants and appointments, depended much too directly upon the benevolence of the administration. If any reproach should be made it could only be that the Collegium acted with a certain reticence in regard to the department; it did not exert its influence with sufficient energy and aggression in a matter in which it had both a strong conviction and strong arguments to back it. How the departments evaluated the situation we do not know, probably the blame would have been placed on the state of the public finances, although this would not have sounded quite convincing.

Shortly after the report of the Collegium appeared, one of Abel's former pupils inserted a reply:

"I have found the observation by Lecturer Boeck to Holmboe's necrology of Abel so very true, and the later statement by the Collegium not in agreement with my own views in this matter.

"It has presumably been the intention of the Collegium to invalidate Boeck's assertion 'that Abel, after the completion of his studies, did not receive the encouragement from the Norwegian university which he was entitled to expect on account of his extraordinary talent.' To my mind, this proof has not been successful.

"It is true that from the time Abel became a student at the university much has been done for him, by honorable private individuals as well as by the authorities; but what was the purpose of all these encouragements when one in the end did not want to hit the nail on the head by securing him a decent living at the university, in accordance with the plan which once had been laid. Due in a large measure to these encouragements, he had exclusively worked with mathematics instead of choosing some study for a living; so he found himself in a very difficult position when he became disappointed in his well-motivated expectations.

"It could never have been the intention to encourage Abel to procure such an education for the purpose of serving at a foreign university. Truly, it seems to me that for such action the university is too young and too poor in superlative talents such as his. It is too great a generosity to donate what one will later need oneself.

"Why was Abel not immediately appointed as lecturer in pure mathematics upon the retirement of Professor Rasmussen?

1. Because he was abroad and the university could not await his return.

2. Because he could not adjust himself to the intelligence of the younger students.

So it was said.

"When the post in question became vacant, Abel had already been abroad half a year, and his whole journey took a year and a half, so it was only a question of a year. Could not some arrangement have been made until he came home? The only professor in chemistry was twice abroad for a longer period, yet a satisfactory arrangement was worked out both times. Let us not touch upon more of these temporary absences,

242

but only observe that the situation at the moment is the same, the only professor in applied mathematics has been away for a year and a half, and still the university manages.

"Thus, the first reason seems insufficient for the appointment of another instead of Abel, precluding the opportunity for a call to the university in his own country.

"The second reason was that he could not adjust himself to the younger students.

"How was this known? And what justified such a prejudice?

"Many who have tutored with Abel have declared that his presentation was very intelligible; personally I have had the same experience. After having tried in vain to profit from a not very gifted teacher's lectures *ex cathedra*, I went to Abel and asked him, if possible, to overcome this malapropos aversion against mathematics which had resulted from my long and fruitless efforts. During a three months' period he proceeded so far that I got into my head algebra, function theory, the rudiments of higher equations, calculus; yes, I even found great delight in applying calculus to prove theorems in solid geometry and trigonometry. It is unnecessary to say that I found his instruction clear and his method very useful.

"You are no more among us, my departed friend! Nor do you need my weak defense. I should gladly have written some lines in your memory, but more forceful voices than mine have already honored you. So I shall only add that I shall never forget the heartfelt kindness which you always showed me when we were together."

Shortly after the Collegium had issued its statement in regard to Abel, the annual report for the preceeding year, 1828, was edited and discussed during a meeting. The group wanted to express its sense of sorrow: "The Collegium regrets to report that through the death of temporary Docent Abel this year, the university, the country, and science have suffered a loss which cannot easily be replaced. At the age of 26 years this talented young man had fulfilled the extraordinary expectations created by his precocious genius for the mathematical sciences. He died at Froland Works on April 6, after 12 weeks of illness."

The report went on to state that Holmboe had taken over Abel's lectures, and the whole seemed a quite natural and appropriate expression of the feelings of the university. This, however, did not prevent the

243

professor of law, Steenbuch, from making the following formalistic comments:

"Since Abel was only a substitute in the place of Hansteen in his absence, it cannot properly be said that the university has suffered a loss which cannot easily be replaced. For it is possible that he never would have received a permanent appointment. The statement also gives the impression that Holmboe, who took over Abel's duties, was not good enough. Also, if Abel is to be mentioned, and to this I have no objection, then I maintain that the words 'the university' should be omitted, for under the terms 'country and science' the university is in any case included."

The discussion of Abel's case continued privately, but after a time the indignation subsided, giving rise to more dispassionate reflections. In a magazine article about Abel's life a few years later the anonymous author commented:

"Here in Norway, there were too few scholars capable of understanding Abel's extraordinary importance. Thus, the recognition of the right of a genius to be excepted from the usual rules could not be established in the public opinion; were this not the case, there would have been many objections to the creation of a post just for the sake of the person.

"If his European fame had had time to become recognized, and to reverberate among our mountains before his death, we believe for the sake of our own honor that everything would have been done not to lose him, as well as many other of the most distinguished sons of the country. But his flight was too rapid — he rose like a brilliant meteor and, before there was time to comprehend its greatness and splendor, vanished just in the moment when it should have displayed itself in all its glory.

"Rumors have circulated that Norway has been ungrateful for the honor which he, like every great man, spread over his country; it has been said that he was to be exiled and that he collapsed under the weight of barbaric ignorance. This is far from true. But if he did not enjoy the encouragement he deserved, it was not from any resentment of his merits; rather it was that no one was yet aware that he was a being created for immortality, and particularly because the conditions of the country — its meager resources — did not permit it to become an appropriate stage for the highest and most liberal scientific activity. The country was small; its conditions restrictive in every way. It is tragic, but almost unavoidable, that the great, sweeping geniuses must move out into the wide world to gain their proper importance and find an arena worthy of their capabilities, where they can expand their activities to full force."

The polytechnic institute in Berlin, which Crelle had advocated so strongly, was created a few years after Abel's death. One of the first scientists to be considered for its faculty was Abel's good friend Steiner, who had long struggled in a modest teaching position. Among the experts consulted was Jacobi, who in strong words impressed upon the minister of education the necessity for action:

"When I have expressed my wish to your Excellency in particularly urgent terms, then this is provoked by the memory of the recently deceased Abel. He never belonged to a university or an academy. A discovery that he presented to the Academy in Paris was so great that it remained incomprehensible and was disregarded. His works in Crelle's mathematical *Journal* have assured an undying reputation for this publication. When they attracted wider attention, it is true that his discovery was again brought to light; the Academy awarded him its Grand Prix, the king of Sweden was requested to make him an ornament for the academy in Stockholm, a call to Berlin assured him a modest, albeit adequate existence. But all this came only to the departed. The honors which are destined for the living cannot succour the dead."

20

THE SEARCH FOR A MANUSCRIPT

౿ FROM THE MOMENT Abel submitted his large memoir to the French Academy, he lived in the constant hope of hearing from "these slow men." Strangely reticent, he never wrote directly to the Academy to expedite the committee, nor did he ask Legendre for information when he entered into correspondence with him.

But Jacobi had seen the footnote in Abel's paper on the hyperelliptic functions, and in his great astonishment wrote to Legendre on March 14, 1829, and put the question directly to him:

"What a discovery by Herr Abel, this generalization of Euler's integral! Has anything like it ever been seen? But how is it possible that this discovery, perhaps the most important in our century, can have avoided the attention of yourself and your colleagues after having been communicated to the Academy more than two years ago?"

To this Legendre was compelled to reply on April 8, two days after Abel's death:

"I cannot conclude this letter without replying to that section of your letter which touches upon Abel's beautiful article in the preceeding issue of Crelle's *Journal*, which had been presented to the Academy by its author during the last months of 1826.

"At the time Poisson was the president of the Academy; Monsieur Cauchy and myself were appointed to examine the memoir. We noticed that the memoir was almost illegible; it was written in very thin ink, the letters were indistinctly formed. It was agreed between us that a new copy, more clear and legible, should be requested from the author.

"It remained in this way. Monsieur Cauchy kept the article until now without occupying himself with it; the author Abel appears to have departed without concern for the fate of the paper, he produced no new copy, and no report was submitted. However, I have requested Monsieur

246

Cauchy to leave the manuscript with me; I have, until now, never had it in my hands, but I shall see what can be done to remedy the negligence which he has shown toward a work which undoubtedly had deserved a better fate."

Legendre's explanation is an excuse which he must have composed in a moment of embarrassment. Perhaps Cauchy had remarked that the paper seemed difficult to read; but it seems hard to believe, for Abel's manuscripts were usually well prepared and written clearly, albeit in a small hand as was customary in that period. Certainly, Abel was never requested to produce a new copy, although he waited in Paris long enough to have been informed.

The difficulties cannot have been overwhelming: after Legendre, on June 22, 1829, had informed the Academy of Abel's death, Cauchy submitted his report at the next meeting, on June 29. It was a quite reserved report, the content was described in Abel's own words from the introduction; it exhibited the same misunderstanding as Legendre in his letter to Jacobi, that the memoir was nearly the same as Abel's paper on the hyperelliptic functions. Thus Cauchy observed that since most of the results had since been published in Crelle's *Journal*, under normal circumstances the article would have been given an oral refusal, but due to the great scientific achievements and tragic death of the author, he would nevertheless recommend that the memoir be printed. Legendre also signed the report, although its terms were quite different from those which he used about Abel's works both before and afterward. His approval, without objections, can only be explained by his wish to see the action promoted as quickly as possible. The Academy accepted the proposal of the committee, and decided to include the memoir in its series of publications designated for the works of foreign scientists. Jacobi arrived in Paris during the fall of 1829; he was well aware that Abel's memoir was a different work from his previous article; in particular, the latter had not contained the theorem which Abel considered the basic result. Jacobi called on Fourier, the permanent secretary of the Academy, and extracted from him the promise that Abel's memoir should be quickly printed. But, unfortunately, Fourier died the following year, and a few months later the July revolution broke out. The members of the Academy became occupied with entirely different matters. Cauchy belonged to the minority who refused to take the oath of allegiance to the new king, Louis Philippe; consequently, he was compelled to follow the royal family into exile. The banishment lasted more than eight years before Cauchy was willing to return to his native Paris.

A few years passed without news of the memoir. In 1832 Jacobi published an article on Abelian transcendentals in Crelle's *Journal,* and in a footnote he expressed deep regret that the *Academy* continued to postpone the printing of Abel's memoir. It was the reverent duty of the Academy to render homage to the eminent young man who, by fate, had been denied academic honors in his lifetime. Jacobi appealed particularly to Fourier's successor as permanent secretary, the physicist François Arago, to fulfill the promise that had already been made.

Norwegian scientists began to take an interest in the article. The university in Oslo had decided to publish the complete works of Abel. Holmboe, named editor in charge, energetically attempted to track down various Abel manuscripts through the Norwegian-Swedish foreign service; Count Löwenhielm made inquiries of the Academy in Paris and of Gergonne's *Annales,* where Abel had indicated that he intended to send more papers. Other inquiries were made through the office of the envoy; the Academy wanted to be informed about Abel's family, and the disbursement of the prize money. Löwenhielm replied on April 11, 1832, probably to Holmboe:

"The letter of January 5 I received in due time. The demands from the French minister for verifications of the legality of the dispositions in the case of the deceased Abel I shall leave unanswered until they are reiterated and then I intend to propose that the Norwegian Department of Justice give him a summary statement that all has been done in legal form.

"Of the posthumous works of the deceased Abel I have only been able to find his *Memoire sur les fonctions transcendentales.* It was discovered among Monsieur Cauchy's papers, and it should just have been copied by Monsieur Libri if he had not taken ill in the common epidemic [cholera] which ravages here. I have also inquired at Gergonne's, but he has not yet replied."

The young Italian mathematician Libri had probably been asked by Legendre to prepare another copy for the printer, and so Abel's manuscript was inadvertently sucked in as a little storm-blown flake in one of the greatest scandals which the scholarly world has ever witnessed.

Guglielmo Icilio Bruto Timoleone Libri, Count of Carrucci della

Somaia, was born in Florence and early showed great mathematical ability. He received an excellent classical education, and acquired great proficiency in the ancient languages. At the age of twenty he became professor at the university in Pisa. During the troubled times in Italy following the July revolution, Libri took part in the patriotic insurrection against Austrian rule. When it failed, he escaped to France.

Libri's mathematical works had received a certain attention, and when Abel and Jacobi were nominated to the vacant foreign membership in the Academy in 1827, Libri's name had also been on the list. Upon his arrival in Paris after the revolution, Libri had been received with open arms as a heroic champion of the cause of liberty. After a short time he was granted French citizenship and was appointed to a position at Collège de France. He ingratiated himself with Legendre, and when the veteran scientist died in 1833, Libri was elected to his vacant seat in the Academy of Science. A few years later he was also named to a professorship at the Sorbonne.

During these years, Libri's scientific interests suffered a change of direction, and it seems probable that there was a transformation in his character as well. From a cultivation of pure mathematics, Libri turned to the study of the history of science, and gained renown particularly for his four-volume work on the development of mathematics in Italy. He soon acquired the reputation of an expert bibliophile. This technical knowledge he applied not only to collecting, but also to trading old books and rare manuscripts on a businesslike basis, and with good profits.

Libri had become interested in Abel through his association with Legendre, and in 1833 he wrote the first fairly extensive account of Abel's life in French. It was presented to the Academy, and shortly afterward was printed in Michaud's biographical dictionary. The strongest point of Libri's biography is his analysis of Abel's mathematical discoveries, but his information on the details of Abel's life was extremely meager. However, as may be seen from the following excerpts, he felt no compunction in letting his fantasy fill the gaps:

"It may have been Abel's unusual modesty or his natural timidity or, as others have believed, the insufficiency of his means which prevented Abel from making any acquaintances. At least on his journey to Italy he met no one and he did not introduce himself to anyone, not even in Milan and Turin, where he would have been appreciated and encouraged by well-known mathematicians. After leaving Italy he traveled to Paris, where he remained for 10 months.

"No one suspected the genius of the young man whose death knell rang mournfully all over Europe two years later, and it was only after many supplications that Monsieur Fourier agreed to present his memoir to the Academy.

"It must be admitted that Abel had no success in Paris. Upon his return home after a journey of 20 months, he could find no position, no help. Devoid of all resources, he had to seek refuge with his poor mother in Oslo, and accept an extremely modest post in order to exist at all. The misery in which he lived gradually undermined his health.

"It was not so much the poverty which burdened Abel, for men of his character have loftier aims than money; it was rather his consciousness of his own superior ability, without finding anyone who could fathom his genius; it was that he could not, through the greatness of his discoveries, conquer the indifference. He lost courage, an immoderate amount of work and sorrow destroyed his constitution.

"Nevertheless, he was constantly spurred on by his love for science; under these conditions of lonesomeness and suffering he composed the beautiful works which have created admiration among the mathematicians."

Libri also reproduced the address to the Swedish king, and commented:

"One should have believed that such a noble and unusual action from deservedly famous men should have made the fortune of the one for whom the aid was intended; but far from it, the letter was never even acknowledged.

"His death, with the deplorable conditions which surrounded and perhaps caused it, was mourned the world over. Through an unparalleled action the Institut de France decided that half its Grand Prix for 1830 should be awarded Abel's mother, and so the unfortunate woman must have felt still more acutely the loss she had suffered."

Libri described Abel's character in terms borrowed from Crelle's necrology, and added that the famous Herr Bessel had called him "the ideal man." But from then on Libri gave free reins to his indignation:

"Finally, after four years, it seems that the Swedish government has heard these exclamations of admiration. It has now entrusted Herr Hansteen with the task of preparing a collected edition of Abel's works.

This shall also contain a complete biography of the writer. All friends of science eagerly await its publication.

"Here we raise our voice to demand an account of all those egotistical men who, by their indifference, have contributed to the shortening of Abel's life; we demand a reckoning for all the discoveries of which his death has deprived us. Some of these he only expressed without proof, and they are astounding to all those who have understood their importance.

"Is it possible that Camoëns' death shall be repeated in the nineteenth century? We address ourselves not only to kings and governments; we address ourselves to one and all in the nations, for it is never asked under what regime did Camoëns perish, but one says: Camoëns died from hunger in Portugal.

"One may observe that the solicitude for famous scholars usually comes at an age when they are no longer in need of it. The protection which brought Galileo to his home town after the persecutions in his youth was nothing more than the desire to buy back for money a part of a great man's honor. A man who would have been an ornament to the name of his country had he been well treated can cover it with shame if he is left to succumb in his sorrow."

The biography by Libri was the only one available to the European public for a number of years, so it is no wonder that strange rumors circulated in regard to Abel's life and poverty. Within the French Academy of Science the behavior of its new members must also have produced rather peculiar feelings. No sooner had Libri placed his foot within its doors than he saw fit to favor the venerable institution with the following kick:

"Through the indifference of the modern mathematicians — from which each one of them has himself suffered, the reason why one almost never has an opportunity to read the works of the younger mathematicians — Abel's memoir long remained buried in the papers of the committee members. Later praise was heaped upon him, but too late."

Perhaps a modern psychologist would find, in part, the cause for Libri's outburst in his personal identification with Abel. He was himself in exile, and felt little appreciated in Italy. He complained bitterly in the foreword to his papers about the inordinate time which the Academy had seen fit to let his articles wait before publication. But, in addition, there was a deep feeling of animosity between Libri and the new secretary of the Academy, Arago. Upon various occasions they aired their resentments in public, and this was an opportunity for Libri to exhibit his asperity toward Arago.

It should be pointed out that Libri's reproaches against the members of the Academy were not the first to be published. Saigey and Raspail had tired of the dreary work for Ferrusac's *Bulletin*; they resigned simultaneously and began publishing their own scientific magazine: *Annales des sciences d'observations*. Immediately upon the arrival of the message about Abel's death, in the issue of May 1829, Saigey wrote an article in memory of his friend. He revealed Abel's disappointments in Paris, the indifference of the Academy members in regard to everything but their own works, and then drew the following gloomy picture of the old men in the Academy:

"The details which I have brought out may be excused on the basis of the interest which the tragic fate of the gifted always creates. It has not been my purpose to throw the blame upon any one member of an organization whose importance is recognized by all scholars in Europe. What I wanted to point out, since there is an opportunity for it, is the fate which will inexorably befall a young man who presents himself to this high scientific court, with no other recommendation than his own works.

"It consists of a small group of scientists, men who have reached the age when thoughts are predisposed to turn toward the past, men who receive scientific innovations with anxiety and rancor. Even if they had been filled with energetic eagerness it would, in reality, be extremely difficult to examine, even in the most superficial manner, the many papers on which they must express an opinion. Thus, often favor or chance will make the choice and pronounce the judgment."

Finally Saigey protested violently against the attempts of the old men to lead scientific studies into those channels which they hoped would attract the greatest attention to their own works:

"Even in the present case it is not the undisputable merits of Abel and Jacobi which the Academy has recognized; rather it is an encouragement to investigate certain fixed problems, outside of which there seems to be neither progress for science nor advantages for the writer.

"Some members will say: Take my own works for the starting point of your studies; cultivate the most abstract domains of analysis, bring to fruition the fertile seeds which I have disseminated. On the contrary, others will say: The questions in the natural sciences are the most valuable; direct your efforts toward these lofty applications which are so essential for human knowledge.

"But we say: Young scientists, do not listen to anything but your own inner voice which tells the tasks best suited for your own inclinations and abilities. Read and contemplate the writings of the men of genius, but never become pliable pupils, or egotistical admirers. The device must be: Objectivity toward the facts and freedom in the choice of views."

The evidence seems to indicate that there existed a strong feeling of bitterness among some of the younger scientists about the dominant position of the Academy in French scientific life. The tragic case of Abel was seized upon as tangible evidence of its perfidy.

In the year 1831, two years after Abel's death, two eminent young scientists were incarcerated in the prison of Ste. Pélagie in Paris, both charged with revolutionary activities. One was Saigey's friend Raspail, the other, Evariste Galois.

Galois was a mathematician who had been inspired by Abel's works. Barely twenty years of age, he had published a couple of papers. Though still almost unknown to the mathematical world, he had succeeded in creating a remarkable new theory for the algebraic equations. It represented both the completion of Abel's main problem and the foundation of group theory, one of the most important branches of modern mathematics.

"Grant him three years," Raspail wrote from jail, "and then one will talk about the scholar Galois." But Galois was granted only one more year of life. The next year he was killed in a duel; it does not seem improbable that he fell victim to the *provocateurs* of the political police. Many years passed before mathematicians realized Galois' importance to science; now the names of Abel and Galois are often mentioned in almost the same breath in the history of science, two youthful, creative giants of mathematics.

Twice Galois had submitted his chef-d'oeuvre to the Academy; as far as he had been able to find out, it had both times disappeared in Cauchy's piles of papers. He wrote a third, and improved, version, which he presented in the hope that it might be eligible for one of the prizes of the Academy; while he was still in the Ste. Pélagie prison the work was returned with a polite refusal. The referees had been unable to understand his reasoning even after consulting Abel's papers and doubted the correctness of his results.

Raspail, in his letters from the jail, tells of his daily association with Galois. Often they talked of the Academy, probably in terms little suited for print; Abel's case they also brought into the discussion. In Ste. Pélagie Galois commenced a new mathematical manuscript, and in the foreword he let loose his fury:

"Let me first state that the second page of this work contains no dedications with names and Christian names, honors and titles, nor some eulogy of a parsimonious prince who opened his purse when he felt a whiff of incense and closed it again when the censer was burned out. It does not honor some person in a high scientific position, a thing so necessary — perhaps I should rather use the term unavoidable — for a young man of 20 who wants to publish. I do not express to anyone that whatever may be found of value in this work is due to his advice and encouragement. I do not say it, because it would be a lie.

"Should I turn to any of the great in this world, or to some of the great in the sciences — nowadays they are about of the same kind — then I swear it would not be in gratitude. To one of these groups I owe that this memoir has been so delayed, to the other that it had to be written in jail. This is a place which has been considered appropriate for cogitation, but incorrectly so. I have often been surprised at my own recklessness when I have been unable to keep my mouth shut to my dumb Zoïlos. I purposely use the name Zoïlos [the author of a malicious criticism of Homer] for that does not run counter to my modesty, so low do I place my opponents.

"This is not the place to explain how and why I am in jail. My publisher will probably say: The author is a republican, he is a member of the party Amis du Peuple, he has indicated by gestures that under certain conditions he considers regicide useful. This ought to be thrice enough to place him in jail, and I am surprised that he finds any reason for complaint.

"However, I must relate how the manuscripts so often disappear in the drawers of the members of the Institute, although it is truly inexplicable how such a practice can still be permitted among men who have the death of Abel upon their conscience. It is not my intention to compare myself to this famous mathematician; it is sufficient to say that my article on algebraic equations in its completed form was submitted to the Academy in February 1830, an extract was sent in 1829, but no report has been made, and it has been impossible to obtain the return of the manuscripts."

No one seems to have protested against Libri's charges at the time they were written; he was known as a keen controversialist and as a man of influence. But many years later, when Libri's reputation was in decline, Arago, still secretary of the Academy, wrote an indignant reply in an article about Abel, included in a series of biographies of famous scientists.

It was obvious that the charges had been unpleasant for Arago personally, and also for the mathematicians in the Academy: "It is understandable that the press has devoted itself to this theme with bombastic eloquence." Arago could correct Libri's information on a few points, but his own was also deficient. In spite of Arago's great show of vexation it was not easy to explain away the main point, the inordinate procrastination of the Academy. Arago placed the blame on Cauchy's self-centered character, but forgot that many years had passed during which the main obstacle to the printing of the memoir must have been the indifference of the secretary.

Even long after the days of Arago, Abel's case was used as a rallying point. As late as 1870, the old radical and veteran revolutionist Raspail rose in the Chambre des Députés to deliver a speech, an attack rendered in "bombastic eloquence," upon the egotistical capitalist bloodsuckers of society:

"It was about 40 years ago, at a time when the rapaciousness of the members of the Institute and the Academy of Science was at its height, when a young Swede presented himself to one of my friends. My friend read the memoir which the young man intended to present to the Institute, and it seemed to him that it showed signs of a remarkable fantasy. [Laughter in the audience.]

"He said to him: My friend, give your memoir to Monsieur Fourier in the Institute, to no one else; go to him personally, he will read it and fix a day. But he [Abel] presented his memoir to Cauchy, who at that time had accumulated positions yielding him as much as 50,000 francs a year, almost as much as the zoologist Cuvier, who managed to make 60,000 francs, while many young men were dying from hunger.

"The young man then went to Fourier, who received him in his small apartment the way he received everyone who worked in the sciences; he treated them with great consideration and never avoided a discussion of the problems which occupied them. Cauchy, the capitalist, on the other hand, to whom the young man had entrusted a copy of his article, managed to mislay it among his papers; Poisson, who had also received a copy, lost it in a similar manner.

"The young man was well received by my friend, who was an expert in this field. He was himself a man who was compelled to work for his living in the same way as he does today, poor and deserted. [Louder! Louder! We do not hear!]

"[Many members: His name, what is his name?]

"His name is Monsieur Saigey. His name may be unknown to many of you, but he is very well known by all who work in the sciences. I believe that there are also several here present who know him.

"Saigey offered the young man money, he invited him to eat at his home; but the young Swede blushed with shame to be supported in this manner at the expense of a friend. One day he told that he was preparing to return to his home country, Sweden. Actually he traveled to Sweden, but he went on foot! [Noise and interruptions.]

"He had left his memoir with Legendre, of whom you have all heard. Legendre had stated: See what a young man can pretend; he believes he has found the solution to a problem which I myself have worked on in vain for 40 years; then he threw the paper on his desk.

"But when he [Abel]traveled through Berlin, he left the work with a scientific journal edited by a scientist who received him with more kindness and understanding. Legendre was a decent man, and as soon as he saw the printed article, his conscience began to bother him. When he arrived home, he sought the manuscript and then exclaimed to himself: Actually, he has found what I was seeking, he has made the most difficult discovery in the world, he has produced the solution I have sought for 40 years.

"Legendre grasped his pen, shaking with sorrow that justice must come so late, and wrote to the minister of education in Sweden, told him what a great scientist he possessed within his realm, and requested that he take him under his care, for Legendre had just been informed that the young man was starving. This was the reply: The young scientist was dead, dead from hunger.

"Do you know who this man was? It was the same Abel whose name today is mentioned everywhere with the greatest admiration, because the whole world knows his memoir. He died when he was 25 years old.

"Here one can see the consequences of the money hoarding among the members of the Institute. [Cries.] If they had not been allowed to accumulate money in this manner, they would have acted as my friend did, they would have taken care of this young man who showed the most eminent, yes, the most brilliant ability."

The holy fervor with which Libri had expressed himself in the biography of Abel would lead us to expect that he would have considered it a personal duty to ensure the publication of Abel's memoir; but no action followed the harsh words.

Holmboe had worked assiduously on the edition of Abel's works, and the manuscript was nearing its completion. The great memoir he had been unable to obtain. In October 1838 he wrote to the Church Department, describing his desperate efforts and appealing for official assistance:

"More than four years ago, when the philosophical faculty had discussed the project of collecting and publishing Abel's works, Professor Hansteen wrote to Arago, asking for a copy of the memoir in question, but to this letter he never received a reply.

"During the summer of last year, the orientalist Mohn was going to Paris, and I directed him to call on Arago to obtain a copy of the memoir. This Mohn promised to do, and upon his arrival in Paris, succeeded in seeing Arago after several unsuccessful attempts. Arago declared that he knew that the manuscript had been turned over to the Institute and from there to the royal printing office. Although he was aware that great confusion reigned in this printing establishment — it might be difficult to find the manuscript — he still believed that Mohn could receive a copy.

"Mohn informed me of this at the end of the last year, saying that he had spared no effort to find the manuscript. However, he did not succeed, because some time ago he wrote me again that all his exertions had been in vain; he was now convinced that without an official request through the envoy it would be impossible to obtain the memoir.

"I have permitted myself most humbly to inform the high department of this, in order to show that I have not failed to do everything in my power to make the edition of Abel's works as complete as possible. I must appeal to the judgment of the department as to whether there is anything more to be done in this matter. If so, I must request the assistance of the high department in obtaining a copy of the memoir."

The Norwegian government now took official cognizance of the affair. After a formal governmental request to the French authorities, the Academy was finally shocked out of its lethargy. A search resulted in the discovery of the manuscript, and the Academy placed Libri in charge of the printing. In 1841 — all of fifteen years after Abel presented his masterpiece and began waiting — the work was made available to the scientific world.

This one would expect to be the end of the adventures of the Paris memoir; the manuscript could be included in the collection of documents of the Academy as a remarkable item. But in a note added to the printed work, Libri explained that he had only been able to read the proofs under the greatest difficulties, for during the printing the original manuscript had disappeared in some mysterious way.

The enterprising Libri had many irons in the fire. In 1840, while Abel's memoir was being printed, he was appointed secretary to a royal commission entrusted with the task of registering and cataloguing the many old manuscripts scattered throughout the French provincial libraries. In the collections of towns and castles, churches and schools, lay hidden inestimable treasures, often neglected and mistreated due to ignorance or indifference.

The renowned bibliophile Libri was considered ideally suited for such a job. He traveled around the country, and reported on his most important finds. At the same time he maintained his own private business; he held large book auctions; as agent for private collections he negotiated sales to various foreign institutions. A unique collection of rare manuscripts was offered to the British Museum; after some hesitation the museum decided that the price was too high for its means. After strictly confidential negotiations, the collection finally went to Lord Ashburnham, for a reported price of 200,000 francs.

There was no doubt about Libri's expert qualifications; he could count many of Europe's most eminent scholars among his friends and acquaintances. On the other hand, there was no dearth of enemies; his caustic tongue and sharp pen had speared many opponents in public controversies and press polemics. Rumors that some of Libri's book treasures were of strange provenance began to circulate; the police

258

even received anonymous tips, indicating a suspicion that some of the manuscripts sold had originally belonged to libraries inspected by Libri; in one specific instance it was charged that an illuminated medieval manuscript had been disguised by new bindings and a false title page.

Such rumors in regard to a most prominent man appeared to be too fantastic to be credible and after a couple of halfhearted attempts by the police to conduct an investigation, the matter was dropped. Several years later the February revolution of 1848 broke out. Libri lost many of his patrons within the administration, and several of his enemies gained power, among them his bitterest foe, Arago, who entered the cabinet as minister of war. The investigations of Libri were resumed; when he felt the ground burning under his feet, Libri hastily boxed and shipped the most valuable parts of his collections and fled to England.

Meanwhile, Libri was indicted in Paris, the bill charging him with the theft of some of the gems of French libraries. Long lists of irreplaceable books and documents, allegedly appropriated by Libri, were presented to the court; among them were mentioned specifically a large number of letters and manuscripts of historical importance which had disappeared from the archives of the Academy of Science. The accounts and correspondence which Libri had left behind seemed to contain much damaging evidence. Libri was sentenced *in contumaciam* to ten years in jail, the maximal legal punishment. However, he remained safely in England, for there existed no treaty between the two countries which could cover his extradition.

Few incidents have produced such excitement in the learned world as the Libri affair. Libri always insisted upon his absolute innocence. He demonstrated a considerable number of errors in the indictment; he documented with bills of sale from bookdealers his purchases of some of the books which were missing from the French libraries; and he ascribed the indictment to malicious persecution by his enemies.

The affair was disputed and eagerly commented upon the world over. Some of Libri's friends, many of them famous men, rallied to his support in newspaper articles and special pamphlets. The bibliophile and historian Lacroix promenaded each day along the bookstalls on the quais of the Seine, and picked up books stolen from the libraries in Paris. Altogether he returned 101 books, each accompanied by an ironical letter, commenting upon the ease with which one could happen to acquire such lost volumes.

The control and cataloguing in French libraries was doubtless very unsatisfactory, and the Libri affair had at least one positive effect: it brought about some improvements in this respect. Libri continued his business in London without impediment, and arranged book auctions which netted him enormous amounts. But the opinion among the book specialists gradually turned against him, and there seems to be little doubt that beside his legitimate purchases of books, Libri had also helped himself quite liberally from the French libraries during his official inspections. Libri spent his last years in Fiesole on the hill overlooking his native town of Florence. A considerable number of the stolen treasures were later brought back to the French institutions through exchanges and purchases. Other manuscripts, and his own posthumous papers, were placed in Italian libraries.

With this background, it is not surprising that it was suggested repeatedly that the disappearance of the manuscript of Abel's memoir during the printing was due to a quite natural and obvious cause. It is easily documented that Libri had a particular affinity for everything connected with Abel and his works; for instance, in March 1859, Libri arranged an auction of rare manuscripts, the receipts of which exceeded 7000 pounds. As was usual at Libri's auctions, the catalogue was a sumptuous publication with numerous facsimiles and illustrations, and bore the imposing title *Catalogue of the extraordinary collection of splendid manuscripts, chiefly upon vellum, in various languages of Europe and the East, formed by Monsieur Guglielmo Libri, the eminent collector, who is obliged to leave London in consequence of ill health and for that reason to dispose of his literary treasures.* Almost all the manuscripts were of a remarkable age; among the Latin ones alone there were more than seventy from before the twelfth century. But among the few contemporary items from recent times one suddenly finds listed two of Abel's original manuscripts:

"N. H. Abel, *Précis d'une théorie des fonctions elliptiques*, 4to, Saec XIX, on paper.

"An autograph manuscript — with the author's signature at the beginning — of this Norwegian mathematician who died at only 26 years of age, and whose admirable discoveries in the elliptical functions will be recorded as long as mathematics are held in honor. This manuscript consists of 56 columns beside 4 pages of introduction, containing many corrections and alterations which have never been printed in the *Journal* de Mr. Crelle, where this *Précis* was published.

"N. H. Abel. *Démonstration d'une propriété générale d'une certaine classe de fonctions transcendantes.* 4to, 1829, on paper.

In the author's handwriting with a short German note, dated Christiania, Jan. 6, 1829, respecting the printing of this *Démonstration*, and the illness of his intended bride [*sic*], also in his autograph with signature. Abel died on April 6, 1829."

Thus Libri had come into possession of two of Abel's original manuscripts, the last two he had composed. Both had been sent to Crelle; therefore, Libri must have acquired them from him under some pretext. It seemed quite probable as well that the manuscript to the Paris memoir had been purloined by Libri from the French Academy. In such case, it was likely that the memoir was still in existence.

In 1942, a manuscript to the memoir turned up in Biblioteca Nazionale in Rome, but the excitement rapidly died down when it was discovered that it was only a handwritten copy of the printed article, probably executed by some student. During the same year, the Italian mathematician Candido published a little book on the subject of Abel's Paris memoir, pointing out that in the Biblioteca Moreniana in Florence there was a manuscript of the same memoir in its collection of Libri papers. Candido presumed that it was the copy prepared by Libri for Legendre.

Candido's book appeared during the war and was little known; but in 1952, a Norwegian expert on Abel's history, Professor Viggo Brun, during a visit to Florence, decided to make a closer scrutiny of the document. He had not held the yellowing pages in his hands for many moments before he realized that this was actually a part of Abel's original manuscript. The papers carried the stamp of the printing office of the French Academy, the signature "Niels Henrik Abel, norvègien," his Paris address, and an apologetic note in Legendre's handwriting on the title page, explaining the delay in the report of the referees. A further search revealed almost all the missing pages; after more than a century of investigations and speculation, the memoir to which Abel had attached so much hope was again brought to light.

21

MONUMENTS TO GENIUS

~§ AFTER NIELS HENRIK'S DEATH, Crelly came to feel that the mansion at Froland held too many tragic memories for her to remain there. In June, the school year over, she traveled to the capital to deposit Abel's posthumous papers with Holmboe; she also sought a new position, but after a fortnight in Oslo she reversed her decision and returned to the Smith family.

Crelly's future had weighed heavily upon Niels Henrik during the last few months of his life. He wrote to his friend Keilhau, imploring him to assist her in whatever way he could. Keilhau, a man who always earnestly discharged the duties which life imposed upon him, had a deep sense of obligation toward his younger friend. Keilhau had never seen Crelly, but a few months after Abel's death he wrote to her, explaining that he had come to feel that the most beautiful way in which the prayer of his friend could be fulfilled would be for her to consent to become his wife. Crelly must have been very surprised, but undoubtedly also a little flattered. She replied coquettishly that she felt certain that her looks most surely would deflect him from his purpose. For this reason she would permit him to visit her at Froland; the Smith family extended an invitation, and stated that he would be welcome.

Keilhau arrived in Froland in January 1830. A week later Crelly wrote nervously to Fru Hansteen, concerned as to how she would receive the news:

"Beloved Fru Hansteen, for a variety of reasons my intentions of writing to you have come to naught, but today I cannot avoid writing a few lines to you about the news which you may have feared as much as wanted: my engagement to Keilhau. Please do not judge me too severely, but love me if you can, after having taken a step which you may think should have been much more deliberated. Still my pen can write nothing to my justification.

"As you know, Keilhau asked my permission to stay in the vicinity awhile, a request which I, for many reasons, believed that I ought to grant him. I was fully convinced that this would be the best manner in which to awaken him to the deceptive illusions of his fantasy.

"After his first call, he was invited by the Smith family to remain for some time; an offer which he accepted since he had heard from Holmboe that I would not oppose it; so he stayed here a whole week. But this time had no other effect upon him than to confirm more strongly the intention he first stated. On account of my poor health I felt compelled to arrive at a decision, for I was too weak to endure my inner struggle for long.

"Please join me in my prayers, dearest Fru Hansteen, that I may be so fortunate as to give him happiness in the days to come. Pray to our common father that he will bless an attachment which is founded on the most pure and most noble intentions.

"Forgive me that I must already conclude, but I shall ask you first, my motherly friend, never to withdraw from me your friendship and love; always let it hover over me as a mild and beneficial angel. I remain in the blessed hope that I shall never prove unworthy of it. Your devoted friend C. Kemp.

"P.S. Yesterday, upon my 26th birthday, our engagement was declared."

Shortly afterward, Keilhau left on another geological expedition. The wedding took place the next fall, and Crelly became "Fru Professor" in Oslo, although not at the side of Niels Henrik, as she had dreamed. The marriage was very harmonious, but childless.

Elisabeth Abel, Niels Henrik's favorite, also fell in love, and became engaged to a capable young German mining engineer, Carl Friedrich Böbert; again the confidante, Fru Hansteen, had to be informed:

"My sweet and dear Fru Hansteen: You have always taken such a part in everything concerning us that I must write to you, although I feel a little embarrassed. I ask you kindly to accept these lines from Elisabeth with your usual goodness and forbearance. You and Hansteen have heard enough of our sorrows; something agreeable you have never, or rarely, experienced from us. Please do not believe, dear Fru Hansteen, that I am ungrateful; it is only that I cannot express in words what I feel in my heart. I do, and always shall, remember with gratitude that you were the first who brought me, the abandoned, into loving care. But when I wanted to thank you, the words died on my lips. In my heart I prayed that God may reward you, but this probably no one could understand; I must have looked as if I were petrified.

"I suppose that you know already, dear Fru Hansteen, that I am engaged to Böbert. Still, I must tell you how glad and happy I am and how indescribably we love each other. I had often decided I wanted no one but Böbert. If this had not happened, I would have become a chaste old maid; for no reason except love could make me accept an engagement, and the way I love Böbert I could never love anyone else. Most people laugh at words like these, and seem to think that all is well if one only can get married. But this is not my opinion. Truly, dear Fru Hansteen, you agree with me — better to remain unmarried than to have a husband one cannot love."

The couple were married in 1833, and some years later Böbert became the director of the silver mines at Kongsberg.

After the death of his brother, Peder Abel had to stand on his own feet. It would have gladdened Niels Henrik's heart had he been able to witness how this gradually made a man of him. He accepted a position as tutor, just as Niels Henrik so often had suggested, and in the natural order of things became engaged to a daughter of the pastor who employed him. After a family council at the vicarage, he returned to his theological studies. This time he was better able to withstand temptations and finally received his degree. He ended his days as minister to a district on the western coast of Norway, and provided for his youngest brother, Thor Henrik, by taking him into his house as a tutor.

At Lunde, life continued in its haphazard way. Pastor Aas wrote an application on behalf of Fru Abel requesting the remittance of the annual obligation to the university, and this time it was granted. Only a few days after the letter was sent, there arrived an official notification from the Academy in Paris that Niels Henrik had been awarded the great prize for his remarkable mathematical works. The letter was reproduced in the newspapers, and the whole community was awed by the strange greatness of Niels Henrik.

To Fru Abel the money came as manna from heaven; 1500 francs were to be paid to her, or, to be exact, "to the surviving family of Monsieur Abel, the learned mathematician from Oslo."

Anxious to receive the money, she turned first to Holmboe, then to Hansteen for assistance. The Academy insisted upon following the wording of the award, and declined to make any disbursement to Fru Abel alone unless she could produce documentary evidence that she was Niels Henrik's sole heir.

However, after some official pressure upon Arago by the envoy, Count Löwenhielm, she finally received the money. Still, the matter was not settled. Whether there had been any complaint from Abel's brothers we do not know, but the French department of finance subsequently refused to reimburse the Academy for the prize money, the reason being that it had not been paid out in satisfactory legal form. The Academy finally resolved the imbroglio by changing the original wording of the prize award, making the money legally Fru Abel's alone.

Hansteen returned safely from his Siberian journey without having discovered the second magnetic pole he had been looking for. In St. Petersburg he was met by Russian mathematicians who were anxious to hear details about the life of the recently deceased mathematical genius Abel. In Stockholm he requested an audience with the king. It was granted with the explicit royal intent of snubbing him. During the audience Bernadotte demonstrated his displeasure by addressing himself exclusively to Hansteen's companion on the trip, Lieutenant Due. But in Oslo the reception was enthusiastic, and the students honored him with a torchlight parade. Hansteen became the ornament of Norwegian science, and was consulted on all questions which in any way touched upon the natural sciences. He was a member of one commission after another, was used and abused "in all the tasks with which an unreasonable government can overwhelm its scientists," as he expressed it himself. He lived until he was nearly ninety years of age, and was considered the grand old man of the university, the only survivor from its first days, honored and respected at home and abroad.

Holmboe's record was solid and useful, but far less spectacular than that of Hansteen. He devoted himself mainly to the improvement of the level of mathematical instruction in Norway, and wrote good mathematical textbooks. The relations between Abel's two university teachers gradually cooled, the final break coming a few years later, when Hansteen tried his hand at a school text in geometry. Holmboe attacked it in a harsh newspaper review, undoubtedly with some justification. The quick-tempered Hansteen could not refrain from an insulting reply, and for an entire year the two mathematicians kept up a running argument in the Oslo newspapers, climaxed by a separate publication in which Holmboe summed up Hansteen's errors. Several laymen entered this mathematical battle royal, and issued statements which could make a modern mathematician rise up in horror; for instance: "Nothing has been more harmful in the domain of science than this exaggerated effort to give exact definitions for the concepts."

Even their departed common friend could not be kept entirely out of the conflict. In the introduction to his book, Hansteen stated in his salty way: "When I see a student who has received his mathematical education in this school draw a circle for me which has the shape of a potato, and then in the corner of this monstrosity place a point, or still worse, only a capital letter to denote what he calls the center, then I can already tell the time of day, and I know that all his geometry is not worth a pipeful of tobacco."

To this Holmboe replied with the following observation: "I must confess that I find this a most peculiar criterion for the value of the geometric knowledge of a student. Niels Abel belonged to this school. By chance, I may still exhibit to anybody interested several instances of circles which he had drawn. He was weak in freehand drawing, so his circles look quite miserable, and could well be compared to potatoes, to say nothing worse. Thus, all his geometry was not worth a pipe of tobacco."

Keilhau remained a few weeks at Froland Works in 1830 after his engagement to Crelly had been announced. Toward the end of February the pair drove to the Froland Church to visit Abel's grave. In a letter to his friend Boeck, Keilhau described his feelings in regard to the departed common friend and proposed a plan to erect a durable monument on Abel's final resting place:

"Yesterday we were at Froland Church, which lies about five miles from here and where, as you know, Abel is buried. He was placed in a family plot not yet enclosed, intended for the Smiths. Next summer it will probably be provided with an iron railing, and Herr Smith and Apothecary Tuxen in Arendal have agreed to raise a little memorial on Abel's grave.

"This, it seems to me, must be the task of those who were closer to him; I mean we, his friends, to whom he really belonged, who will

ABOVE *The Froland Ironworks (watercolor, 1831).* BELOW *The monument erected by Abel's friends at his grave*

place a marker upon his grave not only out of duty, but feel a true urge to do so, and find a dear satisfaction in it.

"I believe it would be easy to obtain by subscription a considerable amount for a monument to Abel, particularly if we turned to the members of the Storting now in session. But such a procedure appears odious to me. The majority will put themselves down for an amount, either from an unwelcome compulsion or for reasons which, whatever they may be, are not those we desire. Furthermore, such subscriptions are, or appear to be, beggary. At least in his grave our friend shall not solicit.

"There can be no question of a pompous memorial. If for no other reason, the locality and modest surroundings would make it inappropriate. The cemetery, except for the Smith family, shelters only the simple departed inhabitants of the poor valley. It encircles the plain annex church, standing on a hill at the turn of the river. Here and there on the bluffs one sees a farm, but otherwise the countryside consists only of wild forests, without the imposing effect which is so characteristic of our great valleys.

"Yet here our friend has such a touching resting place. It will rarely be visited by anyone capable of understanding his worth, but once in a while through the years it will happen, and then only for his own sake. Then let such a wanderer find a secure and imperishable mark on this place of his pilgrimage, a sumptuous one would not be in harmony with his feelings.

"So, I propose a simple and massive memorial, of the type which can be cast here for about 50 to 100 daler. I mention the following persons, who, I believe, will be glad to participate with us, and to whom I ask you to address yourself: Rector Treschow, Fru Hansteen, Professor Schjelderup, Lecturer Holmboe, Professor Rasmussen, Hjort, and you and I, which makes a total of nine participants, if you will not consider it a presumption on my part to reserve two shares.

"If, in addition to those mentioned above, you know of someone who ought not to be excluded from taking part, then I ask you to invite them according to your own judgment, for you understand me, and know what is appropriate. My approaching journey prevents me from being as active in these matters as I should have desired. I must, therefore, as you actually see me do it, leave all to you, who are active and driving. My two votes I cede to you, if I cannot participate in the deliberations of the group.

"My fiancée will remain here until May; later Fru Hansteen or Fru Treschow will know her address. I presume that you will submit the plan to her, and perhaps leave the selection to her, in case there should be more than one project; the good girl has artistic taste. It would be well if you could write to Herr Smith in a preliminary way as soon as possible.

"My good friend Boeck, how gladly I would receive a few words from you. I know I have caused you pleasure since we were last together, and matters stand entirely different for me now than last year at this time when I wrote to you from Berlin. However, you need not write to me only to send your felicitations; those I know. But if you will reply to the present matter, then for a month the letter may be sent to Stavanger. Your devoted Keilhau."

When Keilhau returned from his geological excursion, the arrangements were still not complete. He wrote to Boeck again, urging all possible speed:

"I may appear unduly impetuous, but in addition to what I have mentioned, the delay grieves me on behalf of my fiancée, who will shortly leave Froland. It will be infinitely painful to her to depart without at least having been assured of the execution of this idea, which has pleased her so greatly.

"A long time will pass before your reply can reach me, and I can explain the situation to her. You could do me a great favor and cause her great joy if you would ask Holmboe to write her a couple of words. He would do it gladly, I believe, and it would reassure her. She is not well, poor girl; the heavy moment when she will have to take her leave of the place where her friend rests is imminent.

"You, dear Boeck, Abel's best spokesman, also sympathize with her fate, so I fear not that I shall appear obtrusive to you, or to the good Holmboe."

The memorial was cast in the foundry at Froland Works, and stands to the present day as the remembrance of his friends to Niels Henrik Abel.

In the center of Oslo a more stately monument has been erected in honor of Abel; a youthful figure symbolizing the soaring flight of his conquering genius, appropriately looking toward the old town around which his life revolved.

His friend Holmboe also created a great monument to his former

The statue of Abel in the Royal Park in Oslo (by sculptor Gustav Vigeland, 1908)

pupil; his edition of Abel's collected works cost him many years of painstaking labor. Shortly after the French Academy had been informed, through Legendre, of the death of Abel, it had delegated a member, Baron Maurice, to make an official condolence call upon the Swedish envoy, Count Löwenhielm. He impressed upon the envoy the great scientific importance of an edition of Abel's works, and suggested that his Royal Highness, Crown Prince Oscar, might be interested in such an undertaking. One year later, on July 17, 1831, Baron Maurice repeated his suggestion on behalf of the four members of the Academy who had petitioned the Swedish king. In his letter he emphasized again the scientific importance of making available Abel's articles and manuscripts, pointing out that it would be a highly worthy memorial in Abel's honor, and a credit to his native country. The university in Oslo took charge of the project, and the government promised the necessary grant.

The two volumes appeared in 1839; in the introduction Holmboe paid homage to his friend in the following words:

"The time and care I have expended on the edition of this work I shall always consider the best used in my life, if it in some measure has contributed to the dissemination of this work, the most important of its kind in our day.

"Through the immense expanse of his problems and the severe stringency he used in his methods, following the example of the famous Monsieur Cauchy, the author has given mathematics an increment which it might not otherwise have achieved in a century. He has mapped paths unknown before him, and created a new view on calculus and analysis in general. For these reasons, the works of our author belong to that highest class which no mathematician desiring to know his science can neglect reading."

In 1881 a new and more complete edition of Abel's works appeared. At the centenary of Abel's birth in 1902 the university in Oslo issued a memorial containing a biography and all letters and documents regarding Abel then known.

Mathematicians, in their characteristic manner, have erected many monuments to Abel, more durable than bronze. The custom prevails of marking new results and great ideas by the name of their originator. Today, anyone who reads advanced mathematical texts will find Abel's name perpetuated in numerous branches of his science: Abelian theorems in abundance, Abelian integrals, Abelian equations, Abelian groups, and Abelian formulas. In short, there are few mathematicians whose names are associated with so many concepts of modern mathematics. Niels Henrik would have been greatly surprised at his own importance.

Bibliography and Index

BIBLIOGRAPHY

Abel's complete works and manuscripts have been published twice and a considerable number of biographies have appeared in the Scandinavian countries, in France and Germany. The present life story of Abel, the first account in English, is based upon a large amount of new material gathered from private letters, official documents, and newspaper files examined at various European sources, particularly the archives in Norway and Denmark. Incorporated in this book also are the many facts embodied in the various magazine articles on Abel which have been published through the years since his death. The following are the most important biographies of Abel and works relating to him.

Abel, Niels Henrik. *Mémorial publié à l'occasion du centenaire de sa naissance.* Oslo, 1902.

Abel, Niels Henrik. *Oeuvres complètes de N. H. Abel, mathematicien, avec des notes et développements, rédigées par ordre du roi par B. Holmboe,* Oslo, 1839.

Abel, Niels Henrik. *Oeuvres complètes Nouvelle édition publiée aux frais de l'état norvègien par M. M. L. Sylow et S. Lie.* Oslo, 1881. 2 vols.

Bjerknes, C. A. *Niels Henrik Abel. En skildring av hans liv og vitenskapelige virksomhet.* Stockholm, 1880.

Bjerknes, C. A. *Niels Henrik Abel. Tableau de sa vie et de son action scientifique.* Paris, 1885.

Bjerknes, C. A. *Niels Henrik Abel. En skildring av hans liv og arbeide. Omarbeidet og forkortet utgave i anledning 100 årsdagen for Abels død.* Ved. V. Bjerknes. Oslo, 1929.

Bjerknes, C. A. *Niels Henrik Abel. Eine Schilderung seines Lebens und seiner Arbeit.* Berlin: Julius Springer, 1930.

Candido, Giacomo. *Sulla mancata pubblicazione, nel 1826, della celebre Memoria di Abel.* Galatina, 1942.

Holmboe, B. *Kort fremstilling av Niels Henrik Abels liv og virksomhet.* Oslo, 1829.

Jacobi, C. G. J. *Gesammelte Werke. Herausgegeben auf Veranlassung der königliche Preussische Akademie der Wissenschaften.* Berlin, 1881.

Köningsberger, Leo. *Zur Geschichte der Theorie der elliptischen Transcendenten in den Jahren 1826–29.* Leipzig, 1879.

Köningsberger, Leo. *Carl Gustav Jacob Jacobi. Festschrift zur der hundersten Wiederkehr seines Geburtstages.* Leipzig, 1904.

Legendre, A. M. *Traité des fonctions elliptiques.* Paris, 1827–32. 3 vols.

Mittag-Leffler, G. "Niels Henrik Abel," *Ord och Bild.* 12:65–85, 129–40 (1903).

Mittag-Leffler, G. "Niels Henrik Abel," *Revue du Mois.* (Paris) 4:5–26, 207–29 (1907).

Ore, Øystein. *Niels Henrik Abel. Kurze Mathematiker-biographien.* Beihefte zur Zeitschrift: Elemente der Mathematikk. No. 8, 1950. Basel, Verlag Birkhäuser.

Pesloüan, Ch. Lucas de. *N. H. Abel, sa vie et son oeuvre.* Paris, 1906.

INDEX OF NAMES